Karen Spencer
4 Burrough Street
Ash
Martock
TA12 6NZ

Teacher's resource
150
Numeracy Hour
Lessons

YEAR 4

Contents	Page
Summary of objectives	3
Mental maths starters	6
Autumn Term lesson plans	8
Spring Term lesson plans	28
Summer Term lesson plans	48
Copymasters	68
Homework copymasters	128
Answers	158

First published 2001
exclusively for WHSmith by
Hodder & Stoughton Educational,
a division of Hodder Headline Ltd.
338 Euston Road
London NW1 3BH

Text and illustrations © Hodder & Stoughton Educational 2001

All rights reserved. This work is copyright. Permission is given for copies to be made of pages provided they are used exclusively within the institution for which this work has been purchased. For reproduction for any other purpose, permission must first be obtained in writing from the publishers.

A CIP record for this book is available from the British Library

Author: Helen Orme
Series editor: Paul Broadbent

ISBN-10 0 340 79006 7
ISBN-13 978 0 340 79006 9

Impression 10 9 8 7 6
Year   2008 2007 2006

Typeset by Techset Ltd.
Printed and bound in Spain

Year 4
Summary of objectives

Autumn Term		
Theme	**Topics**	**Objectives – children will be taught to:**
1 Addition and subtraction	Understanding + and − Mental calculation strategies (+ −) Pencil and paper procedures (+ −)	Consolidate understanding of relationship between addition/subtraction. Understand commutative law of addition. Count on or back in repeated steps of 1, 100, 1000. Identify near doubles. Count up through next multiple of 10, 100, 1000. Use informal pencil and paper methods to support, record or explain addition and subtraction.
2 Money	Money and 'real life' problems Making decisions, checking results	Convert £ to p. Choose appropriate number operations and calculation methods to solve money or 'real life' word problems with one/two steps. Explain and record methods. Check with addition in a different order.
3 Measuring length	Measures, including problems	Use, read, write *km, m, cm, mm* and *mile*. Know and use relationships between units. Know $\frac{1}{2}, \frac{1}{4}, \frac{3}{4}, \frac{1}{10}$ of 1 *kilometre* in *m*, 1 *metre* in *cm* or *mm*. Suggest suitable units and equipment to estimate or measure length. Record metres and centimetres using decimals, and other measurements using mixed units. Convert up to 1000 cm to metres and vice versa.
4 Perimeter	Measures, including problems	Measure/calculate perimeter of rectangles and simple shapes (*cm*). Choose appropriate number operations and calculation methods to solve measurement word problems with one or more steps. Explain and record methods.
5 Shape	Shape and space Reasoning about shapes	Describe and visualise 3D and 2D shapes, including tetrahedron, heptagon. Recognise equilateral and isosceles triangles. Classify shapes (right angles, regularity, symmetry). Recognise position on square grids with numbered lines. Investigate general statements about shapes.
6 Number patterns	Properties of numbers Reasoning about numbers	Recognise, extend number sequences formed by counting from any number in steps of constant size, e.g. 25 to 500. Recognise odd and even numbers up to 1000 and some of their properties, e.g. sums, differences of pairs of odd/even numbers. Solve number puzzles, recognise patterns, generalise and predict.
7 Multiplication and division	Understanding × and ÷ Mental calculation strategies (× ÷) Pencil and paper procedures (× ÷)	Extend understanding of × and ÷ and their relationship to each other and to + and −. Use doubling and halving of two-digit numbers, e.g. ×4 = double double, ×5 = ×10 halve, ×20 = ×10 double, ×8 = ×4 double, $\frac{1}{4}$ = half of one $\frac{1}{2}$. Approximating first, use informal pencil and paper methods to multiply and divide.
8 Fractions	Fractions	Use fraction notation. Recognise fractions that are several parts of a whole, and mixed numbers. Find fractions of shapes. Relate fractions to division and find simple fractions of quantities.
9 Time	Understanding + and − Mental calculation strategies (+ −) Pencil and paper procedures (+ −) Time, including problems	Consolidate understanding of subtraction as the inverse of addition. Find a small difference by counting up. Use relationship between + and −. Develop written methods for + and − of whole numbers less than 1000. Use, read, write vocabulary of time. Read time to 1 min. on analogue/12-hour digital clock. Use 9:53, a.m. and p.m. Solve time word problems.
10 Handling data	Handling data	Solve a given problem by collecting, classifying, representing and interpreting data in tally charts, frequency tables, pictograms (symbols representing 2, 5, 10 units). Include use of computer.

Summary of objectives

Spring Term

Theme	Topics	Objectives – children will be taught to:
1 Mental calculation	Understanding + and − Mental calculation strategies (+ −)	Understand principle (not name) of commutative law for + not −. Add several small numbers by finding pairs that total 10, 9 or 11. Partition into tens and units, adding tens first. Add three 2-digit multiples of 10.
2 Money problems	Pencil and paper procedures (+ −) Money and 'real life' problems Making decisions, checking results	Develop/refine written methods for addition/subtraction, include money. Choose appropriate number operations and calculation methods to solve money and 'real life' word problems with one or more steps. Explain working. Check with an equivalent calculation.
3 Measuring mass	Measures and time, including problems	Estimate and check times using seconds, minutes, hours. Measure and compare using kilograms and grams, and know and use the relationship between them. Know $\frac{1}{4}, \frac{1}{2}, \frac{3}{4}$ and $\frac{1}{10}$ of 1 kg in grams. Suggest suitable units and equipment to estimate or measure mass. Read scales. Record measurements to suitable degree of accuracy, using mixed units or the nearest whole/half/quarter unit (e.g. 3.25 kg).
4 Area	Area of shapes	Measure and calculate area of rectangles and simple shapes, using counting methods and standard units (square centimetres). Choose appropriate number operations and calculation methods to solve measurement word problems with one or more steps. Explain working.
5 Shape	Shape and space Reasoning about shapes	Make shapes and discuss properties. Visualise solid shapes from 2D drawings. Identify simple nets. Recognise clockwise, anticlockwise. Start to draw, measure and order angles. Use eight compass points. Recognise horizontal and vertical lines. Solve shape problems or puzzles. Explain reasoning and methods.
6 Number sequences	Properties of numbers Reasoning about numbers	Recognise, extend number sequences formed by counting from any number in steps of constant size, extend beyond zero if counting back. Investigate general statements about familiar numbers. Explain methods and reasoning.
7 Multiplication and division	Understanding × and ÷ Mental calculation strategies (× ÷)	Understand commutative and associative laws of multiplication. Divide a whole number of £ by 2, 4, 5 or 10 to give £p. Use closely related facts, e.g. derive ×9 or ×11 from ×10, or derive ×6 from ×4 plus ×2. Partition and multiply.
8 Solving problems	Pencil, paper procedures (× and ÷) Money and 'real life' problems Making decisions, checking results	Develop and refine written methods for TU × U Choose appropriate number operations and calculation methods to solve money and 'real life' word problems with one or more steps. Explain working. Check with inverse operation.
9 Fractions and decimals	Fractions and decimals	Recognise equivalence of simple fractions. Identify two fractions with total of 1. Compare a fraction with one half, and say whether it is greater or less. Use decimal notation for tenths, hundredths (money, metres and centimetres) and use in context. Round to the nearest £ or metre. Convert £ to p, or metres to centimetres, and vice versa. Order decimals with two places.
10 Bar charts	Handling data	Solve a given problem by collecting, classifying, representing and interpreting data in bar charts; intervals labelled in 2s, 5s, 10s, 20s. Include use of computer.

Summary of objectives

Summer Term		
Theme	**Topics**	**Objectives – children will be taught to:**
1 Mental calculation	Understanding + and − Mental calculation strategies (+ −)	Understand the principles of associative law for addition (not name). Add or subtract the nearest multiple of 10 and adjust. Use number facts and place value to add/subtract mentally any pair of two-digit whole numbers.
2 Money problems	Pencil and paper procedures (+ −) Money and 'real life' problems Making decisions, checking results	Develop, refine written methods for column addition/subtraction. Add more than two whole numbers less than 1000, and money. Choose appropriate operations and calculation methods to solve money and 'real life' word problems with one or more steps. Explain working. Check using knowledge of sums of odd/even numbers.
3 Measuring capacity	Measures, including problems	Use, read, write litre (l), *millilitre* (ml), *pint*. Know $\frac{1}{4}, \frac{1}{2}, \frac{3}{4}, \frac{1}{10}$ of 1 litre in ml. Suggest suitable units and equipment to estimate or measure capacity. Read scales. Record measurements to suitable degree of accuracy, using mixed units, or the nearest whole/half/quarter unit (e.g. 3.25 litres). Choose appropriate number operations and calculation methods to solve measurement word problems with one or more steps. Explain working.
4 Reflection and angles	Shape and space Reasoning about shapes	Sketch reflection of simple shape in a mirror. Read and begin to write the vocabulary of movement. Make and describe patterns involving translation. Begin to measure angles in degrees. Know whole turn, 360°, 4 angles; quarter turn, 90°, 1 right angle; half turn, 180°, 2 right angles. Recognise 45° as half a right angle.
5 Multiples	Properties of numbers Reasoning about numbers	Recognise multiples of 2, 3, 4, 5, 10, up to 10th multiple. Solve number problems and puzzles. Explain methods and reasoning orally and in writing.
6 Multiplication and division	Understanding × and ÷ Mental calculation strategies (× ÷)	Pencil, paper procedures (× and ÷) Understand distributive law. Round up or down after division. Use relation between × and ÷. Use known facts to multiply and divide. Develop and refine written methods for TU ÷ U.
7 Solving problems	Money and 'real life' problems Making decisions, checking results	Choose appropriate operations and calculation methods to solve money and 'real life' word problems with one or more steps. Explain working. Check results by approximating.
8 Fractions and decimals	Fractions and proportion	Begin to use ideas of simple proportion. Recognise the equivalence of decimal, fraction forms of one half, one quarter and tenths.
9 Time problems	Understanding + and − Mental calculation strategies (+ −) Pencil, paper procedures (+ and −) Time, including problems	Consolidate understanding of addition and subtraction. Add/subtract mentally any pair of two-digit whole numbers. Refine column addition and subtraction. Read timetables and use this year's calendar. Solve problems involving time.
10 Handling data	Sorting diagrams	Solve a given problem by collecting, classifying, representing and interpreting data in Venn and Carroll Diagrams: two criteria. Use a computer and a branching tree program to sort shapes or numbers.

Year 4
Mental maths starters

1. Each pupil starts with 10 points. Write numbers from 1 to 10 on the board and + and − signs.
   Point to a number and a sign. Pupils add or subtract that number from their starter number. Pupils have to remember the total as they go on.
   Repeat for up to 10 times then ask pupils to write the total on a piece of paper and hold it up. Repeat as required.

2. Write a starter number on the board. Go round the class asking pupils to tell you 10 more, 6 less etc.

3. Play *On and off the bus*. A bus leaves the bus station with 20 passengers. At the first stop 5 get off and 3 get on. How many passengers are there now? Continue until each pupil has had the opportunity to answer.

4. Count round the class. Begin with 1 and count in ones. Ask pupils to tell you their number. At an appropriate time specify steps of 2, or count on in odd numbers, steps of 10 etc. Continue counting until pupils have difficulty in saying the numbers. How high can you count in this way?

5. Write 3 digits on the board and ask pupils to tell you all the numbers they can make using these digits.
   Repeat with 4 digits and possibly 5 if appropriate.

6. Doubles. Say a number and ask pupils to tell you the double +1. Repeat with doubles +3, or doubles +5.

7. Target numbers. Write a number on the board. Ask pupils to give you sums for which this is the answer. Ask for: pairs of numbers, 3 numbers which total the target, a pair of numbers which multiplied give the target etc.

8. Measurement numbers. Write 10, 100, 1000 on the board and ask pupils to say a statement about these involving units of measure, e.g. 100 pennies in a pound, 100 centimetres in a metre. Add some more 3-digit numbers and extend this e.g. 125 pence in £1.25.

Mental maths starters

9. Shape and solid statements. Draw several shapes on the board or demonstrate with several solids. Indicate a shape or solid and ask pupils to make a statement about it. Continue until no more statements are possible then choose another shape.
Alternatively make a statement and ask pupils to identify which shape or solid fits this statement.

10. Facts about numbers. Write the numbers 1–20 (or 1–30) on the board. Ask pupils to tell you interesting facts about each number, e.g. any number $\times 1$ stays the same. Continue until no one can think of any more facts then move to the next number.

Theme 1 — Addition and subtraction

Objectives
- Consolidate understanding of the relationship between addition and subtraction
- Understand the commutative law of addition
- Count on and back in repeated steps of 1, 100, 1000
- Identify near doubles. Count up through next multiples of 10, 100, 1000
- Use informal pencil and paper methods to support, record or explain addition and subtraction

Vocabulary
add, addition, more, plus, increase, sum, total, altogether, double, near double, subtract, take away, minus, decrease, between, half, halve, equals, difference between, how many

Resources
Sets of number cards (two-digit numbers, 12 cards per set for each pair of pupils)
Copymasters 1 and 2, Homework copymaster 1

Assessment
At the end of this theme is the pupil able to:
- Understand and use the vocabulary needed to describe addition and subtraction;
- Recognise that addition is commutative;
- Add any pair of two-digit numbers mentally;
- Find the difference between any pair of two-digit numbers mentally?

Mental maths starter 3

Lesson 1

Introduction
Quick fire questions – check number pairs adding to 20. When satisfied that these are secure, move to number pairs adding to 200 using multiples of 10. If pupils have difficulties with any of these, demonstrate the link between the multiples and numbers below 20, e.g. *How many is 15 and 5? How many is 150 and 50?* Use a variety of instructions, e.g. *What's the sum of ...? If you add...? How many...?* depending on the vocabulary already familiar to the pupils.

Activities
Whole class
Work with a number line. Ask pupils to suggest pairs of numbers less than 100. Demonstrate how the pairs can be added by counting on in jumps of 10 then adding the units. Think of a number – ask what number you get if you add four tens, six tens etc. Repeat using multiples of 100.

Individual/pair
Pack of number cards for each pair – twelve cards per pair, with two-digit numbers. Pupils deal the cards between them. Each pupil picks a card from their set. Pupils write the sum and draw a number line to show how they worked out the answer following the method shown in the whole class work. Investigate what number lines look like if you write the number pairs the other way, i.e. 48 + 25 or 25 + 48.
Pairs can swap sets if required but a simple re-deal will give additional combinations.

Differentiation
Low Attainers – Could work with sets of cards which have only multiples of ten or multiples of 5.
High Attainers – Challenge pupils to beat the clock. One of pair to make up sums for the other.

Plenary
Does it make a difference if you write the numbers in a different order? Can you think of a rule for this? Did anybody find pairs which gave a different answer if reversed? Reiterate different ways of asking about addition. Ask pupils to demonstrate using a number line and explaining their method.

Lesson 2

Introduction
Quick fire questions – check doubles to 20. When satisfied that these are secure, move to doubles adding to 200 using multiples of 10. Check doubles of multiples of 5. Move to doubles of other numbers when appropriate.

Activities
Whole class
Ask pupils to suggest a number between 20 and 100. Ask what is the nearest multiple of 10 to the suggested number. What number doubled gives this multiple? Show that the suggested number is a double plus a single digit. Continue with this pattern until pupils can suggest doubles plus quite easily. Introduce the idea of a half. Demonstrate the relationship between halving and doubling.
Ask prepared questions which give a rule and answer introducing subtraction as well as addition, e.g. *'I think of a number and double it. I add 5 and the answer is 45. What is my number?'*
'I think of a number and double it. I take away 3 and the answer is 47. What is my number?'
'I think of a number and halve it. The answer is 18. What is my number?'

Individual/pair
Resource sheet on double patterns, Copymaster 1.

Differentiation
Harder problems for *high attainers*. Stick to doubles of multiples of 10 for *low attainers*.

Plenary
Add pairs of consecutive numbers by recognising these are near doubles. Write a pair of consecutive numbers on the board. Use the words *near doubles*. How does recognising these numbers as near doubles make the adding process easier? Are some numbers easier to double? If you wanted to add 49 and 50, which number would you choose to double?
Ask pupils to put into their own words the relationship between doubles and halves.

Autumn Term

Lesson 3

Introduction
Target numbers. Ask pupils to suggest a number between 0 and 20. Ask for pairs of numbers which total the target number. Ask for examples of simple number puzzles which have the target number as an answer. Relate this to the previous lesson on doubles. Ask for simple subtraction sums which would give the target number.

Activities
Whole class
Target numbers. Ask pupils to suggest a number less than 100. Ask for suggestions for pairs of numbers which total the given target number. Write the pairs as addition sums. Point out that target numbers can be achieved by taking away. Ask for suggested target numbers and write a sum which involves taking away from 100. Write the subtraction sums on the board.

Individual/pair
Investigate ways of forming a given target number using the ideas already discussed. Set target numbers for each child or pair according to ability.

Differentiation
Low Attainers – Should be given target numbers appropriate to their ability.
High attainers – Could be given tasks with specified constraints e.g. *no use of multiples of ten; only use numbers greater than 50.* They could also be encouraged to use target numbers greater than 100.

Plenary
Ask how the children set about the task. Look for systematic methods. Look for examples of commutativity.

Lesson 4

Introduction
Quick fire questions – check subtraction number facts with numbers less than 20. When satisfied that these are secure, move to two digit subtractions which do not cross the 10s boundary, e.g. *48 – 31.* Ensure that questions are phrased in a variety of ways.

Activities
Whole class
Write a subtraction sum on the board, e.g. *76 – 68.* For the initial sums choose numbers which have a difference of ten or less. Ask for ideas for approaches to this sum. Focus on the concept of counting on. If this is not introduced by a pupil then introduce it as something you have noticed pupils doing. (Almost all pupils will use this at times – usually counting on on their fingers.) Demonstrate the process of counting on using a number line. Provide a few more examples where the technique can be demonstrated clearly. Extend the questions using numbers with greater differences. Demonstrate how the counting on process can be used by making jumps of 10.
Discuss how this process could be used with larger numbers – making jumps of 100s as well as 10s if necessary.

Individual/pair
Use the packs of number cards provided for lesson 1, or provide additional cards. Pupils divide the set of cards between them. Each pupil turns over a card and both write down the sum for and the answer to the question: 'What is the difference between these two numbers?' It will be necessary to explain that 'difference between' means taking the lower number from the higher.
Ask the pupils to compare their sums and answers once all the cards have been used. Pupils with a high success rate could be provided with additional cards. Pupils with poor success rates should be encouraged to draw number lines to demonstrate their counting on process.

Differentiation
Lower ability pupils will need more practice with numbers with smaller differences.
Higher ability pupils can use this method with sums involving numbers to 1000.

Plenary
Ask pupils to explain their methods. Did they count on to a multiple of 10 first? Do you always have to start with the smaller number? Why?

Lesson 5

Introduction
Quick fire subtraction sums taking away from 100. Use these to demonstrate the relationship between pairs of numbers summing to 100. Ask: 'What is 100 minus 48? What is 100 take away 52?'

Activities
Whole class
Investigate other ways of using the number line for subtraction. Count backwards in jumps of 10s or 100s.
Refer to the initial introductory activity and discuss the links between the pairs of numbers. Demonstrate that subtraction can be seen as the inverse of addition. Introduce the word *inverse*. Remind pupils that addition is commutative. Ask if this is true of subtraction.

Individual/pair
Resource sheet on missing numbers, Copymaster 2.

Differentiation
Lower ability pupils may need support to ensure their understanding of the new ways of using the number lines. These pupils could repeat the card activity used in lesson 4 but be asked to draw appropriate number lines.
Higher ability pupils should work with numbers to 1000.

Plenary
Check that all pupils understand and can use the vocabulary introduced. Ask pupils to find different ways of expressing a written sum in words.

Theme 2 — Money

Objectives
- Convert £ to p
- Choose appropriate number operations and calculation methods to solve money or real life word problems with one or two steps
- Explain and record methods. Check with addition in a different order

Vocabulary
money, coin, note, penny, pence, pound, price, cost, buy, bought, sell, sold, spent, spend, pay, change, costs more, costs less, cheaper, less/least expensive, how much, how many, total, amount, value

Resources
Copymasters 3 and 4, Homework copymaster 2, further appropriate examples of money problems, coins or coin cards

Assessment
At the end of this theme is the pupil able to:
- Write an amount of money, given in pence, in pounds;
- Identify an appropriate sum to solve a money problem;
- Calculate change?

Lesson 1

Introduction
Identify the set of coins in use. Quick fire questions – hold up cards, with the coin amounts written on, and ask how much money they represent. This could be extended by introducing £5.00 and £10.00 notes.

Activities
Whole class
Establish that 100p = £1.00. Discuss the relevance of the decimal point. Ask how many pence in £2.00, £5.00 and so on. Ask how many pence in £2.50 and continue to extend using different amounts until all pupils are able to offer a correct answer. Write up some of these conversions and look at the patterns formed.
Give a sum of money in pence and ask how many pounds this sum contains. Relate to coin cards if necessary. Continue giving sums of money as pence and ask how these would be written with the £ notation.

Individual/pair
Copymaster 3 with one set of coin cards per pair. Choose one of the squares to use for the game. Spread the coin cards out so the amounts cannot be seen. The pupil selects three cards and adds up the value. If that value appears on the game card the pupil colours in the square. Cards are put back on the desk and mixed up. The second pupil repeats the process. If the amount does not appear on the card or if the square has already been coloured in, the other pupil has their turn. The game continues until one player has coloured in three squares in a row (vertical, horizontal or diagonal). The game can be played until all the squares have been coloured in, or for a set time. The winner in this case is the person who has the most coloured squares.

Differentiation
Lower ability pupils could play a similar game with a reduced set of coins. You would need to produce an appropriate game card.
Higher ability pupils could play with both number squares at the same time. This will cover nearly all the possible combinations of coins. They may also be asked to investigate whether there is any sum of money they are unable to make with this set of coins.

Plenary
Review the work on changing from pounds to pence. Ask pupils to look at the set of cards used in the game. Why was this set chosen?

Lesson 2

Introduction
Quick fire questions – 'If I have ten 20p coins how much money have I got?' Repeat this with other coin amounts. Concentrate initially on multiplying by 10 then extend this using tables with which pupils are secure. Extend this activity by introducing other sums of money up to £1.00.

Activities
Whole class
Shopping – ask pupils to give examples of items which their families buy regularly. Ask pupils to suggest appropriate prices for these items. Write a list of items and prices on the board. Ask questions about these items. 'If I buy... and... how much will they cost?' 'If I buy 5 of... how much will I spend?'

Individual/pair
Ask pupils to create their own shopping lists from those on the board. Pupils should write a list and work out the total cost. You may prefer to prepare a price list of common items in advance and to use this list for the individual activity.

Differentiation
Lower ability pupils should be told to limit the number of items on their list. If you have provided a price list, you could also provide an appropriate shopping list.
Higher ability pupils should be encouraged to include multiple items on their lists e.g. 6 packets of crisps. They could be asked to write shopping lists for a partner to evaluate.

Plenary
Ask pupils to discuss the methods they used to work out the total costs of their lists.

Autumn Term

Lesson 3

Introduction
Use some of the shopping lists produced by the pupils in lesson 2. Discuss the mathematical processes involved in working out the total cost of the list. Review the work from lesson 2 on buying multiples of an item. Quick fire questions of the type: 'If I buy 6 stamps costing 30p each how much will I spend?' Prepare these questions in advance.

Activities
Whole class
Work on real-life questions. Identify examples of the need to buy large quantities, *e.g. items needed to decorate a room; food for a class party*. Discuss the best ways of approaching these problems. Review appropriate pencil and paper working. Discuss methods of setting out problems and showing working.

Individual/pair
Copymaster 4 – money problems.

Differentiation
Higher ability pupils could be asked to make up similar real-life problems for each other. *Lower ability* pupils could be provided with the sums written out, either at the bottom of the copymaster or on a separate sheet, and asked to match up the sum with the written problem.

Plenary
Discuss the ways in which the problems were approached. Is there more than one approach for a two-stage problem? Focus on the fact that prices are often given as £1.99 etc. and discuss easy ways of dealing with such amounts in calculation.

Lesson 4

Introduction
Giving change. Quick fire questions of the type: 'If I buy a stamp for 27p how much change will I get from 50p, £1.00?' 'I spend £9.25 on a book. How much change will I get from a £10.00 note?' If necessary link this to the work done on counting on (Theme 1 lesson 4).

Activities
Whole class
Provide pictures of everyday items and a set of appropriate prices on cards. Show pupils pairs of items and ask: 'Which costs more? How much more? Which is cheapest? How much cheaper? If I bought this what change would I get from...? I am saving up to buy this. I have saved... How much more do I need? Which of these items could I buy with...? How many of these could I buy with...?'

Individual/pair
Provide a set of questions which relate to the items and prices you have been using for the whole class activity. Ask pupils to write down the appropriate sums.

Differentiation
Higher ability pupils should be able to cope with more complex questions and deal with larger sums of money.
With *lower ability* pupils it is important to focus on the reasoning so they should be provided with relatively easy calculations.

Plenary
Discuss the sums written in answer to the problems. Is there any variation in the way these sums are set out. Ask individual pupils to explain their reasoning.

Lesson 5

Introduction
Discuss areas of everyday life where a lot of money transactions occur, *e.g. shops, banks*, and try to introduce the idea of a café.

Activities
Whole class
Ask pupils to list common items of food and drink that they would expect to find in a café. Make a list of these and draw up a price list.

Individual/pair
Ask pupils to produce a menu for their café giving prices. Ask them to work out a selection of 'set meals' and calculate a price for each which is slightly cheaper than buying the same items individually.

Differentiation
Lower ability pupils may only be able to work out one 'set meal'.
Higher ability pupils could draw up a ready-reckoner to help calculate multiple orders.

Plenary
Ask pupils to explain their reasoning and methods when asked to calculate the cost of more than one item, or a list of items. Did anyone use pen and pencil methods?

Theme 3 — Measuring length

Objectives
- Use, read and write km, m, cm, mm and mile
- Know and use relationships between units
- Know $\frac{1}{4}$, $\frac{3}{4}$, $\frac{1}{10}$ of one kilometre in metres, of one metre in cm or mm
- Suggest suitable units and equipment to estimate or measure length
- Record metres and centimetres using decimals and other measurements using mixed units
- Convert up to 1000 cm to metres and vice versa

Vocabulary
length, width, height, depth, breadth, long, short, tall, high, low, wide, narrow, deep, shallow, thick, thin, longer, shorter, taller, higher, longest, shortest, tallest, highest, edge, kilometre, metre, centimetre, millimetre, ruler, measure, measuring, estimate

Resources
Set of cards showing lengths (to 2 m) in m, cm and mixed units, Copymasters 5 and 6, Homework copymaster 3

Assessment
At the end of this theme is the pupil able to:
- Measure lengths in centimetres accurately;
- Discuss appropriate units of measurement;
- Understand fractions of a metre in centimetres;
- Estimate lengths using appropriate units?

Mental maths starter 8

Lesson 1

Introduction
Write the abbreviations cm, mm, m and km on the board. Ask the pupils if anyone recognises them. Write the words centimetre, millimetre, metre and kilometre. Discuss the meanings of the prefixes. Ask if anyone can give an example of something which is 1 cm long and one metre long. Ask for examples of things measuring 10 cm, 15 cm etc. Discuss ways of making sensible estimates. A finger width may be near 1 cm. Is anyone close to 1 m tall? Is there anything in the classroom which would make a good standard measure for comparison?

Activities
Whole class
Discuss ways of measuring accurately. What units do we use to measure longer distances? Discuss the use of miles for measuring distances between places. Give some examples of distances between places in miles and in kilometres and try to establish a rough relationship between the two different units of measure, i.e. a mile is less than 2 km but more than 1 km; or a kilometre is a bit more than half a mile.

Individual/pair
Estimate and then measure items in the classroom.

Differentiation
Lower ability pupils should be given a more structured task. Identify which items they should measure.
Higher ability pupils could be asked to estimate and measure in metres, centimetres and millimetres.

Plenary
Recap on appropriate units for measuring. Ask pupils to decide what units would be appropriate to measure items in the classroom. Ask in what ways they could describe measurements between one and two metres.

Lesson 2

Introduction
Establish that there are 100 cm in a metre. Use a metre rule with the divisions covered with paper. Mark 10 cm, 50 cm and 75 cm clearly but do not write on numbers. Ask pupils to estimate the distances shown by the marks. Indicate other appropriate measures and ask for estimates.

Activities
Whole class
Review work done in lesson 1 on estimating and measuring items in the classroom. Compare answers. Ask how many centimetres there are in half a metre, a quarter of a metre etc. Ensure that all pupils can tell you the equivalent in centimetres for $\frac{1}{4}$ m, $\frac{1}{2}$ m and $\frac{3}{4}$ m.

Individual/pair
Draw two horizontal 20 cm lines on paper. Each pupil should give 6 measurements, taking it in turns. After each one the partner estimates where the point will be, marking the point on their line and writing the measurement. At the end of the game pupils measure the accuracy of their partner's guess.

Differentiation
Lower ability pupils could be provided with a list of appropriate lengths for them to measure.
Higher ability pupils should be encouraged to work in fractions of a centimetre ($\frac{1}{2}$ cm) and in millimetres.

Plenary
Ask how accurate the estimates were. Did anyone have strategies they employed to help them, *e.g. a known length, using fingers*?

Autumn Term

Lesson 3

Introduction
Review that 100 cm = 1 m. Establish that 10 mm = 1 cm, 1000 m = 1 km. Review meanings of prefixes covered in lesson 1. Write six measures in mixed metre/centimetre measures e.g. 150 cm, 1 m, $1\frac{1}{4}$ m, $\frac{3}{4}$ m, 80 cm, 130 cm. Ask pupils which is the shortest. Arrange measures in length order. Repeat with measurements in centimetres/millimetres and metres/kilometres as appropriate.

Activities
Whole class
Point to pairs of objects in the classroom. Which is longer? Which is shorter? Which is taller? Ask 4 pupils to stand up, one at a time. Ask the rest of the class to write down their names in height order. Ask the four to stand up again and arrange themselves in height order. Measure their heights if appropriate. Repeat with other groups of pupils as appropriate. Ask 'Who is tallest? Who is shortest? Is... taller than...?' Estimate the difference in height between any two pupils.

Individual/pair
Make several sets of cards with lengths in the units as discussed in the lesson. Pupils work in pairs. Each pupil picks a card and turns the card face up. Pupils have to answer the question: 'Which is longer?' Ask pupils to write a sentence for the pair of cards they have picked up, e.g. *1 m is longer than 75 cm*. Point out that it is possible that the lengths could be the same, in which case they should write e.g. *50 cm = $\frac{1}{2}$ m*.

Differentiation
Higher ability pupils could be asked to calculate by how much one is longer.

Plenary
Ask pupils to discuss various items in the classroom using the vocabulary introduced in this lesson. How good were they at putting people in size order when they were not next to each other? What strategies could they employ to decide whether items are longer or shorter?

Lesson 4

Introduction
Review appropriate measures for measuring longer distances. Discuss why it would be inappropriate to measure these in metres etc. Discuss why we use miles as a standard measure. Ask for estimates of distances to nearby towns or well-known places of interest.

Activities
Whole class
Construct a distance table in kilometres. Use the information as discussed in the introductory activity or provide suitable information for use. Discuss appropriate ways of tabulating this information. Discuss why this type of table could be useful. Provide an example from a book of road maps or similar.

Individual/pair
Copymaster 5 – longer distances.

Differentiation
Lower ability pupils may need additional support in interpreting the tables.
Higher ability pupils could be asked to draw simple maps and produce distance tables themselves.

Plenary
Review the methods pupils used to answer the questions. Ask pupils to explain how they used the two types of table on the sheet. Discuss how useful these tables are in a real life situation.

Lesson 5

Introduction
Ask pupils how they would draw a straight line to an accurate given measure. Demonstrate how they should set about this task. The process seems obvious but it is worth reiterating this as a preparation for further work on measuring and construction. Discuss how to measure any given line accurately. Discuss possible real-life situations where accurate measurement is necessary, e.g. *home decorating, building a bridge*.

Activities
Whole class
Set various tasks according to pupils' skill levels and ability. Some pupils could be asked to produce posters relevant to this topic. Others could be asked to produce a height chart which could be used in subsequent lessons. Some could provide measuring apparatus to show the measurements of various objects in the classroom.
Lines should be accurately drawn and marked into appropriate units. A height chart, for example, could show one metre from the ground and centimetres from there on.

Individual/pair
Copymaster 6 – real-life problems.

Differentiation
Lower ability pupils may need careful observation and additional support to ensure accurate drawing.
Higher ability pupils could be asked to devise appropriate measuring tools for longer distances.

Plenary
Discuss the problem sheet. Ask pupils what methods they used to solve the various types of problem. Focus on the vocabulary of comparison. How do you decide whether $1\frac{1}{2}$ m is taller than 135 cm?
The final puzzle is open ended and you may like to approach this as a class exercise.

Theme 4 — Perimeter

Objectives
- To calculate the perimeter of rectangles and simple shapes
- Choose appropriate number operations and calculation methods to solve measurement word problems with one or more steps
- Explain and record methods

Vocabulary
length, width, breadth, long, short, wide, narrow, longer, shorter, longest, shortest, edge, perimeter, kilometre, metre, centimetre, millimetre, ruler, measure, measuring, estimate

Resources
Copymasters 7 and 8, Homework copymaster 4

Assessment
At the end of this theme is the pupil able to:
- Explain what is meant by the perimeter of a shape;
- Measure or calculate a perimeter;
- Explain how to approach problems involving length and measurement?

Lesson 1

Introduction
Introduce the word *perimeter*. Ask for examples of perimeters *e.g. perimeter of a playing field or park*. Ensure that pupils understand that the word perimeter can be applied to irregular shapes as well as regular shapes.

Activities
Whole class
Review work done on accurate measuring. Draw a rectangle on the board. Measure the sides and write the measurements beside the rectangle. Ask how the pupils would work out the measurement of the perimeter. Write the sum on the board.
Draw an irregular quadrilateral on the board. Write on appropriate measurements and ask for the sum needed to calculate the perimeter. Draw other irregular polygons and repeat the process. Continue with this activity until all pupils are confident with the process.

Individual/pair
Copymaster 7 – measuring perimeters. Accurate measuring is part of the process with this copymaster. Pupils should be told to measure, in centimetres, to the nearest centimetre.
Pupils should write the sum and calculate the answer.

Differentiation
Lower ability pupils may need support with the measuring. They could be limited to measuring only quadrilaterals and triangles.
Higher ability pupils could be asked to measure and calculate in millimetres for some of the polygons.

Plenary
Review the vocabulary used in the lesson. Ask pupils to give a definition of perimeter in their own words. Were there any problems with measuring the perimeters? Ask pupils to explain their methods in their own words.

Lesson 2

Introduction
Review previous lesson's discussions. Draw a rectangle on the board. Write the measurements beside the rectangle. Ask how the pupils would work out the measurement of the perimeter. Write the sum on the board. Write the sum again with the numbers grouped to highlight the fact that the numbers are repeated *e.g.* a + b + a + b or a + b + a + b
Ask if pupils can think of another way of calculating the perimeter. Try to draw out the idea that it is possible to add two sides and double the answer. Discuss what other shape this rule would work for (a square).

Activities
Whole class
Extend this concept to calculating the perimeters of larger spaces using metre measurements as well as centimetres, or smaller spaces using millimetres.

Individual/pair
Copymaster 8 – calculating perimeters. The copymaster has no dimensions printed on it to allow measurements to be written in as appropriate, using a range of units.

Differentiation
Lower ability pupils could be asked to calculate the perimeter of the regular shapes and to measure the perimeter of the more complex shapes.
Higher ability pupils should be provided with measurements in various units for the calculations.

Plenary
Discuss the processes used by pupils in their calculations. Ask pupils to explain how they calculated the perimeters. Did they all use addition or did some use multiplication?

Autumn Term

Lesson 3

Introduction
Explain that pupils are to investigate patterns formed with squares and the perimeter.

Activities
Whole class
Explain the activity in detail. The investigation is to use a given number of squares, with sides of 1 cm, arranged in various patterns to see how much space can be contained within a given perimeter. 3 squares can be arranged in 2 ways, both giving a perimeter of 8 cm. Investigate possible arrangements with 4, 5 or 6 squares.

Individual/pair
Pupils undertake the investigation.

Differentiation
Lower ability pupils may need to work with prepared gummed squares.
Higher ability pupils could draw the squares.

Plenary
What arrangement always gives the minimum area (rectangle)? Discuss ways in which information can be presented.

Lesson 4

Introduction
Review the strategies for calculating perimeters of rectangles from lesson 2. Draw a variety of regular polygons on the board. Establish that a regular polygon has sides of the same length. Establish that the perimeter of a regular polygon can be calculated by a multiplication sum. It may be necessary to work through the stage that multiplication can be seen as repeated addition.

Activities
Whole class
Continue with the work begun in the introduction. Draw polygons on the board. Establish whether a polygon is rectangular. If so, how do you calculate the perimeter? Ask pupils to provide answers and to explain their reasoning.

Individual/pair
Provide a copymaster of problems. It is possible to use the copymaster from lesson 1 with new measurements written on. Use a variety of units. Ask pupils to write down their sums.

Differentiation
It may be more appropriate to provide *lower ability* pupils with examples involving polygons with up to 6 sides.

Plenary
Discuss the copymaster results and ask pupils to explain their methods in selected examples.

Lesson 5

Introduction
Review the work done for the investigation in lesson 3. Establish that it is possible for a given perimeter to enclose a variety of different shapes. Ask 'What sort of shapes can be contained within a perimeter of...?' Begin by using perimeters derived from the previous investigation.

Activities
Whole class
Explain that pupils are to investigate new shapes which can be contained by a given area. Ask for suggestions as to how pupils might attempt the task. Some pupils might benefit from the provision of strips of card in varying lengths and paper fasteners to hold these in place.

Individual/pair
Pupils undertake the investigation.

Differentiation
Lower ability pupils could be given pieces of string cut to appropriate lengths and asked to form these into rough approximations of the polygons before trying to draw them.
Higher ability pupils could be asked 'What square can you draw to fit the shapes into?' This could be done as a practical activity by cutting out shapes, or as a drawing activity.
Higher ability pupils should be expected to draw triangles, quadrilaterals and figures with right angles accurately but *lower ability* pupils could be asked to provide a sketch with given measurements.

Plenary
Ask 'What is the biggest amount of space enclosed by a given perimeter?'

Theme 5 Shape

Objectives:
- Describe and visualise 3D and 2D shapes including tetrahedron and heptagon
- Recognise equilateral and isosceles triangles
- Classify shapes (right angles, regularity, symmetry)
- Investigate general statements about shape

Vocabulary

shape, pattern, flat, line, curved, straight, round, hollow, solid, corner, point, pointed, face, side, edge, end, sort, make, build, construct, draw, sketch, centre, radius, diameter, net, surface, angle, right-angled, base, square based, vertex, vertices, layer, diagram, regular, irregular, concave, convex, open, closed, 3D, 2D, three-dimensional, two-dimensional, cube, cuboid, pyramid, sphere, hemisphere, spherical, cone, cylinder, cylindrical, prism, tetrahedron, polyhedron, circle, circular, semicircle, triangle, triangular, equilateral, isosceles, square, rectangle, rectangular, oblong, pentagon, pentagonal, hexagon, hexagonal, polygon, quadrilateral, heptagon, octagon, cross section

Resources

Copymasters 7, 8, 9 and 10, Homework copymaster 5, selection of shapes or shape cards, cards with polygon names for display, 12 cm squares of paper or card, set of solids

Assessment

At the end of this theme is the pupil able to:
- Identify a polygon by name;
- Identify a polygon by its properties;
- Describe and draw a named polygon?

Mental maths starter 9

Lesson 1

Introduction

Quick fire questions naming 2D shapes. Show a set of shape cards to pupils. Look for triangle, square, rectangle, quadrilateral, oblong, circle. Introduce, if necessary, pentagon, hexagon, heptagon, octagon. Ask for examples of various shapes from around the room.

Activities

Whole class

Demonstrate simple shapes with a 30 cm square piece of card. Fold the square in half to form a rectangle. Fold one corner to the centre to form a pentagon. Fold the opposite corner to the centre to form a hexagon. Fold in half diagonally to form a triangle.

Individual/pair

Give pupils a piece of card 12 cm square and ask them to investigate how many different shapes they can make by folding. If pupils work in groups they can then produce a poster showing the shapes made. The squares can be folded in any way but should not be cut or torn.

Differentiation

Group *lower ability* pupils with those of *higher ability* to encourage discussions. *Lower ability* pupils may need additional support with the manipulative skills involved.

Plenary

Review all the shapes constructed. How many different pentagons, hexagons etc. have been formed? Ensure that all pupils are familiar with the names you have introduced in the lesson.

Lesson 2

Introduction

Review the names of shapes. Work with a set of shape cards. Select a set of cards, *e.g. those with right angles,* and ask what they all have in common. Repeat with various sets – triangles, regular shapes, quadrilaterals etc. Classify 2D shapes.

Activities

Whole class

Introduce the words *regular, right-angled, equilateral* and *isosceles* and illustrate with as many examples as possible. Discuss how it is possible for some shapes to have more than one property.

Individual/pair

Work with Copymaster 7. Give each pair a copy of the sheet. Ask the pair to produce a table which identifies each shape by name. Ask pupils to identify two or three set criteria, as discussed in the class activity, and to find an appropriate way of presenting this information.

Pupils could colour code, cut out and reorder or draw lines around the sets.

Differentiation

Lower ability pupils may need help to decide on appropriate criteria for their sets.

Higher ability pupils could investigate two sets with two properties, *e.g. shapes which are regular and have right angles or shapes which are members of more than one set.*

Plenary

Review vocabulary. Ask pupils to give examples of the various criteria they used in deciding which shapes could be grouped together *e.g. quadrilaterals, regular polygons etc.* Did some belong to more than 1 set?

Autumn Term

Lesson 3

Introduction

Quick fire questions naming polyhedra. Use various solids and ask for names. Look for cube, cuboid, pyramid, sphere, prism. Introduce tetrahedron, cone, cylinder, if necessary. Ask for examples of various solids from around the room. Ensure that pupils are familiar with the terms 2D, 3D, two-dimensional, three-dimensional.

Activities

Whole class

Describe various 2D and 3D shapes to the class using vocabulary learnt and reviewed so far. Where possible describe the shapes by listing 3 or 4 properties. Initially stop after the first property and ask for suggestions:

My shape has 4 sides – what might it be?
My shape has a right angle (or 4 right angles)
My shape is regular – what might it be?

Continue with descriptions. Ask pupils to guess what shape you are describing. If you have sufficient sets of shape cards, pupils could be encouraged to hold up the card they think is correct.

Individual/pair

Copymaster 9. Pupils could be asked to draw some examples of their own, or to look through household catalogues to find pictures which approximate to mathematical solids.

Differentiation

Higher ability pupils could be asked to provide sets of statements about a solid to be used to allow others to guess the solid, following the model from the earlier part of the lesson.

Plenary

Ask pupils to share their copymaster ideas with the rest of the class. Ask for descriptions of solids and shapes and encourage pupils to use the vocabulary covered in the lesson.

Lesson 4

Introduction

Define faces, edges and vertices of solids. Use the set of solids and ask how many faces, edges and vertices each solid has. Ensure that pupils can identify the solid by name.

Activities

Whole class

Continue as with the introductory activity. Look at the faces of various solids. Are all the faces the same shape? What 2D shapes can you see as a face of a solid? If you covered one face of the solid with paint and used it to print, what shape would it be? Ensure that all pupils understand and can use the associated vocabulary.

Individual/pair

Copymaster 10 – name the solid.

Differentiation

Higher ability pupils could be asked to attempt to draw some of the solids.

Plenary

Ask what facts pupils have established about prisms, *e.g. the cross section is the same along the whole length*. What different shapes can you find on a prism? For example, a cuboid may have two square faces and four rectangular faces.

Lesson 5

Introduction

Recap facts covered in this theme. Ensure that pupils are able to classify shapes and solids according to given criteria, *e.g. Can you name a solid which has six square faces? What name do we give to a triangle with two sides the same length?*

Activities

Whole class

Investigation into shape using tessellations. Pupils will need a selection of shapes to use as templates. Pupils should be asked to investigate: Which shapes fit together without gaps? Are there any shapes which tessellate but leave regular gaps? Do only regular shapes tessellate?
Pupils should also be asked to investigate what happens if you put two shapes together to form a different shape, *e.g. two rectangles can be put together to form a square, another rectangle or an octagon. Two hexagons will make a decagon.*

Individual/pair

Pupils should be asked to draw examples of the tessellation patterns they make and should write down any interesting facts from their investigation.

Differentiation

Higher ability pupils could investigate ways of fitting 3D shapes together. Make 3D shapes using centimetre cubes and investigate which would fit together.

Plenary

Review vocabulary. You might like to look at the work of Escher.

Theme 6 — Number patterns

Objectives
- Recognise and extend number sequences formed by counting from any number in steps of constant size, *e.g. 25 to 500*
- Recognise odd and even numbers up to 1000 and some of their properties, *e.g. sums, differences of pairs of odd/even numbers*
- Solve number puzzles, recognise patterns, generalise and predict

Vocabulary
number, count, odd, even, every other, multiple of, digit, next, consecutive, sequence, continue, predict, pattern, pair, rule, relationship, sort, classify, property

Resources
Copymasters 11 and 12, Homework copymaster 6

Assessment
At the end of this theme is the pupil able to:
- Identify a rule which generates a sequence;
- Make statements about odd and even numbers;
- Recognise, describe and extend a number sequence?

Mental maths starter 4

Lesson 1

Introduction
Quick fire questions of the type: What number is 100 more than 300? Ask questions involving multiples of 10 initially then extend to other numbers. Choose an appropriate starting number and write it on the board. Ask 'What number do we get if we add 15?' 'What do we get if we add another 15?' Write down the series as it is formed. Repeat this as necessary.

Activities
Whole class
Write a series of numbers on the board. Ask pupils for the next numbers in the sequence. Ask how they worked out what the next number should be. Establish a procedure for working out the sequence, i.e. look at the difference between any pair of numbers and use this to add on.

Individual/pair
Copymaster 11 – number snakes. Complete the number sequences. Pupils could be asked to make up sequences for themselves and to ask a friend to find more terms.

Differentiation
Provide similar copymasters for *high attaining* pupils with more difficult tasks.

Plenary
Ask pupils to give an example of a number sequence and express the rule in words. Discuss alternative approaches to finding a rule from a given sequence.

Lesson 2

Introduction
Recap and define odd and even numbers. Give a number, between 1 and 20 initially, and ask whether the number is odd or even. Establish that all pupils are able to respond quickly and accurately. Extend this to numbers to 100. Note any pupils who have difficulty with this.
Ask how pupils work out whether a number is odd or even. Look for answers such as: even numbers end in 2; odd numbers end in 1; even numbers are in the two times table. Extend this to numbers to 1000.

Activities
Whole class
Pose the questions: 'What type of number do you get if you add even numbers together?' 'What type of number do you get if you add odd numbers together?' 'What type of number do you get if you add an odd and even number together?'

Individual/pair
Pupils are asked to investigate the answers to these questions. You may or may not wish them to make predictions before they undertake the investigation.
Pupils should work from a 100 square. One pupil picks two numbers from the square. The other writes the sum and the answer. Each pupil should end with 10 written sums. Identify which of the three possible sums has been produced (e + e, o + o or e + o) and for each decide whether the answer is odd or even.
Pose the questions: 'What type of number do you get if you take an even number from another even number?' 'An odd number from an even number?' 'An even number from an odd number?' 'An odd number from an odd number?' Ask pupils to make predictions based on their results from the first activity. Ask them to construct sums and investigate by taking pairs of numbers from the 100 square.

Differentiation
Higher ability pupils should investigate larger numbers.

Plenary
Establish rules for odd and even numbers and formulate these in words.

Autumn Term

Lesson 3

Introduction
Write a number on the board. Ask for the next number in the counting sequence. Ask for the next number. Introduce the term *consecutive numbers*. Repeat this several times. Ask pupils for starting numbers. Show that you can obtain consecutive numbers by counting backwards or by adding one to and subtracting one from the starting number.

Activities
Whole class
Ask for three consecutive numbers between given limits. Ask for the total of the three numbers. Repeat this several times. Ask if the pupils can see any patterns in the totals they have calculated.

Individual/pair
Investigate whether the sum of two consecutive numbers is odd or even. Investigate the sum of three consecutive numbers in the same way. What happens if you add four consecutive numbers? Can you find a rule? Does it make a difference whether you start with an odd or an even number?

Differentiation
Higher ability pupils could be encouraged to make predictions about sums of more than four consecutive numbers. Can they work out a rule by writing odd or even in place of the real numbers? (write o + e + o + e instead of 5 + 6 + 7 + 8).

Plenary
Establish general rules and formulate these in words.

Lesson 4

Introduction
Ask pupils to guess the number you are thinking of. Clues could be of the type: I think of a number and add 5 tens. My answer is 56. What number did I start with? I think of a number and double it. I add 8 and the answer is 58. What number did I start with? I think of a number and double it. I double it again and the answer is 16. What number did I start with? Choose numbers and rules appropriate for the level at which the pupils are working.

Activities
Whole class
Provide each pupil with some scrap paper. Ask one pupil to write a starting number between any given limits, *e.g. 1 – 10, 20 – 50, less than 100*. Ask another pupil to write down a rule. Pupils should give you the paper without letting anyone else see. Putting an empty circle as the starting number, write a sequence of four or five numbers on the board which demonstrate the rule. Pupils have to offer both the missing number and the rule.

Individual/pair
Provide each pupil with a copy of Copymaster 11, with the numbers blanked out. Write in a rule and ask pupils to fill in the snakes. You could provide starting numbers if you wish, which could be filled in on the sheets or written on the board. If different groups were to work with different starting numbers this could provide the basis for some work on extending the number sequences.

Differentiation
Choose rules appropriate for various ability levels.

Plenary
Discuss effective ways of working out the rule. Do you have to have worked out the rule to guess the starting number?

Lesson 5

Introduction
Review work done during the week. Focus on the methods the pupils have used in their investigations. Discuss how pupils identify a rule. What ways do they use to test their hypotheses?

Activities
Whole class
Introduce the concept of a magic square to pupils and demonstrate how to set about finding the solution. Teachers should look for examples of magic squares to use or should develop some of their own. It is easy to produce magic squares using the fact that the sum of the rows, columns and diagonals is three times the centre number.
Other possibilities for investigation could include looking for patterns in a multiplication square. Which tables are all even numbers? Why is this?

Individual/pair
Copymaster 12 – number puzzles.
The three number squares on the copymaster derive from sets of consecutive numbers. Pupils are asked to identify number sequences and should be encouraged to investigate the diagonals and the centre rows and columns.

Differentiation
Higher ability pupils could be asked to develop quick ways of adding consecutive numbers, working from the fact that the sum of three consecutive numbers is three times the middle one.

Plenary
Focus on each type of number puzzle individually. Ask pupils to explain their methods and approaches to the solutions.

Theme 7 — Multiplication and division

Objectives
- Extend understanding of × and ÷ and their relationship to each other and to + and −
- Use doubling and halving of two-digit numbers, e.g. ×4 = double, double; ×5 = ×10 halve; ×20 = ×10 double; ×8 = ×4 double, $\frac{1}{4}$ = half of $\frac{1}{2}$
- Approximate using informal pencil and paper methods to multiply and divide

Vocabulary
lots of, groups of, times, product, multiply, multiplied by, multiple of, once, twice, three times, four times, times as (big, long, wide etc.), repeated, addition, array, row, column, double, halve, share, share equally, one each, two each, three each etc., group, in pairs, threes, tens, equal groups of, divide, divided by, divided into, divisible by, remainder, factor, quotient, inverse

Resources
Copymasters 13 and 14, Homework copymaster 7

Assessment
At the end of this theme is the pupil able to:
- Understand and explain inverse operations for addition and multiplication;
- Double and halve numbers and understand the process of repeated doubling;
- Calculate divisions using known tables facts?

Mental maths starter 10

Lesson 1

Introduction
Quick fire questions on basic tables skills. Use a variety of ways of asking the question, e.g. 'What is 4 times 5?' 'If you multiply 7 times 5 what is the answer?' 'What is the product of 3 and 9?' 'What number is 10 times bigger than 4?'

Activities
Whole class
Write an example of an addition sum and ask for a subtraction sum using the same numbers. Recap on the concept of inverse. Ask if anyone can suggest the inverse of multiplication. Say or write a multiplication sum and ask for the corresponding division sum.

Individual/pair
How many sums can you write from one fact, e.g. 4 × 8 = 32: related sums 32 ÷ 8 = …, 8 × 4 = …, 32 ÷ 4 = …

Differentiation
Give sums to *lower attainers* as above but give starter numbers to *higher attainers* and ask them to identify a range of possible sums.

Plenary
Encourage use of all appropriate vocabulary in discussion. Ask pupils to explain the task in their own words and explain their approaches.

Lesson 2

Introduction
Quick fire questions on doubles and halves. Ensure that the questions are phrased in a variety of ways. e.g. What is double…? What is twice…? What is half of…? etc.

Activities
Whole class
Ensure that pupils are confident with doubles and halves of all numbers to 20, doubles of multiples of 5 to 100 and doubles and halves of multiples of 10 to 1000. Demonstrate that a doubling sum can be written as multiplication, e.g. 40 × 2, or addition, e.g. 40 + 40.

Individual/pair
Work out repeated doubles and draw up tables, e.g. twice 30 = 60; four times 30 = twice 60 = 120 etc.

Differentiation
Lower attainers may need more guidance and support in the individual work.

Plenary
Ask for examples which result from repeated doubles. Is there any way of identifying such numbers quickly?

… Autumn Term

Lesson 3

Introduction
Check multiplication by 10, 100 and 1000 by quick fire questions.

Activities
Whole class
Write multiples of 10, 100 or 1000 on the board and ask pupils to suggest a sum involving one of those multiples which would give this answer. Establish that 500 could be the answer to the sum 5 × 100 or 50 × 10. Establish related division facts.
Explain the need for a reasonable estimate of the answer to a multiplication sum. Give examples close to multiples of 10, e.g. *21 × 4 approximates to 20 × 4; 48 × 3 approximates to 50 × 3*. Ask pupils to give approximate answers to various sums. Write the sums on the board as some pupils may have difficulty in deciding on the nearest multiple of 10 and would benefit from a little additional time. Having established the concept of approximation, demonstrate approaches to multiplication through partitioning, or other informal methods appropriate to the class.

Individual/pair
Copymaster 13.

Differentiation
Higher ability pupils could be provided with additional questions of a similar type, or make up questions to ask partners.

Plenary
Discuss how pupils approached the questions on the copymaster.

Lesson 4

Introduction
Halving chains. Write a number on the board and establish whether it is odd or even. Explain that the rule for the chain is: If the number is even, halve it and write the answer. If the number is odd, add 1 then halve it and write down the answer. Continue until you get to 1.

Activities
Whole class
Review work done on estimating answers from the previous lesson. Review previous work on division. Discuss the concept of sharing. Ask pupils to suggest ways in which they might approach a problem involving sharing. Discuss these methods and try to establish an appropriate method for use in this lesson.
Write a sum on the board, e.g. 38 ÷ 4. Ask pupils to apply the strategy established in the previous lesson to estimate a reasonable answer. Ask if they would expect the answer to be greater or smaller than their estimate. Demonstrate how pupils can use known tables facts to find the answer, i.e. 9 × 4 = 36 so the answer will be near 9 but this is not exact. Discuss the concept of a remainder.
Repeat this process until pupils are confident with this method.

Individual/pair
Copymaster 14.

Differentiation
Lower ability pupils would benefit from having access to a tables square. They may try to use drawing methods. Try to discourage this at this point and encourage use of a tables square instead.

Plenary
Review and discuss pupils' individual approaches to division. Establish rules which all pupils will be able to apply to future tasks. Ask pupils to explain their approaches to the tasks, especially those with remainders. What methods did they use?

Lesson 5

Introduction
Explain that the task for the lesson is to find some rules about number which will help them when they are asked to do multiplication sums. Review work done on number patterns to establish appropriate ways of formulating the rules.

Activities
Whole class
Establish rules for multiplication by 1 and 0. Ask what other rules pupils can suggest which are helpful for checking answers. Establish that all doubles are even numbers and all multiples of 2 are even numbers. Establish the relation between doubles and multiples of 2. Establish that all multiples of 10 have 0 in the units column.

Individual/pair
Provide each pair with a tables square and ask them to write out multiples of given numbers and look for patterns and rules similar to those discussed.

Differentiation
Lower ability pupils should be asked to look for rules involving:
Multiples of 5 Rule: multiples of 5 end in 0 or 5.
Multiples of 4 Rule: all multiples of 4 are double doubles.
Higher ability pupils could be asked to consider:
Multiples of 9 Rule: sum of digits is always 9 → if sum of digits in a number is 9 that number is divisible by 9.
Multiples of 3 Rule: sum of digits is 3, 6 or 9.

Plenary
Ask pupils to give details of any rules they discover and to explain their working and methods.

Theme 8 — Fractions

Objectives
- Use fraction notation
- Recognise that fractions are several parts of a whole, and mixed numbers
- Find fractions of shapes
- Relate fractions to division and find simple fractions of quantities

Vocabulary
part, equal parts, fraction, one whole, half, quarter, eighth, third, sixth, fifth, tenth, twentieth

Resources
Copymasters 7, 15 and 16, Homework copymaster 8

Assessment
At the end of this theme is the pupil able to:
- Identify a fraction of a shaded shape;
- Write fractions;
- Order fractions in terms of size;
- Calculate fractions of a number?

Lesson 1

Introduction
Discussion on halves and quarters. What do pupils understand by these terms? Can anyone define a half? Look for two parts, equal parts. Ask how you would find half of a cake, a bag of sweets etc. How many people are there in the class? How many in half the class? Can anyone define a quarter? How do you find a quarter of...?

Activities
Whole class
Draw a circle on the board. This represents a cake. Draw a line which cuts the circle into two obviously unequal parts. If I give you this – the smaller section – have I given you a half? Why not? Introduce the concept of equal shares.
Introduce and discuss thirds, fifths, sixths etc.

Individual/pair
Copymaster 15 – shade in named fractions.

Differentiation
Lower attainers may need additional support.

Plenary
Check the work done on the copymaster. Discuss what is shown when more than one area is shaded.

Lesson 2

Introduction
Understand relationships between $\frac{1}{4}$ and $\frac{3}{4}$ i.e. $\frac{3}{4}$ is $3 \times \frac{1}{4}$.
Halving numbers: What is half of...? What is half of that?

Activities
Whole class
Draw a number line on the board. Mark the line into 8 equal sections and write in 0, 1 and $\frac{1}{2}$. Indicate various points on the line and ask what fraction you are indicating.
Repeat with other lines divided into 10 sections and 12 sections.

Individual/pair
Copymaster 15. Write a fraction in each box and ask pupils to draw more lines and to shade in the appropriate areas to show these fractions. Demonstrate what they have to do by taking the first square – give the fraction $\frac{5}{6}$. Show where pupils would need to draw the lines.

Differentiation
Lower attainers will probably need more detailed explanation of the task.

Plenary
Discuss the relationships between fractions with the numerator 1 and those with the same denominator but increasing numerators. Ask pupils to identify fractions in terms of size. Establish that fractions with a larger denominator are smaller. Ask pupils to explain this in their own words.

Autumn Term

Lesson 3

Introduction
Draw shapes on the board and ask the class to estimate how much of each shape is shaded. Use irregular shapes as well as regular shapes. Use shapes divided into tenths.

Activities
Whole class
Investigate simple equivalent fractions through drawing. Shapes divided into twelve are particularly useful for this but continue to include tenths. Use diagrams of different sizes to illustrate that a half is a concept not a quantity, i.e. half of a metre square is not the same as half of a 10 cm square.
Individual/pair
Use Copymaster 7 and investigate what fractions can be easily illustrated with this sheet.

Differentiation
Some of the shapes can be cut into fractions more easily. Identify these and ask *low attainers* to work only with these. You could specify which fractions they should illustrate. *Higher attainers* may be asked to look for more than one way to cut the shapes.

Plenary
Discuss which shapes could easily be used to show fractions. Which ones were not suitable? Why not? Did all pupils choose to show the same fractions on the same shapes. Reiterate work on equivalent fractions if appropriate.

Lesson 4

Introduction
Ask how many people there are in the class. How many in half the class? How many in a quarter of the class? Demonstrate this by writing appropriate sums on the board using fraction notations.
Ask how pupils would go about working out how many people there are in half the class. Would they physically move people around? What sort of sum would they do?
Quick fire questions round the class on simple division.
Write some mixed numbers on the board. Ask pupils which part is the whole number and which the fraction.

Activities
Whole class
Oral work on simple problems involving numbers. 'A packet of sweets has 24 sweets in it. If I share it with two of my friends, how many do we get each?' 'What is a quarter of 44?' 'Half a kilo of apples is 3 apples. How many would I get in one kilo?'
Individual/pair
Copymaster 16 – fractions of numbers.

Differentiation
Lower attaining pupils might be asked to focus on fractions with numerator 1.

Plenary
Focus on the problem on the copymaster. Ask pupils to explain their reasoning and methods.

Lesson 5

Introduction
Draw three identical pictures of pencils on the board. Ask how many there are. Draw a picture of a half-size broken pencil. Ask 'How many now?' Pupils should say $3\frac{1}{2}$. Explain that the three full pencils are whole ones.
Repeat the process with a variety of shapes and easily identifiable fractional parts. Expect answers such as $4\frac{1}{4}$ or 4 whole ones and $\frac{1}{4}$.

Activities
Whole class
Write several mixed numbers on the board and ask pupils to tell you what they are. Give some examples of mixed numbers and ask pupils to write them down.
Discuss how you can tell which numbers are bigger, e.g. Which is bigger – $2\frac{1}{2}$ or $2\frac{1}{4}$?
Write several fractions, with numerator 1, on the board. Ask pupils to identify the largest and smallest. Ask if pupils can decide on a rule which can be applied to all fractions, i.e. that the larger the denominator the smaller the fraction.
Discuss the relative sizes of fractions with the same denominator and different numerators.
Individual/pair
Ask pupils to draw a number line from 0 to 3, with spacing to allow for eighths.
Write several mixed numbers on the board and ask pupils to mark these on the number line.

Differentiation
Higher attaining pupils could be asked to draw fraction strips to compare the relative sizes of various fractions.
If necessary, *low attaining* pupils could compare fractions by drawing and shading methods.

Plenary
Review any rules established which will help put fractions in size order. Ask pupils how they made decisions about the positioning of mixed numbers on the number line.

Theme 9 — Time

Objectives
- Consolidate understanding of subtraction as the inverse of addition
- Find a small difference by counting up. Use the relationship between + and − to develop written methods for + and − of whole numbers less than 1000
- Use, read and write the vocabulary of time
- Read time to 1 min on analogue/12-hour digital clock
- Use digital time, am and pm
- Solve time word puzzles

Vocabulary
time, Monday, Tuesday…, January, February…, spring, summer, autumn, winter, day, week, fortnight, month, year, leap year, century, millennium, weekend, birthday, holiday, calendar, date, date of birth, morning, afternoon, evening, night, am, pm, noon, midnight, today, yesterday, tomorrow, before, after, next, last, now, soon, early, late, earliest, latest, quick, quicker, quickest, quickly, fast, faster, fastest, slow, slower, slowest, slowly, old, older, oldest, new, newer, newest, takes longer, takes less time, how long ago? how long will it be? how long will it take to? timetable, arrive, depart, hour, minute, second, o'clock, half past, quarter to, quarter past, clock, watch, hands, digital/analogue clock, timer, how often? always, never, sometimes, usually

Resources
Copymasters 17 and 18, Homework copymaster 9, time dominoes or similar game, analogue clock for display

Assessment
At the end of this theme is the pupil able to:
- Read the time on a digital and analogue clock;
- Use and understand am and pm;
- Read and write times in words and numbers?

Lesson 1

Introduction
Quick fire questions — 24 add 13 makes 37. What is 37 take away 13? Extend this to larger numbers. When pupils demonstrate that they are confident, ask how they know what the answer is. Discuss the link between addition and subtraction.

Activities
Whole class
Review the work done in Theme 1 lesson 4 (counting on). Draw a number line on the board. Show, for example, 62 as a jump of 19 and 81. Ask what sums this number line could represent. It could be 62 plus 19, or 81 minus 62 if the question is phrased as 'How many more than 62 is 81?' Write the sums on the board. Draw more number lines to demonstrate subtraction by counting on and ask pupils to identify appropriate sums.
Review written methods of addition. Ensure that pupils can set out written sums in columns. Check pupils are secure in additions which involve crossing the tens boundary.

Individual/pair
Use appropriate books or other printed materials to consolidate.

Differentiation
Set work at levels appropriate for varying ability range.

Plenary
Discuss examples worked by the pupils. Ask them to describe the methods they used. Ask them to describe and demonstrate any pencil and paper methods.

Lesson 2

Introduction
Quick fire questions — add single digit numbers to any 3 or 4 digit number crossing the tens boundary. Review basic subtraction number bonds of numbers to 20 and subtraction of a single-digit number from any 3 or 4 digit number crossing the tens boundary. Ask 'How did you work out these sums?' Relate to their knowledge of the basic number bonds.

Activities
Whole class
Develop written subtraction methods for subtraction of 3 or 4 digit numbers without carrying. Demonstrate standard written methods of subtraction involving decomposition.

Individual/pair
Use appropriate books or other printed materials to consolidate.

Differentiation
Set work at levels appropriate for varying ability range.

Plenary
Discuss examples worked by the pupils. Ask them to describe the methods they used. Ask them to describe and demonstrate any pencil and paper methods. Ask pupils to demonstrate their approaches on the board.

Autumn Term

Lesson 3

Introduction

Discuss your plan for the day's lessons. Ask what time the school day starts. What time is play time? What time is lunch time? Show these times on an analogue clock face. Discuss the use of digital clocks. Which do pupils find it easier to read? Check understanding of units: how many minutes in an hour etc.

Activities

Whole class

Check pupils' understanding and ability to read times on an analogue clock face.

Individual/pair

Daily diary – how long did you spend on various activities?

Differentiation

Provide additional sheets for *low attainers* which indicate appropriate blocks of time e.g. hour or half hour intervals. *Higher attainers* pupils should be encouraged to consider time blocks in other intervals.

Plenary

Discuss and compare diaries. Check understanding of am and pm.

Lesson 4

Introduction

What do we mean by am and pm? Recap on digital and analogue clock faces. Ensure understanding of the relationship between 10.30 and half past 10, 6.45 and a quarter to seven, 12.15 and a quarter past 12.

Activities

Whole class

Measuring time. How do we measure time? What other ways are there of measuring time (kitchen timers, egg timer, sundials etc.)? How long is a minute? Ask the class to try to measure a minute. Sit quietly with your eyes closed. Put up your hand when you think a minute has passed. Who gets closest? Did those people have a way of working this out (*e.g. counting*)?

Individual/pair

Copymaster 17 – reading times. Once pupils have written in the appropriate times they could be asked questions based on times shown, *e.g. How long is it from the time shown on* a *until the time shown on* b? *How many minutes before 2 o'clock does clock* g *show? What time does clock* f *show? How long is it until...?*

Differentiation

Lower ability pupils could be provided with cards giving appropriate 'time' words. When attempting the final task they could cut out the clock faces and order in this way. *High attainers* should be asked to read times to minutes, particularly using an analogue clock face.

Plenary

Check that lower attainers are secure with reading analogue clocks. Discuss the final task. Why does it specify times between 8 am and 8 pm. What differences might there be in the order if this had not been specified?

Lesson 5

Introduction

Quick fire questions – What time is 10 minutes after 10.30? What time is 3 minutes before 11 o'clock? How many minutes is it from 2.55 to 3.04?

Activities

Whole class

Discuss time: adding minutes and hours and minutes. Use an analogue clock to ask pupils questions about time. Set times and ask for answers to the nearest minute. Demonstrate how an analogue clock face can help solve problems of the type 'How long until..?' 'How long ago was..?'

Individual/pair

Copymaster 18 – on time puzzles. Time dominoes game to allow practice in matching digital and analogue times.

Differentiation

Lower ability pupils would benefit if they could have access to analogue clocks as demonstrated in the earlier part of the lesson.

Plenary

Discuss the problems from the copymaster. Ask pupils to explain how they worked out the answers.

Theme 10 Handling data

Objectives
- Solve a given problem by collecting, classifying, representing and interpreting data in tally charts, frequency tables and pictograms (symbols representing 2, 5, 10 units)

Vocabulary
count, tally, sort, vote, survey, questionnaire, data graph, block graph, pictogram, represent, group, set, list, chart, bar chart, tally chart, table, frequency table, Carroll diagram, Venn diagram, label, title, axis, axes, diagram, most popular, most common, least popular, least common

Resources
Collection of pictures of forms of motor transport (encourage pupils to collect a variety of pictures of cars, agricultural vehicles, lorries etc.), Copymasters 19 and 20, Homework copymaster 10

Assessment
At the end of this theme is the pupil able to:
- Construct and interpret a tally chart;
- Decide on an appropriate symbol for a pictogram;
- Display information on a pictogram;
- Read and interpret information from a pictogram?

Lesson 1

Introduction
Focus on the information from pupils' daily diaries (Theme 9 lesson 3). Identify four of the most common activities. List these on the board.

Activities
Whole class
Draw a tally chart on the board to demonstrate the format. Ask each pupil to say which of the four activities they would most like to do and mark responses on the tally chart.

Demonstrate how this information could be displayed on a pictogram. Discuss appropriate symbols.

Individual/pair
Copymaster 19 – interpreting data from a pictogram on favourite activities.

Differentiation
More able pupils could be asked to collect data from the class on favourite subjects and could produce a pictogram of their own following the copymaster model.

Plenary
Discuss what symbols are appropriate for display. Identify the half symbol and discuss what it means.

Lesson 2

Introduction
Discuss what sort of data would be appropriate for display on a pictogram.

Activities
Whole class
Use the collections of pictures of vehicles. Display some of the pictures and ask pupils to identify appropriate groupings. List these groups on the board and recap on how to construct a tally chart. Hold up each picture and ask which group it should be placed in. Mark each on the tally chart. Ensure that marks are grouped in fives to enable pupils to count up tally marks easily at the end. Show how the information from a tally chart can be displayed on a frequency table. Decide, as a class, what symbol would be appropriate for a pictogram to display this information.

Individual/pair
Ask pupils to copy the frequency table and draw a pictogram to display the information.

Differentiation
More able pupils could be asked to identify other sets from the pictures and to construct their own tally chart and frequency table for these new sets.

Plenary
Discuss how effective this method is for displaying information: how you can read a pictogram; the need for titles etc.

Autumn Term

Lesson 3

Introduction
Ask each pupil to draw two basic house shapes on squared paper. Write a list on the board of features the houses may have, e.g. 1 chimney, 2 chimneys, no chimney, 2, 3 or 4 windows, 1 or 2 doors etc. Ask children to add some of these features to their drawings.

Activities
Whole class
Decide, with the class, which information you want to display on a pictogram. Do you want to include all the features you have listed or only some of them? Use a tally chart to collect the data on the house pictures. This could be done by a simple count of hands. Draw the tally chart on the board. Decide on an appropriate symbol for the pictogram.

Individual/pair
Construct a frequency table from the tally chart and draw a pictogram to show this information.

Differentiation
Lower attaining pupils may need support to transfer the information from the tally chart to the frequency table.

Plenary
Review the vocabulary used. Ask pupils to explain the terms in their own words. Ask pupils to explain the link between the numbers on the frequency table and the symbols on the pictogram.

Lesson 4

Introduction
Draw a tally chart on the board. Ask questions which relate to this. The tally chart could be based on work done in the previous lessons or could relate to entirely new data.

Activities
Whole class
Review drawing a pictogram. Refer to any point from the plenary session of the previous lesson. Review the choice of an appropriate symbol.
Give the copymaster to the pupils and discuss the information given on the tally charts.
Discuss the results on the class frequency table. What symbol will be appropriate for this pictogram? In what ways might it need to be different from the pictogram for the group results?

Individual/pair
Copymaster 20. Construct a tally chart and frequency table. Draw pictograms from the given data.

Differentiation
Lower attaining pupils may need support when dealing with the larger numbers of the class frequency table.
Ask *higher attaining* pupils to work in pairs to produce a set of questions which could be answered by using the pictogram of the class results. Refer back to Copymaster 19 to see the sorts of question they could ask.

Plenary
Ask pupils to explain how they transferred the data from the tally chart to the frequency table.
Ask questions which need pupils to refer to the pictograms to provide the answers, or use any questions produced by the higher attaining pupils.

Lesson 5

Introduction
Explain to pupils that they have to work in groups to decide on a topic on which to collect information and to think of the best way to display this information.

Activities
Whole class
Discuss possible appropriate topics and decide on a final list from which pupils select the most appropriate for their group. Topics could be: shoe sizes, heights (although this may be too complex as it would be more appropriate to use grouped data), favourite sports, favourite TV programmes or favourite books. (For these last three, provide a list of options and ask pupils to choose from the lists or the data may be too widespread to be of use.) You may like to collect weather data over a long period of time and use this at a later date.

Group/pair
Each group should decide on the topic most interesting to them. They should collect data from the rest of the class and should present the data appropriately. Use all stages for classroom display work.

Differentiation
Lower ability pupils may need greater guidance in selecting an appropriate topic and also in the collection of the data.

Plenary
Ask pupils to tell you why they selected their chosen topic; how they collected their data; what symbol they chose to represent the numbers on their pictogram. Discuss any difficulties they had. Encourage pupils to use appropriate vocabulary when they are explaining their approaches.

Theme 1 — Mental calculation

Objectives
- Understand the principle of the associative law for + not −
- Add several small numbers by finding pairs that total 10, 9 or 11
- Partition into tens and units, adding tens first
- Add 3 two-digit multiples of 10

Vocabulary
add, addition, more, plus, increase, sum, total, altogether, double, near double, subtract, take away, minus, decrease, between, half, halve, equals, inverse, difference between, how many?

Resources
Copymasters 21 and 22, Homework copymaster 11, set of single digit cards per group

Assessment
At the end of this theme is the pupil able to:
- Understand and explain that addition is associative but subtraction is not;
- Find pairs of numbers which sum to 9, 10 and 11 and use these in calculation;
- Partition numbers into tens and units and use this to add 2 digit numbers?

Mental maths starter 1

Lesson 1

Introduction
Quick fire questions on addition and subtraction of numbers to 20. Check understanding of adding a single digit number to 10, 9 and 11.

Activities
Whole class
Write several single digit numbers on the board in random order. Ask pupils to say which pairs equal 10, which pairs equal 9, which pairs equal 11. Expect fast responses. When pupils are secure with the identification of such pairs, say a single digit and ask what you would need to add to get the answer 10, 11 or 9.
Move to adding 3 digit numbers. Use the digits written on the board and identify 3 digits to be added. Demonstrate the technique of appropriate selection by choosing two numbers which equal 10, or nearly 10. Oral practice using this technique.

Group/pair
Work in groups of 3. Each group will need a pack of digit cards shared between the members of the group. Each pupil turns over and displays a card. The first pupil to say the correct answer scores a point. Groups should play until one person scores 10 points.

Differentiation
Lower ability pupils may need additional support whilst playing the game.
Higher ability pupils could identify all possible combinations of 3 single digit numbers and their totals.

Plenary
Ask pupils to explain their strategies for quickly adding 3 single digits. Ask pupils if they could have played this game as a subtraction game. Ask for reasons why it wouldn't have worked.

Lesson 2

Introduction
Recap on previous lesson on pairs of numbers summing to 9, 10 and 11. Ask for sums giving numbers in reverse order. Point out that answers to addition sums will be the same irrespective of order. Can the same be done for subtraction? Sums involving three numbers can be done in any order. Demonstrate. Can the same be done for subtraction?

Activities
Whole class
Review work on adding 3 numbers. Write 20 single digit numbers on the board. Give a target number and ask pupils to suggest 3 numbers to make the target. This is quite a challenging exercise for some pupils and teachers may need to demonstrate approaches several times.

Individual/pair
Copymaster 21 – number cards. Make as many sums as you can involving 3 of these number cards. Write down the sums showing how you could use your knowledge of pairs summing to 10 to make them easy.

Differentiation
Lower ability pupils would be helped by giving them 3 counters to put on the cards so they know which cards they are working with at the time.
Higher ability pupils could be asked to investigate highest and lowest sums for their given set of cards.

Plenary
Ask pupils how they set about doing the copymaster task. Did they construct sums at random or did they work through in a logical order? If the latter, what sorts of techniques did they apply?

Spring Term

Lesson 3

Introduction
Quick fire questions of pairs of numbers involving multiples of 10 to 100.

Activities
Whole class
Check understanding of place value. Write a selection of numbers to 100 on the board and ask 'Which of these numbers has a twenty in it?' 'Which has a fifty in it?' 'Which have a two in them?' etc. Point to a number and ask for a pair of numbers which give this as an answer. Say that one of the numbers must be the biggest possible multiple of 10. Ask for the similar pairs which sum to the other numbers on the board.
Write two two-digit numbers on the board and demonstrate the method of adding by partitioning. Ask pupils to split the numbers into tens and units. Add the tens and note the answer, then add the units. Use examples which do not cross the tens barrier initially, then move on to these as pupils develop a competency.

Individual/pair
Copymaster 22 – partitioning numbers.

Differentiation
Lower attaining pupils could be set further questions similar to those in the first section before moving on to the addition sums.

Plenary
Discuss the similarities of techniques in adding single digit numbers and multiples of 10. Review the techniques pupils used to work out the addition sums on the copymaster. Note any areas of difficulty and focus on these in the next lesson.

Lesson 4

Introduction
Recap on partition of numbers. Ask 'What number is in the tens column of...?' Quick fire questions adding multiples of 10. Ask 'What number is in the units column of...?' Quick fire questions – addition of a 2-digit number plus a single digit number crossing the tens boundary.

Activities
Whole class
Demonstrate the techniques of adding partitioned numbers. Review the work done in the previous lesson. Use a number line if necessary. Focus on any areas of difficulty noted in the previous lesson.

Individual/pair
Set appropriate addition examples which need partitioning. Encourage pupils to find ways to record their answers.

Differentiation
Ensure *lower ability* pupils are confident with place value.

Plenary
Review the techniques used by the pupils. Ask pupils to explain how they set about the tasks. What methods did they use to make it easier to do these sums?

Lesson 5

Introduction
Review the techniques used to add 3 single digit numbers and apply this to multiples of 10. Use this to add 3 two-digit multiples of 10. Quick fire questions.

Activities
Whole class
Ask pupils to draw a 3 × 3 square. Tell pupils to choose 9 numbers (which should be multiples of 10) within the range 30 to 200. Call out sums which involve adding 3 such numbers. Pupils cross off any answers which occur in their squares. The winner is the first to cross off all the numbers. It is useful to have a set of sums prepared in advance.

Individual/pair
Ask pupils to draw another square and complete with a further set of numbers. You could use the same restrictions or numbers in a different range. Each pupil passes their square to a partner and the partner is asked to write a sum for each number on the square.

Differentiation
Lower attaining pupils could be limited to sums which involve adding only 2 numbers.
Higher attainers might be asked to look for numbers to add which are not multiples of 10.

Plenary
Discuss the possible sums which will give you the answers required.

Theme 2 — Money problems

Objectives
- Develop and refine written methods for addition and subtraction including money
- Choose appropriate number operations and calculation methods to solve money and 'real life' problems with one or more steps
- Explain working. Check with equivalent calculation

Vocabulary
money, coin, note, penny, pence, pound, price, cost, buy, bought, sell, sold, spent, spend, pay, change, costs more, costs less, cheaper, less/least expensive, how much how many? total, amount, value

Resources
Copymasters 23 and 24, Homework copymaster 12, money cards, examples for practice in adding and subtracting TU

Assessment
At the end of this theme is the pupil able to:
- Add and subtract sums of money using mental and written methods;
- Work out how much more money is needed to buy an object;
- Work out how much change should be given;
- Work out money problems?

Lesson 1

Introduction
Check understanding of money. Establish that 100p = £1.00. Quick fire questions – 'How many pennies in £…?'

Activities
Whole class
Oral questions using small sums of money, e.g. 'If I spend 45p and 20p, how much do I spend altogether?' 'I have £1.00 and I spend 28p. What change will I get?' When pupils are secure, introduce sums involving whole £1.00 including £5, £10 and £20. Finally move to questions using sums of money involving £p appropriate to the level at which the class is working.

Individual/pair
Use cards with various sums of money from 10p to £1.00. Provide each pair with 16–20 cards. Pupils work individually and take 2 cards. The pupil writes the sum and the answer. This could be extended by asking pupils to calculate how much change they would have from £5.00. Set a time limit and challenge pupils to see how many sums they can do within that time.

Differentiation
Higher ability pupils could pick 3 or more cards. Cards provided for *lower ability* pupils could be limited to multiples of 5 or in other appropriate ways.

Plenary
Discuss the strategies pupils used to work out the answers. Did any use the partitioning methods they learnt in Theme 1?

Lesson 2

Introduction
Quick fire questions on adding pairs of single digit numbers. Review adding 3 single digit numbers.

Activities
Whole class
Write any sum involving 2 numbers to 100 on the board and ask pupils how they would set about doing the sum. Establish the method of working in TU with carrying. Demonstrate this several times, offering opportunities to all pupils to participate. Ensure that all pupils are secure with the concept of carrying.

Individual/pair
Provide appropriate examples for practice.

Differentiation
Lower ability pupils should be provided with examples involving carrying in only the T or the U column.
Higher ability pupils could be asked to sum three TU numbers.

Plenary
Review the ways in which pupils tackled the sums. Establish that the numbers can be written in any order. Ask why it is necessary to carry numbers when a column sums to more than 10.

Spring Term

Lesson 3

Introduction
Quick fire questions on subtracting single digit numbers from 10.

Activities
Whole class
Write any subtraction sum involving 2 numbers to 100 on the board and ask pupils how they would set about doing the sum. Ensure that in the initial sums it is not necessary to cross the tens boundary.
Review methods involving decomposition.
Demonstrate this several times, offering opportunities to all pupils to participate. Ensure that all pupils are secure with the concept of decomposition.
Individual/pair
Provide appropriate examples for practice.

Differentiation
Higher ability pupils should be provided with examples involving HTU – TU.

Plenary
Ask pupils to explain how they set about the calculations provided for them. Discuss why we need to use decomposition.

Lesson 4

Introduction
Quick fire questions on money sums. Giving change – 'I have a £5.00 note and I spend … How much change will I get?' 'Billy collects 2p pieces. He has 10. How much money does he have?' 'Gemma collects 10p pieces. She has £1.20. How many coins does she have?'

Activities
Whole class
Review the work done on shopping lists in the Autumn term. If the price lists produced for those lessons is appropriate it could be used for this lesson. Otherwise you may like to provide a new list with more difficult prices for use. Set problems based on the price lists, e.g. 'I buy a… costing… and a… costing… What sum do I need to write?' Write the sum and demonstrate following the method used in lesson 2.
'I had… in my purse when I went shopping and I spent… How much money did I have left? What sum do I need to write?' Write the sum and demonstrate how to do it following the method used in lesson 3.
Show how money sums need to be set out.
Individual/pair
Copymaster 23 – adding and subtraction sums with money. You may like to cut the copymaster in two.

Differentiation
Higher ability pupils could be asked to do sums involving subtraction from £10.00, £20.00 etc, although this involves more complex decomposition.

Plenary
Ask which sums were easy and which were hard. Ask pupils to recap on the methods used and to link their working with the work done in previous lessons.

Lesson 5

Introduction
Write a set of coins on the board and a list of appropriate prices. Ask quick fire questions relating to these: 'Which item is dearer, costs most, costs least…?' 'Which of these could I buy if I had £1.00…?' 'What coins could you use to pay for…?'

Activities
Whole class
Recap on addition and subtraction using money from the previous lesson. Set a simple problem in words and ask pupils to identify the type of sum they would need to do. Ask some simple questions which involve multiplying. Ask simple division questions if appropriate.
Ask pupils to explain how they would approach the problems you have set. Ensure that pupils are secure with the methods needed before starting on the copymaster.
Individual/pair
Copymaster 24 – real life problems.

Differentiation
Provide *higher attaining* pupils with similar problems which involve more difficult calculations.

Plenary
While pupils are working on the sheet, note any problems and concentrate on these during the plenary session. Ask pupils to explain their methods and working.

Theme 3 — Measuring mass

Objectives
- Estimate and check times using seconds, minutes, hours
- Measure and compare using kilograms and grams and know and use the relationship between them. Know $\frac{1}{4}, \frac{1}{2}, \frac{3}{4}$ and $\frac{1}{10}$ of a kilogram in grams
- Suggest suitable units and equipment to estimate or measure mass
- Read scales
- Record measurements to a suitable degree of accuracy, using mixed units or the nearest whole/half/quarter unit

Vocabulary
seconds, minutes, hours, mass, big, bigger, small, smaller, balances, weight, heavy/light, heavier/lighter, heaviest/lightest, weigh, weighs, kilogram, half-kilogram, gram, balance, scales

Resources
Copymasters 25 and 26, Homework copymaster 13, scales and assorted weight, cards with weights in mixed units, cards with shopping items and their weights, product labels collected in advance, one or more simple recipes

Assessment
At the end of this theme is the pupil able to:
- Read time from an analogue or digital clock;
- Know that there are 1000 g in 1 kg and compare weights written in either (or mixed) units;
- Read weights from various scales;
- Understand balancing?

Lesson 1

Introduction
Review previous work on time. How many minutes in an hour? Days in a week? Seconds in a minute? Review other associated vocabulary, e.g. *o'clock, half past, quarter to, ten past, forty-five etc.* Ensure pupils can read and say these times.

Activities
Whole class
Devise appropriate word problems for oral work. Review telling the time on an analogue clock. Ask pupils to draw the hands on an analogue clock face when given a digital clock face. Look at digital displays with seconds. Look at the role of the second hand on an analogue clock. Establish that there are 60 seconds in a minute.
Ask questions involving 'How long is it...?' e.g. 'What is the time now? ... What time is playtime? ... How long until playtime?' 'What time do we go home? ... How long until we go home?'
Ask questions involving 'What time will it be in...' e.g. 'What time will it be in 10 minutes?' 'What time will it be in half an hour?' 'What time will it be in two hours?'

Individual/pair
Set problems which ask pupils to work out how long between two given times. These could be real life problems of the type 'It is half past eight. John takes 10 minutes to get to school. What time will he arrive?'

Differentiation
Lower attaining pupils should be secure with digital times.
Higher attaining pupils should be able to read an analogue clock to the nearest minute.

Plenary
Discuss how you work out how long from one time to another. Ask pupils to explain how they calculate differences in time. Focus on any difficulties pupils have in reading analogue clock faces.

Lesson 2

Introduction
Measuring mass – what units do we use to measure mass? How many grams in a kilogram? What is the clue in the word kilogram which tells us this? Explain that we can use both weight and mass in everyday conversation. You may like to stick with the word weight but pupils should be introduced to the word mass.

Activities
Whole class
Ask the question 'What sorts of things do we need to measure?' Write a list on the board of items given by pupils. Ask for suggestions for the approximate mass for these items. Ask how many grams in a kilogram, how many grams in $\frac{1}{2}$ kilogram, in $\frac{1}{4}$ kilogram, in $\frac{3}{4}$ kilogram.
Pupils could be asked to collect examples of product labels for display work.

Individual/pair
Game – how heavy is my shopping basket? Have prepared cards for use. Use labels from everyday items if appropriate, or make up suitable items and weights if preferred.
This activity could be played as a game with pupils picking just two cards and giving the total orally, or as a paper and pencil exercise where pupils pick up to 5 cards and write the list with the weights before calculating the total.

Differentiation
Lower attaining pupils should be encouraged to work out $\frac{1}{4}$ by halving then halving again.

Plenary
Discuss the need to change weights over 1000 g to kg. Are there any difficulties involved in working with numbers to 1000? Ask pupils if there are any strategies they use to make adding easier.

Spring Term

Lesson 3

Introduction
What do we use to measure mass? Look at different types of scales – pupils could be asked to collect pictures from catalogues. It would be helpful to obtain large scale pictures or posters.

Activities
Whole class
Reading scales. Look at various types of scales. Pupils should be given the opportunity for practical activities if possible. Look carefully at different ways of measuring, different scales etc.

Individual/pair
Copymaster 25 – reading different types of scales.

Differentiation
Lower attaining pupils will need much practice, both with practical activities and reading scales.

Plenary
Discuss any difficulties with reading various types of scales. Review the need to measure mass and discuss which units are appropriate measures for given items. Consider different types of scales and balances as discussed in the first part of the lesson.

Lesson 4

Introduction
Quick fire questions on comparison of weight using everyday items, e.g. 'The tin of beans is 250 g, the tin of tomatoes is 200 g. Which is heavier? How much heavier?' 'My bar of chocolate is 125 g. The next size is twice as big. What will that one weigh?'

Activities
Whole class
Continue work on comparisons. Write a set of weights on the board and ask pupils to put these in size order. Write a list of everyday items on the board and ask pupils to suggest a list in size order.

Individual/pair
Set of cards with appropriate mass written in mixture of grams and kilograms.

Pupils work in pairs. Each pupil takes a card. The pupil with the greater mass scores a point.
Pupils could be asked to write the pair of weights and record either the total or the difference between the two.

Differentiation
Lower ability pupils should be asked to add the masses, *higher ability* pupils should be asked to work out what should be added to make them the same.

Plenary
Review comparisons of mass. Review the use of mixed units and changing from grams to kilograms or mixed units. Ask pupils to explain how they did this. Ask pupils to explain how they made decisions about size order.

Lesson 5

Introduction
Review work done in lesson 2 on fractions of a kilogram. Establish that 500 g = $\frac{1}{2}$ kg and the number of grams in $\frac{1}{4}$ kg and $\frac{3}{4}$ kg. Ask pupils to change a given mass in kg to g, including fractions of a kg.

Activities
Whole class
Write a list of everyday items on the board, e.g. those used in the game in lesson 2. Ask pupils to suggest appropriate weights for these. Write a further list including much heavier items and repeat.

Write a recipe on the board, e.g. a cake recipe. Ask pupils to calculate appropriate measurements for two cakes.

Individual/pair
Copymaster 26 – problem solving. Pupils should work in pairs. They should be told that there may be more than one approach to solving these problems.

Differentiation
Pair *higher attainers* with *lower attainers* for the pair work.

Plenary
Ask pupils to explain their approaches to solving these problems. Discuss various options where pupils have suggested different ideas.

33

Theme 4 Area

Objectives
- Measure and calculate areas of rectangles and simple shapes, using counting methods and standard units (cm^2)
- Choose appropriate number operations and counting methods to solve measurement word problems with one or more steps
- Explain working

Vocabulary
length, width, height, depth, breadth, long, short, longer, shorter, longest, shortest, kilometre, metre, centimetre, millimetre, ruler, measure, measuring, estimate, area, covers, surface, square, centimetre, cm^2

Resources
Copymasters 27 and 28, Homework copymaster 14, transparent cm^2 grid or tracing paper marked in cm^2, A5 paper and appropriate shapes

Assessment
At the end of this theme is the pupil able to:
- Discuss appropriate units for the measurement of area;
- Measure area by counting;
- Calculate the area of a square or rectangle;
- Calculate the area of a complex shape which can be cut into 2 or more rectangles?

Lesson 1

Introduction
What is area? How do we measure flat surfaces? Recap of linear measurement. Why might we need to measure areas?

Activities
Whole class
Explain that pupils are going to investigate ways of measuring area. Ask for suggestions as to how they might go about this task. Explain that we need to find ways of covering a flat surface that can be used to make comparisons.

Individual/pair
Provide an A5 sheet of paper for each child and an appropriate card or plastic shape to draw round. Ask the pupils to fill their sheet with the shape – leaving no spaces, or as little space as possible.

Differentiation
Lower ability pupils should be given square or rectangular shapes.
Higher ability pupils could be given circles or more complex shapes.

Plenary
Discuss which shapes were appropriate for the task. Ask pupils to tell you their answers. Point out that they all started with the same sized piece of paper. How could they have ensured that their answers were consistent?

Lesson 2

Introduction
Review work done in plenary session of previous lesson. Introduce the term *square centimetre*.

Activities
Whole class
Introduce the concept of measuring in square centimetres. Draw a rectangle on the board and demonstrate how it can be divided into square centimetres. Draw an irregular shape on the board. Discuss ways of finding the area of this shape. Draw squares over the shape and shade in and count all the complete squares. Ask what can be done about the part squares. Look for half squares. Explain that the convention is to count as one a square which is more than half covered and ignore those which are less than half covered.

Individual/pair
Finding areas of irregular shapes by drawing and counting. Pupils could be given prepared shapes to use or could be asked to find the area of classroom objects by drawing round them. Use the perimeter sheet to find areas by drawing.

Differentiation
Lower ability pupils might be given grids predrawn on tracing paper or acetate. Commercially produced grids are available.

Plenary
Discuss the methods pupils used for recording the squares they have counted. How sure are they of the accuracy of their counting? If pupils have measured the same objects, or all the class has been working on the same pre-drawn shapes, their answers could be compared. This could then lead to a discussion on the level of accuracy of the counting method.

Spring Term

Lesson 3

Introduction
Ensure that pupils are confident with the terms *length* and *width*. Check measuring skills are secure. Introduce the notation *cm²*.

Activities
Whole class
Explain to the class that they are going to find the areas of square and rectangular shapes. Give pupils the measurements of 6 appropriate rectangles and ask them to draw these on cm squared paper. Draw a results table on the board with columns for length, width and area.
Individual/pair
Pupils should draw the rectangles and find the area by counting. Copy the table from the board and complete by filling in the columns as appropriate.

Differentiation
Lower attaining pupils could be provided with a pre-prepared table.
Higher attaining pupils should be encouraged to extend this activity. Ask them to try to establish a rule.

Plenary
Discuss the relationship between the measurements in the columns and the number given for the areas. Establish that the area is the product of the length and width. Establish that the linear measures are in centimetres and the area is in square centimetres.

Lesson 4

Introduction
Review notation. Reinforce the work done in the previous session. Quick fire questions – 'What is the area of a rectangle measuring 5 cm by 2 cm?' 'What is the area of a rectangle with length 8 cm and width 3 cm?' Ensure that all pupils are secure with the concept of finding area by multiplication.

Activities
Whole class
On the board, draw a polygon which can be cut into two rectangles. Ask how pupils would set about finding the area of this shape. If the suggestion is made that it should be done by counting, ask how it could be done by calculation.
Demonstrate that the shape can be split into two rectangles. Establish the measurements of the two rectangles then calculate the area of the whole. Repeat the process as necessary to ensure all pupils understand the concept.
Individual/pair
Copymaster 27 – areas by calculation.

Differentiation
Lower attaining pupils could be asked to draw these shapes onto squared paper and measure by counting. They should be encouraged to investigate cutting the shape into 2 or more rectangles.
Higher ability pupils could investigate ways of calculating areas of more complex shapes.

Plenary
Ask pupils to explain the process involved in calculating areas of more complex shapes. Ensure that they can use and understand the terms length, width and square centimetre.

Lesson 5

Introduction
Extend the idea of units of area when linear measure is in mm, m and km. Point out that if the measurements of a shape are given in cm, then the area is measured in cm². Ask what you might use for a square of side 1 m. How many cm squares would there be in this shape? Why is a measurement in cm² a problem for larger areas? What would be more sensible measurement?

Activities
Whole class
Real life problems. Discuss situations when it is necessary to understand and use area, *e.g. in the home, at school*.
Individual/pair
Copymaster 28 – building a patio with m² slabs. Investigate various arrangements. Pupils could be provided with further copies of the garden blanks if necessary.

Differentiation
Higher ability pupils could investigate relationships between slabs 50 cm square and slabs 1 m square, or could be set the same problem with various constraints.

Plenary
Discuss the various possibilities and patterns which could be made. Ask pupils to explain their methods and decisions. Check that all arrangements conform to the requirement that the areas remain unchanged.
The results of this investigation would provide good display material.

Theme 5 — Shape

Objectives
- Make shapes and discuss properties
- Visualise solid shapes from 2D drawings
- Identify simple nets
- Recognise clockwise and anticlockwise
- Begin to draw, measure and order angles. Use eight compass points
- Recognise vertical and horizontal lines
- Solve shape problems or puzzles. Explain reasoning and methods

Vocabulary
shape, pattern, flat, line, curved, straight, round, hollow, solid, corner, point, pointed, face, side, edge, end, sort, make, build, construct, draw, sketch, centre, radius, diameter, net, surface, angle, right-angled, base, square based, vertex, vertices, layer, diagram, regular, irregular, concave, convex, open, closed, 3D, 2D, three-dimensional, two-dimensional, cube, cuboid, pyramid, sphere, hemisphere, spherical, cone, cylinder, cylindrical, prism, tetrahedron, polyhedron, circle, circular, semicircle, triangle, triangular, equilateral, isosceles, square, rectangle, rectangular, oblong, pentagon, pentagonal, hexagon, hexagonal, polygon, quadrilateral, heptagon, octagon, turn, rotate, whole turn, half turn, quarter turn, right angle, straight line, degree, ruler, angle-measurer, set square

Resources
Copymasters 7, 8, 29 and 30, Homework copymaster 15, prepared treasure map for lesson 4

Assessment
At the end of this theme is the pupil able to:
- Describe a 3D solid;
- Name appropriate solids;
- Identify nets for a cube;
- Describe a turn in terms of compass points;
- Recognise the terms clockwise, anticlockwise, horizontal, vertical?

Mental maths starter 9

Lesson 1

Introduction
Review work on shapes and solids from previous term. Draw a selection of 2D shapes on the board and ask pupils to name them. Use an appropriate selection of solids and ask pupils to name them. Ensure that pupils are familiar with the terms *2D* and *3D*. Review the terms *face*, *side* and *vertex*.

Activities
Whole class
Draw a square on the board. Say that this is one face of a solid. Ask for suggestions for names for the solid. Look for cube and cuboid. If necessary, point out that this could be the base of a pyramid. Ask pupils to offer suggestions to describe this pyramid, e.g. number of faces, shape of face, number of vertices. Ask pupils to describe a cube and a cuboid in words.

Draw a net for a cube on the board. Ask pupils what solid this could be made into if cut out and folded.

Individual/pair
Copymaster 29 – nets. A further net is to be found on Copymaster 30. There are two nets to cut out and construct the solid and six nets which may form a cube. Pupils should make the solids first. They should then be asked to identify which of the remaining nets would give a solid. If time allows they could copy those which would give a solid onto squared paper and construct the cubes.

Differentiation
Lower attainers may have difficulty in making this decision and could be allowed to attempt to make the cubes first.

Plenary
Review the vocabulary used. Discuss which nets would and would not make cubes and discuss the reasons why.

Lesson 2

Introduction
Ask three pupils to come out to the front of the class. Ask them to stand facing front. Ask the first to turn round. The likely outcomes are either that the pupil will turn through 360° or 180°. If the pupil has turned through 360°, make the instruction to the next pupil 'Turn half way round'.
If the first pupil turned through 180° make the instruction to the next pupil 'Turn all the way round'. Ask the third pupil to turn a quarter of the way round.

Activities
Whole class
Demonstrate these turns on the board. Show a full turn, a half turn and a quarter turn. Demonstrate that a quarter turn can be in one of two directions, leading to a different end point. Explain that we need to be able to measure turns accurately and that the amount of turn is measured in degrees. Demonstrate the notation.

Tell pupils that a whole turn is 360° and ask how many degrees there are in a half turn, how many in a quarter turn.
Explain that a quarter turn is called a *right angle*. Ask pupils to identify right angles in the classroom. Point out that right angles can be found in three dimensions, e.g. *corners of the room*.

Individual/pair
Identify all the right angles on Copymasters 7 and 8. Classify the shapes into those with 0, 1, 2 ... 4 right angles etc. Put the results into a table.

Differentiation
Lower attaining pupils will need help to construct an appropriate table.
Higher attaining pupils should design their own.

Plenary
Review the vocabulary used. Discuss any tests pupils made to decide whether an angle was a right angle. Ask pupils to make general statements about shapes with 4 right angles.

Spring Term

Lesson 3

Introduction
Repeat the introductory exercise from the previous lesson. Ask the first pupil to turn a quarter turn. Ask how many degrees they have turned through. Ask the next pupil to turn a quarter turn. Ask 'Did ... turn the same way as ... or the other way?' Ask the third to turn a quarter turn in the opposite direction from the second.
Ask other pupils to decide which pupil should turn, how much (a whole turn, a half turn or a quarter turn) and in which direction.

Activities
Whole class
Discuss the difficulties of being precise about direction. Look at the way pupils face after a quarter turn. Ask if pupils can suggest any object which turns regularly. If necessary draw their attention to the clock. Explain that we use the term *clockwise* to describe a turn moving the same way as the hands of a clock and *anticlockwise* to describe a turn in the other direction.
Demonstrate and discuss the compass and its use in relation to maps. Check pupils' understanding of the terms and concepts of north, south, west and east. Explain common use of initials. Introduce terms such as north-west etc.

Individual/pair
Draw a compass rose for display.

Differentiation
Lower attaining pupils will need a high level of support with the individual task.

Plenary
Review vocabulary. Ask pupils to describe the construction of the compass rose using appropriate vocabulary.

Lesson 4

Introduction
Draw a blank compass rose on the board. Ask pupils to tell you where to put the various labels.

Activities
Whole class
Draw a grid on the board and position a stick man in the centre. Ask pupils to describe movements of the stick man in terms of compass points, making turns clockwise or anticlockwise, the number of squares moved vertically or horizontally etc. Establish one side of the classroom as north and ask a pupil to move according to a given route and number of steps.

Individual/pair
Provide each pupil with a blank treasure map. Each pupil should decide which square contains their treasure and mark it without letting their partner see. They should then decide on a route to get to the treasure and write this down. Starting point should be the bottom left hand corner of the grid.
Each pupil then describes their route to their partner who marks it on their own map and identifies the treasure square. Once both pupils have had a turn, they compare maps.

Differentiation
Lower attaining pupils should be limited to fewer instructions.
Higher attaining pupils should be encouraged to find more complex routes.

Plenary
Discuss how effective pupils were with their instructions. Ask pupils to give short routes and draw them on the board. Encourage all pupils to use appropriate vocabulary.

Lesson 5

Introduction
Review work done in the previous lesson. Recap on the vocabulary used. Ask questions involving turning.

Activities
Whole class
Draw a grid on the board with a modified plan of the classroom. Include things like the door, teacher's desk and significant furnishings. There should be about 6 items spaced around the grid. Put a spot in the middle of the plan. Ask questions such as 'I am facing the door. I make a half turn clockwise. What will I see?'

Individual/pair
Copymaster 30. Ask pupils to choose a plan of their own and to place items on the grid. This could be the classroom, a room in their house or a fantasy viewpoint. Ask them to write routes to get from the shaded square to points on their grid using various instructions as covered in the previous lessons.
They may like to design treasure maps or islands as a follow-up to the previous lesson.

Differentiation
Differentiation will be by outcome in this task.

Plenary
Ask pupils to describe their plans to the rest of the class using appropriate vocabulary. Some of the work could be used as display material.

Theme 6 — Number sequences

Objectives
- Recognise and extend number sequences formed by counting from any number in steps of constant size
- Extend beyond zero if counting back
- Investigate general statements about familiar numbers
- Explain methods and reasoning

Vocabulary
number, count, odd, even, every other, multiple of, digit, next, consecutive, sequence, continue, predict, pattern, pair, rule, relationship, sort, classify, property, integer, positive, negative, minus, above/below zero

Resources
Copymasters 31 and 32, Homework copymaster 16, 1–100 number squares

Assessment
At the end of this theme is the pupil able to:
- Find a rule for a number sequence;
- Extend the number sequence by following the rule;
- Make general statements about numbers and number patterns;
- Continue counting back using negative numbers?

Mental maths starter 6

Lesson 1

Introduction
Go round the class giving each pupil a number, e.g. 5, 10, 15. Ask the next pupil what their number should be. Tell the class that they will be counting in steps of 10, 100 etc. and ask each pupil to say their number. Repeat counting backwards, giving a starting number and asking them to count down in 2s, 5s etc.
Write a starting number and rule on the board and pick pupils in random order to give the next number in sequence.

Activities
Whole class
Draw a number line on the board and divide into ten equal parts. Put 30 at the start of the number line and 40 at the end. Point to the intermediate points in random order and ask what the number should be at that point. Write the numbers 100 and 200 at the ends of the line. Establish what jumps are indicated and ask for missing numbers as before.
Use other appropriate end numbers to demonstrate jumps of different size.
Write 0 in the middle of the line and 5 at the end. Ask for suggestions as to what numbers could be put in the spaces, i.e. numbers below zero. It is likely that pupils will offer fractions, in which case ask questions such as 'If I've got a cake, would you rather have half/a quarter/a tenth of it or would you rather have none?'
It is possible that some pupils may have met the concept of a negative number – in the weather forecast, for example. If not, explain that we can count beyond zero and introduce and explain the terms *negative* and *minus*.
Relate this to standing at the top of a flight of stairs and moving down. The importance of zero in the counting process should be established.

Individual/pair
Ask pupils to draw ladders, flights of steps or number lines to demonstrate the process of counting down (back).

Differentiation
Lower attaining pupils may experience some difficulties with this concept.

Plenary
Ensure that pupils understand and can use the vocabulary appropriately. Ask pupils to demonstrate and to comment on their drawings.

Lesson 2

Introduction
Go round the class counting backwards in steps of 1, counting through zero.
Repeat this in steps of varying size. Ensure that pupils are secure with the vocabulary.

Activities
Whole class
Draw a series of number lines on the board, with number patterns which go through zero. Ask pupils to identify the missing numbers.

Individual/pair
Write sets of 5 or 6 numbers on the board in random order. Include some sets with negative numbers. Ask pupils to order each set in ascending or descending size.

Differentiation
More able pupils could be asked to identify a rule for each set of numbers and add more terms to the sequence.

Plenary
Ask pupils to explain how they decide which number should be next in the sequence. Discuss how they can find a rule which describes the sequences. How many terms do you need to be sure of a rule?

Spring Term

Lesson 3

Introduction
Ask quick fire questions based on adding or subtracting in 10s, 100s and 1000s, e.g. *'Tell me a sequence I can get by starting with 4 and adding on in tens...'*

Activities
Whole class
Have a large 1–100 number square for display on the board. Ask pupils to tell you even numbers. Shade in or circle numbers as pupils tell you what they are. Point out patterns. Ask pupils to suggest other criteria which might provide patterns.
Explain that pupils are going to undertake an investigation into patterns.

Individual/pair
Give each pupil three 1 – 100 number squares to investigate number patterns.
Investigate patterns in tables: write answers to the 9× table in a column. Identify patterns and describe in words the 11× table and 12× table.

Differentiation
Ask *higher attaining* pupils to write down number sequences formed and the rule they use.

Plenary
Discuss the patterns pupils have found.

Lesson 4

Introduction
Review number statements from last term's work on adding odd and even numbers and summing consecutive numbers. Quick fire questions involving adding three consecutive numbers.

Activities
Whole class
Ask pupils to investigate adding three consecutive numbers – begin with single digit numbers and move to 2-digit numbers. Construct a table on the board and ask pupils to give examples of numbers and their totals. Ask if anyone can suggest a rule to help with this.
Try to establish that the addition of three consecutive numbers is 3× the middle number. Explain that this can be seen as repeated addition or multiplication.

Individual/pair
Copymaster 31.

Differentiation
Higher attaining pupils could be asked to return to the whole class activity and investigate if the rule is true for much larger numbers.

Plenary
Discuss the examples on the copymaster. Ask pupils to explain how they decided on the next terms. How did they identify the rule?

Lesson 5

Introduction
Write a number sequence on the board. Ask for a description in words. Look for a given starter number and a rule. Demonstrate how a rule can be written in mathematical form as well as words, *e.g. add 4 each time or +4 ... numbers in the 3× table or ×3.*

Activities
Whole class
Repeat until all pupils are able to describe a sequence in words. Sequences should involve counting on and back and should include the use of negative numbers.

Individual/pair
Copymaster 32 – writing sequences.

Differentiation
Higher attaining pupils could be asked to make up rules of their own.

Plenary
Discuss the sequences produced as answers to the copymaster. Did anyone have any difficulty with these?

39

Theme 7 — Multiplication and division

Objectives
- Understand commutative and associative laws of multiplication
- Divide a whole number of £ by 2, 4, 5 or 10 and give the answer in £p
- Use closely related facts e.g. derive $\times 9$ or $\times 11$ from $\times 10$ or derive $\times 6$ from $\times 4$ plus $\times 2$
- Partition and multiply

Vocabulary
lots of, groups of, times, product, multiply, multiplied by, multiple of, once, twice, three times, four times...ten times, times as (big, long, wide and so on), repeated, addition, array, row, column, double, halve, share, share equally, one each, two each, three each..., group in pairs, threes... tens, equal, divide, divided by, divided into, divisible by, remainder, factor, quotient, inverse

Resources
Copymasters 33 and 34, Homework copymaster 17

Assessment
At the end of this theme is the pupil able to:
- Explain why multiplication is commutative and associative and give examples to support this;
- Calculate division sums based on related multiplication facts;
- Use partition to multiply TU by U;
- Estimate and calculate multiplication sums by using related known number facts?

Lesson 1

Introduction
Use a display tables square. Ask pupils to give examples of tables facts they are sure they know or can work out easily, e.g. $2\times$, $5\times$, $10\times$ tables. Review the fact that multiplication is commutative and discuss the implications of this, e.g. *if you know that $8 \times 2 = 16$ then you know that $2 \times 8 = 16$*. Establish which number facts are known in the 6, 7, 8 and $9\times$ tables.

Activities
Whole class
Write a multiplication sum involving three single digit numbers on the board. Ask pupils to give you the answer then ask for an explanation of the process. Establish that the answer is the same irrespective of the order of the calculations. Pupils may need to use pencil and paper methods in some cases.

Individual/pair
Copymaster 33 – investigations into commutativity and associativity in multiplication. What other calculations are the same as $\times 10$, $\times 4$, $\times 6$ etc?

Differentiation
Lower attainers may need some support in completing the tables square.
Higher attaining pupils could be set a time challenge for the completion of the tables square.

Plenary
Discuss the examples on the copymaster. Ask pupils to describe how they approached the various types of sum.

Lesson 2

Introduction
Review work done on division. Ensure that all pupils are secure with the vocabulary *divide*, *share* and *remainder*. Quick fire questions based on known tables facts. Ask pupils sums based on division of multiples of 100 by 4, 5 or 10.

Activities
Whole class
Write a sum of money on the board (each digit should be divisible by 2). Ask pupils to tell you half of this amount. Ask how they derived this answer. Ask pupils to tell you half of £5.00, £9.00 etc. Establish that if the number of £s is odd then the remainder must be changed to pence to continue.

Divide sums of money by 2, then by 2 again and establish that this is the same as dividing by 4.
Continue with sums to be divided by 4, 5 or 10.

Individual/pair
Provide appropriate examples of sums for pupils to work on individually.

Differentiation
Find examples appropriate for the various ability levels.

Plenary
Review vocabulary and methods used. Focus on some of the examples set for individual work and ask pupils to explain in their own words how they tackled these. While pupils are doing the individual work, look for any areas of difficulty and concentrate on these.

Spring Term

Lesson 3

Introduction
Quick fire questions on tables facts, doubling and halving. Introduce two stage questions, *e.g. 'I start with 5 and double it. I multiply the answer by 3. What do I get?'*

Activities
Whole class
Review the relationship between multiplication and addition, i.e. that 12 × 4 can be written as 12 + 12 + 12 + 12. Write some multiplication sums on the board and ask pupils to tell you an addition sum which would give the same answer. Write a 2-digit number on the board in a sum such as 68 × 9. Explain that you are going to look for an easy way to do this. Ask for an estimation of the answer. Pupils should be able to suggest 680. Ask pupils to explain how they derived this estimated answer. Write the sum 68 × 10 = 680 on the board. Establish the addition equivalent of this sum. Write the sum 68 × 9 and establish the addition equivalent for this sum. Ask pupils if they can explain how they could derive the answer to the sum 68 × 9 from these known facts.
Establish that 68 × 9 can be calculated by knowing 68 × 10 and subtracting 68.
Repeat this process using other 2 digit numbers. When pupils are secure with the process, derive the fact that multiplication by 11 can be approached in a similar way.

Individual/pair
Copymaster 34.

Differentiation
Find or devise further examples appropriate for the various ability levels.

Plenary
While pupils are doing the individual work look for any areas of difficulty and concentrate on these. Ask pupils to explain their working with reference to specific sums.

Lesson 4

Introduction
Review partitioning of 2-digit numbers. Give a number and ask 'How many tens?' or 'If I write this number what should go in the tens column? What should go in the units column?'

Activities
Whole class
Review previous work done on pen and pencil methods of multiplication of TU. Establish that 16 × 5 can be solved by calculating 10 × 5 and 6 × 5 and adding. Develop a standard method for multiplication by partitioning. Encourage pupils to make a reasonable approximation of the answer before they begin.

Individual/pair
Copymaster 34.

Differentiation
Find or devise further examples appropriate for the various ability levels. Ensure that *lower attaining* pupils are secure with calculations which involve crossing the 1–tens boundary.

Plenary
While pupils are doing the individual work look for any areas of difficulty and concentrate on these. Ask pupils to explain their working with reference to specific sums. Discuss those examples which involve crossing the tens boundary.

Lesson 5

Introduction
Write a number on the board, *e.g. 12*. Ask pupils to tell you any facts they know about the number *e.g. it is even, 12 May is someone's birthday, it is the answer to the sum 3 × 4, 12 items are called a dozen.* When you have as many facts as you wish, choose another number and repeat the process.

Activities
Whole class
Explain that the class is to make a number facts book. You want them to think of as many facts as they can for numbers between 1 and 20. The facts can be purely mathematical but can include other items where appropriate.

Individual/pair
Give each pair two or three numbers to work on. Each pair should be asked to find as many facts as possible about their numbers and record these on paper.

Differentiation
Give easier numbers to *lower attaining* pupils. If necessary, *high attainers* could be asked to find facts for selected larger numbers.

Plenary
Review and record all the facts. Decide if all facts are appropriate for a number book. If some are rejected, ask pupils to argue for or against their inclusion. Ultimately the book should be produced using the results from the pair work. This could be compiled as a class book or as group work.

Theme 8 — Solving problems

Objectives
- Develop and refine written methods for TU × U
- Choose appropriate number operations and calculation methods to solve money and real life word problems with one or more steps
- Explain working. Check with inverse operation

Vocabulary
lots of, groups of, times, product, multiply, multiplied by, multiple of, once, twice, three times, four times…ten times, times as (big, long, wide and so on), repeated, addition, double, halve, share, share equally, one each, two each, three each…, group in pairs, threes… tens, equal groups of, divide, divided by, divided into, divisible by, remainder, factor, quotient, inverse

Resources
Copymasters 35 and 36, Homework copymaster 18

Assessment
At the end of this theme is the pupil able to:
- Use pencil and paper methods for multiplication of TU by U;
- Choose appropriate operations to solve real life money problems;
- Use pencil and paper methods for multiplication of money?

Lesson 1

Introduction
Quick fire questions – tables facts for 2, 3, 4, 5 and 10× tables.

Activities
Whole class
Write some 2-digit numbers on the board. Ask pupils to identify the tens and units. Recap on multiplying a multiple of 10 by one of the digits practised in the introduction. Review the fact that multiplication by a multiple of 10 means that there will be a 0 in the units column of the answer.
Review the work done in the previous theme on the partition of TU numbers. Focus on any problem areas identified in that lesson. Discuss ways of multiplying by using partition. Use the work done in the previous theme to develop written methods into a standard method. Ensure that pupils are secure when presented with sums which involve crossing the tens boundary.

Individual/pair
Provide appropriate examples of sums for pupils to work on individually.

Differentiation
Lower ability pupils should be provided with plenty of practice examples which do not involve crossing the tens boundary.

Plenary
Ensure that pupils are secure with the reasoning involved in the concept of using partitioning to calculate multiplication sums. Ask pupils to describe the methods they used in their own words. Ask pupils to discuss any particular difficulties they encountered. Ask why it is necessary to 'carry' tens into the next column when using standard written methods. Link this with the informal methods and approaches previously used.

Lesson 2

Introduction
Quick fire questions – tables facts for 6, 7, 8 and 9× tables. Review known tables facts established in previous lessons.

Activities
Whole class
Review the work done in the previous lesson. Focus on any problem areas identified in that lesson. Review ways of multiplying by using partition. Review the written methods developed and reviewed. Ensure that pupils are secure when presented with sums which involve crossing the tens boundary.

Individual/pair
Copymaster 35 – multiplication of TU.

Differentiation
Provide similar but more challenging examples for *high ability* pupils.

Plenary
Ask pupils to describe the methods they used in their own words. Ask pupils to discuss any particular difficulties they encountered.

Spring Term

Lesson 3

Introduction
Quick fire questions – review all four rules involving simple money sums, working in pence or pounds.

Activities
Whole class
Review changing amounts in pence to an amount in £p. Ensure that all pupils are secure with this activity. Write a multiplication problem involving pence on the board and ask pupils how they would calculate this. Establish that the calculation could be done by partitioning, either using informal or formal methods. Ask pupils to convert the answer to a sum involving £p.

Individual/pair
Copymaster 36 – problems.

Differentiation
Provide additional example for *higher attaining* pupils.

Plenary
Focus on the questions on the copymaster and ask pupils to explain their methods and reasoning.

Lesson 4

Introduction
Quick fire questions involving money sums as in lesson 3.

Activities
Whole class
Provide examples of more complex two-stage problems. Ask pupils to identify the appropriate calculation methods and to explain how they would work out the sum. Investigate alternative approaches where possible, e.g. repeated addition instead of multiplication. Which method is more efficient? Which is easier? Why?

Individual/pair
Ask pupils to write word problems attached to various sums. Pupils could be asked to solve each other's problems or this could be done orally with the whole class contributing to the task.

Differentiation
Lower ability pupils will find it more complex.
Higher ability pupils should be able to undertake this task fairly easily.

Plenary
Ask pupils to tell you the problem they have worked out for the sums. Discuss different approaches.

Lesson 5

Introduction
Write a sum on the board and ask pupils to identify all related number facts.

Activities
Whole class
Make a simple statement, e.g. 'I think of a number and double it. The answer is 24. What was my starting number?' Ask the pupils to explain in words the process they employed to solve the puzzle. Write the sum on the board, choosing an appropriate symbol to stand for the starting number, e.g.
? doubled is 24 ... 24 halved is 12 or 24 ÷ 2 = 12
'I think of a number and add 10. The answer is 38. What was my starting number?'
? + 10 = 38 ... 38 − 10 = 28

When pupils are secure with the methods involved, establish that each operation used has an inverse and that this inverse provides a method of solving a problem. Ask pupils to tell you the opposite of addition, multiplication etc.

Individual/pair
Provide examples of various sums for pupils to attempt and ask them to check their accuracy by doing a sum involving the inverse operation, e.g.
40 ÷ 8 = A   so   A × 8 = 40

Differentiation
Higher attaining pupils could be given more complex sums.

Plenary
Review vocabulary and ensure pupils' understanding of inverses.

43

Theme 9 — Fractions and decimals

Objectives
- Recognise equivalence of simple fractions
- Identify pairs of fractions which total 1
- Compare a fraction with $\frac{1}{2}$ and say whether it is greater or less
- Use decimal notation for tenths, hundredths (money, metres and centimetres) and use in context. Round to the nearest £ or metre
- Convert £ to p or metres to cm and vice versa
- Order decimals with two places

Vocabulary
part, equal parts, fraction, one whole, half, quarter, eighth, third, sixth, fifth, tenth, twentieth, proportion, in every, for every, decimal, decimal fraction, decimal point, decimal place, equivalent

Resources
Copymasters 15, 37 and 38, Homework copymaster 19

Assessment
At the end of this theme is the pupil able to:
- Identify equivalent fractions;
- Order fractions by size;
- Order decimal fractions by size;
- Recognise decimal fractions of money and length?

Lesson 1

Introduction
Review fractions work from Autumn term (Theme 8). Identify those diagrams which had $\frac{1}{2}$ shaded. Ask pupils to write the fractions written for those diagrams. Discuss the fact that $\frac{1}{2}$ is also represented by $\frac{2}{4}$.

Activities
Whole class
Ask pupils to identify which diagrams can be used to show $\frac{1}{2}$ of the shape and to shade in the sections needed to do this. Ask pupils to give the fractions shaded, e.g. $\frac{3}{6}$, and write these on the board. Ask pupils if they can see any relation between the numerator and denominator. They should be able to express the relationship in terms of doubles, or the two times table. Draw a 3 × 4 rectangle and demonstrate different ways of showing $\frac{1}{4}$.

Individual/pair
Copymaster 37 – shading equivalent fractions.

Differentiation
Higher attaining pupils could take the investigation of equivalent fractions further.

Plenary
Discuss individual examples from the copymaster. Ask pupils to explain their reasoning.

Lesson 2

Introduction
Quick questions to introduce the concept of adding fractions to make one whole. 'I have a bar of chocolate and I eat half of it. If you eat the rest, how much do you get?'
'Mum had $\frac{1}{4}$ of the cake left. How much had we eaten?'
'What fraction must I add to $\frac{1}{3}$ to make a whole?'

Activities
Whole class
Draw several rectangles on the board. Mark the rectangles to show different fractions. Ask pupils to identify the fractions needed to show 1 whole. Write an addition sum for each one.

Individual/pair
Find pairs of fractions totalling 1 – use Copymaster 15 and identify shaded and unshaded fractions. Construct a table to show the relationship between the shaded and unshaded parts.

Differentiation
Ask *higher ability* pupils to decide on appropriate ways of demonstrating pairs of fractions summing to one. *Lower ability* pupils would benefit from having a prepared table to fill in. *Higher ability* pupils could be asked to identify other, less commonly discussed pairs of fractions.

Plenary
Write several simple fraction pairs on the board and ask pupils to identify which pairs add to one. Ask pupils to describe their methods of identification. Try to establish that the denominators must be the same.

Spring Term

Lesson 3

Introduction
Write the fractions $\frac{1}{4}$, $\frac{1}{2}$ and $\frac{3}{4}$ on the board. Which is the biggest? Which is the smallest? Write further fractions on the board. Choose those with which pupils have become familiar, e.g. $\frac{1}{3}$, $\frac{1}{6}$ etc. Which is the biggest? Which is the smallest? Establish the rule that the greater the denominator, the smaller the fraction.

Activities
Whole class
Write several fractions on the board, some less than $\frac{1}{2}$ and some greater than $\frac{1}{2}$. Ask pupils to identify which are which. Ask pupils how they made the decision whether a fraction is bigger or smaller than $\frac{1}{2}$. Many will just have applied guesswork at this stage.
Write the fractions $\frac{4}{10}$ and $\frac{6}{10}$ on the board. Ask if they are both less than $\frac{1}{2}$ or both more than $\frac{1}{2}$. Ask pupils how they decided. Review work on equivalent fractions. What fraction in tenths is equivalent to $\frac{1}{2}$? Continue to demonstrate this process.

Individual/pair
Write a set of fractions on the board and ask pupils to decide whether each is larger or smaller than $\frac{1}{2}$. Answers could be written in a table.

Differentiation
More able pupils could be asked to write the fraction equivalent to a half for each fraction given. They could also be asked to consider ways in which they could order the fractions. *Less able* pupils are likely to need a greater level of support. A card with a list of appropriate fractions equivalent to $\frac{1}{2}$ might be provided for these pupils to enable them to make sensible attempts.

Plenary
Why do fractions with large denominators represent very small parts? Review the method of finding fractions equivalent to $\frac{1}{2}$.

Lesson 4

Introduction
Write several fractions in tenths on the board and ask pupils to order these. You may like to start by identifying those less than $\frac{1}{2}$ and those greater than $\frac{1}{2}$. Establish that ordering is easy when the denominators are the same.
Ask where we might find it helpful to work in $\frac{1}{10}$s. Establish that it is useful for measures.
Write several fractions in hundredths on the board and ask pupils to order these.
Ask where we might find it helpful to work in $\frac{1}{100}$s. Establish that it is useful for money.

Activities
Whole class
Explain that a system of writing fractions in $\frac{1}{10}$s and $\frac{1}{100}$s has been developed for ease of calculation and that we call this the *decimal system*. Establish that $\frac{1}{10}$ is written as 0.1. Discuss the concept of writing numbers in columns if appropriate. Ask pupils to suggest decimal fraction equivalents for all other fractions in tenths.
Demonstrate some simple addition sums involving decimal numbers which will total less than 1. Ask pupils to identify pairs of decimal fractions which will total 1. Relate this to the previous work on pairs of fractions which will total to 1. If pupils are secure with this concept, move to addition of decimals which will total more than 1. Discuss the relevance of the number in the units column.

Individual/pair
Look for games involving fraction and decimal cards. Decimal domino sets would provide a good follow-up activity for this lesson.

Differentiation
Low attaining pupils may need additional support during the game.

Plenary
Observe pupils during the pair work session and focus on any areas of difficulty.

Lesson 5

Introduction
Quick fire questions – how many pennies in £1.00, £1.20 etc? How many cm in 1 m, $1\frac{1}{2}$ m etc?

Activities
Whole class
Ensure that all pupils are secure with the change from £ to p and m to cm. Establish that any amount of money greater than 100p can be written as a decimal fraction of £. Recap on the concept of a decimal fraction from the previous lesson and demonstrate the relevance to money. Using money as a model, demonstrate how measurements in cm can be written as decimal fractions of a metre.
Demonstrate how sums of money less than £1 can be written in this notation. Discuss the relevance of the digit to the left of the decimal point. Establish that this represents the number of whole £. Write several sums of money less than £1 on the board and ask pupils to put these in order. Repeat until pupils are secure. Using money as a model, demonstrate how measurements in cm, less than 100 cm, can be written as decimal fractions of a metre.

Individual/pair
Copymaster 38 – decimal fractions as £ or m and ordering decimals to 2 places.

Differentiation
Lower attaining pupils may need more practice with ordering decimals.

Plenary
Discuss the copymaster problems. Ask pupils to discuss their approaches to the problems.

Theme 10 — Bar charts

Objectives
- Solve a given problem by collecting, classifying, representing and interpreting data in bar charts with intervals of 2s, 5s, 10s and 20s

Vocabulary
count, tally, sort, vote, survey, questionnaire, data graph, block, graph, pictogram, represent, group, set, list, chart, bar chart, tally chart, table, frequency table, label, title, axis, axes, diagram, most popular, most common, least popular, least common

Resources
Copymasters 19, 20, 39 and 40, Homework copymaster 20

Assessment
At the end of this theme is the pupil able to:
- Read a bar chart and comment on the information shown by the chart;
- Construct a bar chart choosing appropriate labels for the axes?

Mental Maths starter

Lesson 1

Introduction
Write a list of popular books on the board. Ask pupils to decide on their three favourite books from the list and to write down their favourites. Their top choice should be given 3 points, their second 2 points and their third 1 point. Construct a tally chart for the book list and ask each pupil to tell you the number of points for the books they have chosen.

Activities
Whole class
Transfer the information from the tally chart to a frequency table. Recap on the vocabulary. Explain that you are going to display this information in a new way called a *bar chart*. Draw an appropriate pair of axes and label the horizontal axis to show the book titles. Number the vertical axis in steps of 1. Ask pupils to suggest an appropriate label for this axis. Ask pupils to suggest how they would approach the next step – reiterate that this is called a bar chart.
Discuss ways of making the information easy to read, e.g. a title, clear use of labels, use of colour etc.

Use Copymaster 19. Explain that you want this information displayed on a bar chart. What is the first thing they will need to do (find the totals)? Decide which set of data to use. Discuss an appropriate way to set out this information and decide on the scale to use.
Individual/pair
Ask pupils to construct a bar chart from the chosen pictogram.

Differentiation
Lower ability pupils may need assistance in drawing and labelling the axes. If necessary, provide sheets with appropriate axes already constructed and, possibly, labelled. *Higher ability* pupils could be asked to draw bar charts from both pictograms.

Plenary
Did pupils have any difficulties with constructing the bar charts? Does everybody's chart look the same? Could we reconstruct the frequency table from the bar chart? Why is it so important to put proper labels on the charts?

Lesson 2

Introduction
Review the previous work done on collecting and classifying data. What sort of information could we show on a bar chart?

Activities
Whole class
Prepare a frequency table for favourite sweets. This should be display size. Keep this hidden. Draw an appropriate bar chart on the board. Give the chart a title: Favourite Sweets. Mark the horizontal axis with spaces for sweet names but don't fill in the names. Number the vertical axis appropriately. Point out the title and ask what labels you might use for the axes.
Display the frequency table. Ask pupils which sweet names should be written in the spaces. Encourage discussion to establish that the sweet names must be put in to match with the data given in the frequency table.

Ask questions relating to the bar chart you have drawn: Which was the favourite sweet? Which was the least favourite sweet? How many more people liked ... than liked...?
Individual/pair
Copymaster 39 – interpreting a bar chart. Ask pupils to complete the numbering on the vertical axis of the second chart. Further work could be done by asking pupils to provide data for these two and drawing new graphs incorporating this class information.

Differentiation
There are several other questions based on the two graphs which should be set at a level appropriate to pupils' ability levels. *Higher attaining* pupils could be asked to construct frequency tables.

Plenary
Discuss the questions set and ask pupils to explain how they read the information from these charts.

Spring Term

Lesson 3

Introduction
Focus on appropriate labels for axes and discuss how you can draw a bar chart to fit your page if you have to deal with larger numbers. Draw a vertical axis on the board and ask for appropriate steps to display frequencies up to 20, up to 40 etc. Ask why the graduations need to be the same size.

Activities
Whole class
Use Copymaster 20. Tell the pupils they are to draw a bar chart from the information on the frequency table. Look at the numbers involved. What would be a sensible scale to use for the horizontal axis? How many bars will the chart have to display? What measurements should you use on the vertical scale (*e.g. jumps of 1 cm/2 cm*)? If you work in larger jumps, how will you cope with the smaller numbers (*e.g. 1, 3*)?
Individual/pair
Ask pupils to draw the bar chart according to the decisions made by the class.

Differentiation
Lower ability pupils may need support in reading a scale which is in jumps of 10.
Higher ability pupils may be asked to draw a bar chart based on the numbers from the five tally charts on that sheet.

Plenary
Ask pupils to display and comment on their work.

Lesson 4

Introduction
Review work done in the previous term and revisit the data collected.

Activities
Whole class
Look at the subjects of the data collection exercise and the frequency tables produced. Tell pupils which set of data to use and if possible ensure that pupils are working with a different set of data from that previously used.
Individual/pair
Pupils work in pairs to produce a piece of work for display. Pupils should choose one of the pieces of work done in Autumn term Theme 10 (lesson 5) and should produce a large bar chart from that information. If the previous work is no longer on display, you might like to consider which pieces of work should also be displayed. Would it be appropriate to display the pictogram as well?

Differentiation
Differentiation will be by outcome although *low attainers* may need additional support.

Plenary
Discuss the ways in which pupils tackled their task. Examine labels and appropriate choice of axes. Ask pupils to display their work and comment.

Lesson 5

Introduction
Class collection of data. Discuss the type of information which can be displayed satisfactorily on a bar chart. Ask pupils to make suggestions for information to be collected. Discuss ways of collecting the data. Focus on appropriate questions.

Activities
Whole class
Choose a subject that can be researched in the classroom. Devise appropriate data collection methods. Collect data and draw a graph.
Individual/pair
Copymaster 40 is provided for use if it is inappropriate for pupils to collect information for themselves. If this option is chosen, some class discussion and guidance will be necessary. The data provide information which could be used in a variety of ways.

Differentiation
Lower ability pupils will need greater guidance and a more prescribed task.
Higher ability pupils should be encouraged to do their own data collection and decide on appropriate presentation methods if at all possible.

Plenary
Ask pupils to describe all the stages in the process, from the data collection to the finished graph. Ask if there are any difficulties inherent in the data collection process and how pupils overcame these.

Theme 1 — Mental calculation

Objectives
- Understand the principles of the associative law for addition
- Add or subtract the nearest multiple of 10 and adjust
- Use number facts and place value to add/subtract mentally any pair of 2 digit whole numbers

Vocabulary
add, addition, more, plus, increase, sum, total, altogether, double, near double, subtract, take away, minus, decrease, between, half, halve, equals, inverse, difference between, how many?

Resources
Copymasters 41 and 42, Homework copymaster 21

Assessment
At the end of this theme is the pupil able to:
- Understand the associative law and use this in calculations;
- Recognise and use multiples of 10;
- Use known number facts to add and subtract mentally?

Mental maths starter 2

Lesson 1

Introduction
Check understanding of place value in numbers to 1000. Write a number on the board and ask 'How many 10s in this number?' 'What number does the digit 4 represent?'

Activities
Whole class
Ask questions involving 100s and 1000s, e.g. 'What number is 1000 more than…?' 'What number is 1000 less than…?' 'If I add 200 to 120 how many will I have?' 'What is 450 – 30?' Continue until all pupils are secure with this type of calculation. Write an example of this type of sum on the board and ask pupils to explain the method they use to find the answer.

Individual/pair
Game: in pairs have two sets of number cards – a random selection of up to 20 two digit numbers, the other multiples of 10 and 100. Two cards are turned over and the pupil who says the answer first scores a point. If there is a disagreement about the correct answers both pupils work out the sum and the one who was correct scores the point. The pupil with the most points at the end of the session is the winner. Pupils should be directed to add or subtract as appropriate.

Differentiation
More able pupils could be provided with sets of cards which will produce more challenging sums.

Plenary
Review adding and subtracting multiples of 10 and ask pupils to explain how they used this knowledge to help their calculations. Set questions and ask pupils to talk through their own methods.

Lesson 2

Introduction
Quick fire questions – add multiples of 100 and multiples of 10 to single digit numbers, e.g. 'add 400 and 5', 'What is the total of 200, 50 and 2?'

Activities
Whole class
Review adding three single digit numbers by looking for pairs which sum to 10. Write three single digit numbers on the board and ask pupils to explain their methods for working out an answer. Check that all pupils are secure with the concept of associativity. If any are not, write a selection of sums on the board then rewrite them in a different order and ask pupils to check that the answers are the same irrespective of the order.
Write several two digit numbers on the board and ask pupils to partition them. Choose two where the units add to 10. Ask pupils to tell you the answer to the addition sum. Check that pupils are secure with the concept of crossing the 10s boundary. Ask pupils to explain their reasoning and methods. Did anyone use the concept of partitioning to help them do the sum? Focus on this method and discuss its advantages.

Individual/pair
Ask pupils to investigate ways of adding three 2 digit numbers by using partition. Write a range of sums on the board and ask pupils to do these sums, recording the stages they go through. Ask them to try to do the sums in a variety of ways and to decide which are easiest.

Differentiation
Higher attaining pupils should be given more difficult examples.

Plenary
Ask pupils to explain their methods of working and establish, as a class, appropriate ways of calculating the sum of three 2 digit numbers, which they can use on a regular basis for mental calculation. Ask pupils how they can check the accuracy of their answers and encourage the concept of giving an estimated answer.

Summer Term

Lesson 3

Introduction
Check understanding of number names. Ask pupils to write numbers given in words. They could either be invited to write on the board or could write several on paper. Write 2 or 3-digit numbers on the board and ask pupils to say the numbers in words.

Activities
Whole class
Check subtraction facts of numbers to 20. Write a subtraction sum on the board. Ensure that it is not necessary to cross the 10s boundary at this stage. Ask pupils to give an answer and to describe how they did the sum.
Write a subtraction sum where the smaller number is easily recognisable as a near multiple of 10. Demonstrate subtraction using near multiples and compensating.
Repeat this process until all pupils are able to suggest an appropriate method for the calculation.
Individual/pair
Copymaster 41.

Differentiation
Ensure that *lower attaining* pupils are secure with the concept of subtraction which crosses the 10s boundary. They should have shown this by successful completion of the first section before they attempt the more difficult sums. *High attaining* pupils could be set more sums which involve this.

Plenary
Discuss the examples on the copymaster. Ask pupils to explain their methods with reference to specific sums. Ask similar questions for them to attempt without the need for pencil and paper.

Lesson 4

Introduction
Review work done in the previous lesson on subtraction.

Activities
Whole class
Check addition and subtraction using two or three 2-digit numbers for addition and two 2-digit numbers for subtraction. Write several appropriate numbers on the board and use these to form sums.
Check that pupils are aware that subtraction is not commutative. If pupils suggest partitioning as a method for subtraction, ensure that they are aware that both parts of the number need the minus sign.
Ask a mixture of addition and subtraction sums and ensure that you use a wide range of vocabulary in the questioning.
Individual/pair
Copymaster 42.

Differentiation
Encourage *higher attaining* pupils to make more sums than the minimum number suggested. They could work with three number sums or ignore the restriction on one from each set and choose any numbers.

Plenary
Discuss why pupils could make fewer subtraction sums and the limits to this part of the activity.

Lesson 5

Introduction
Recap on different ways of writing sums and the relationship between addition and subtraction. Ask quick question addition sums – ask one pupil for an answer then two others to tell you a sum using the inverse, e.g. 'What is 16 add 12?' 'Now tell me another sum using those numbers.'

Activities
Whole class
Continue with the introductory task but extend the concept to 2-digit numbers.
At each stage ask pupils to explain their methods and reasoning.
Individual/pair
Write six appropriate numbers on the board and ask pupils to write as many addition and subtraction sums as they can using those numbers. Point out that they may use three numbers in the addition sums.
Depending on the time available, pupils could be asked to find either a given number of sums or as many as they can. Pupils could then attempt their own sums or could give them to other pupils.

Differentiation
Higher ability pupils could be given some 3-digit numbers in the set, and could be asked to write more complex addition sums, i.e. adding more than three numbers.

Plenary
Ask pupils to explain how they decided which numbers to use in which order. Were any number pairs not appropriate for subtraction sums? Why?

Theme 2 — Money problems

Objectives
- Develop and refine written methods for column addition/subtraction
- Add more than two whole numbers less than 1000, and money
- Choose appropriate operations and calculation methods to solve money and 'real life' word problems with one or more steps
- Explain working

Vocabulary
money, coin, note, penny, pence, pound, price, cost, buy, bought, sell, sold, spent, spend, pay, change, costs more, costs less, cheaper, less/least expensive, how much? how many? total, amount, value

Resources
Copymasters 43 and 44, Homework copymaster 22

Assessment
At the end of this theme is the pupil able to:
- Add two or more numbers to 1000;
- Add money;
- Decide on appropriate calculations for money problems and do them?

Mental maths starter 8

Lesson 1

Introduction
Review previous work done on written methods of addition. Review sums involving crossing the 10s boundary. Discuss the need to carry a 10 into the next column. Check that all pupils are able to write a sum in column format. Ask why we write in columns. Relate to place value and establish, by referring to past work on addition, that it is more efficient to add multiples of 10 then units etc. Establish that the standard method when working in columns adds the units column first.

Activities
Whole class
Demonstrate the standard method for addition using numbers to 1000. Discuss the need to cross the hundreds boundary. Work through a number of examples on the board and ensure that all pupils can comment, at each stage, on the reasoning behind this approach.
Ask pupils who are secure to demonstrate to the class and to explain what they are doing. Repeat the process of column addition using three numbers. Relate the addition of three digits to previous work.

Individual/pair
Provide appropriate examples for practice.

Differentiation
High attaining pupils should be offered more challenging examples.

Plenary
Ask pupils to write a sum on the board and to nominate another pupil to do the sum. The pupils nominated should do the sum as a demonstration, explaining the process used and the reasoning at each stage. Ask other pupils if they think this is the right way, or if they could have done it more easily. Repeat the process. You may like to write less challenging sums and nominate lower attainers to ensure they are presented with an appropriate opportunity to display their knowledge. Review any difficulties pupils may have experienced with adding three numbers.

Lesson 2

Introduction
Review previous work done on written methods of subtraction. Review sums involving decomposition.

Activities
Whole class
Demonstrate the standard method for subtraction using numbers to 1000. Discuss the need to adjust from tens to units and from hundreds to tens.
Work through a number of examples on the board and ensure that all pupils can comment, at each stage, on the reasoning behind this approach.
Ask pupils who are secure to demonstrate to the class and to explain what they are doing.
Individual/pair
Provide appropriate examples for practice.

Differentiation
Provide more challenging examples for *higher attainers*.

Plenary
Check methods of working and approaches while the class is working individually. Focus on any areas of difficulty and ensure that all pupils are secure with the methods used.

Summer Term

Lesson 3

Introduction
Quick questions involving money – 'I have 50p and 30p. How much is that altogether?', 'I go into a shop with £5.00 and spend ...What change will I get?', 'I'm saving up to buy a bike costing £... I have £... How much more do I need?'

Activities
Whole class
Link techniques for formal pencil and paper methods of addition and subtraction to money sums.
Focus on the use of the decimal point. What does this indicate? Link to previous work on decimals.
Check that all pupils can write column sums correctly and stress the importance of this when doing money sums. Review methods used for both addition and subtraction and apply this to examples involving money. Discuss the need to adjust from tens to units in the pence columns and from pounds to pence.

Individual/pair
Copymaster 43 – standard money sums, addition and subtraction

Differentiation
Provide similar but more challenging examples for the *higher attainers*. *Lower attainers* may need further help in setting out the sums for the first part of the copymaster.

Plenary
Discuss individual examples from the copymaster. Ask pupils to explain their reasoning.
Ask what methods pupils could use to check the accuracy of their answers, particularly with reference to the section on getting change.

Lesson 4

Introduction
Review changing pence to pounds and pounds to pence. Review the need to set out money sums correctly and to ensure that decimal points are in a line. Write £1.5 on the board and ask what amount this is. Point out the ambiguity and demonstrate that money should have two digits in the pence columns.

Activities
Whole class
Pose problems of the type set on Copymaster 44. Discuss approaches to solving these. Identify appropriate operations to solve problems. Discuss appropriate written methods.

Individual/pair
Copymaster 44.

Differentiation
Lower attainers should be asked to solve problems with easier calculations and should be encouraged to focus on methods.

Plenary
Discuss the examples from the copymaster. While pupils are working individually, take note of any errors in calculation and difficulties experienced in deciding on the operation. Use these for areas of discussion. Ask pupils to explain how they set about the tasks. Ask pupils to identify any areas of particular difficulty.

Lesson 5

Introduction
Quick fire questions on adding larger sums of money – working in pounds.

Activities
Whole class
Discuss the use of money at home. Who gets pocket money? What sorts of things do you spend your money on? How long does your money last?
What items would you buy if you had £100 to spend? If you had £200 to spend?
Explain that the individual task is to furnish a new bedroom. Ask for items pupils would like in their bedrooms. Make a list of these and construct a list of appropriate prices. Point out that most items will be available in a range of prices and add a choice of price to your list so that pupils can choose to buy a cheaper item or a more expensive item.

Individual/pair
Investigation – how much will it cost to furnish your new room? Pupils should be given a fixed amount of money and asked what they would buy. They should list the items with the prices and calculate totals. Pupils could be asked to draw plans of their ideal bedroom, with costings, for display work.

Differentiation
High attainers could be asked to consider other factors, *e.g. new curtains or the cost of decorating the room*.

Plenary
Discuss the choices that pupils have made. How did they decide which items to buy? Did they start off with a list which cost too much or did they keep track of how much they spent as they went along?

Theme 3 — Measuring capacity

Objectives
- Use, read and write litre (l), millilitre (ml), pint
- Know $\frac{1}{4}$, $\frac{1}{2}$, $\frac{3}{4}$, $\frac{1}{10}$ of a litre in ml
- Suggest suitable units and equipment to estimate or measure capacity
- Read scales
- Record measurements to a suitable degree of accuracy, using mixed units or the nearest whole/half/quarter unit (e.g. 3.25 litres)
- Choose appropriate number operations and calculation methods to solve measurement word problems with one or more steps
- Explain working

Vocabulary
big, bigger, small, smaller, capacity, half full, empty, holds, contains, litre, half litre, millilitre, pint, container, measuring cylinder

Resources
Copymasters 45 and 46, Homework copymaster 23, 1 l and 2 l milk containers, other appropriate containers for comparison, equipment for practical work, appropriate recipes for lesson 4

Assessment
At the end of this theme is the pupil able to:
- Compare liquid measures and decide which is greater;
- Know standard units;
- Solve problems involving capacity?

Lesson 1

Introduction
Have a selection of plastic containers for display – 1 litre and 2 litre milk containers, lemonade bottles or drinks cans which indicate capacity. Ask which will hold the most liquid. Ask if anyone can tell you how much any of these might hold. Expect litres, but you may get pints as well. If anyone suggests pints, ask what they would expect to see measured in pints.

Activities
Whole class
Show pupils the litre container. Explain that this holds one litre and write the word on the board. Compare with smaller containers. Ask if anyone knows the units used to measure smaller quantities. If necessary introduce the word *millilitres*. Focus on the prefix and ask if anyone can link this with other forms of measurement. Establish that 1000 ml = 1 l.

Individual/pair
Construct a chart showing how many ml in $\frac{1}{4}$, $\frac{1}{2}$, $\frac{3}{4}$, $\frac{1}{10}$ of a litre.

Differentiation
Lower attaining pupils may need support in calculating the fractions of a litre.

Plenary
Check charts produced by pupils. Discuss any difficulties pupils may have experienced. Ask quick questions relating to these, e.g. how many ml in 1 l, 2 l, $2\frac{1}{2}$ l etc.

Lesson 2

Introduction
Consider the selection of containers used in lesson 1. Is it always possible to tell how much something holds just by looking? Show pupils pairs of containers and ask them to judge which has the greater capacity.

Activities
Whole class
Pupils should undertake practical measuring activities if possible, using a measuring jug or cylinder. Ask pupils to investigate the capacity of various containers. If practical work is not appropriate, demonstrate how capacity is measured. Focus on reading scales on the measuring jug or cylinder.

Individual/pair
Copymaster 45. This copymaster can be reused by blanking out the numbers and replacing them with other appropriate amounts. Further work can be done by asking questions such as 'How many cans of cola would fill the measuring cylinder?' or 'How much space is left in the cylinder?'

Differentiation
Higher attaining pupils should be asked to estimate the capacity of various containers. If possible, allow checking by practical methods otherwise use containers of known capacity so pupils can check their answers. Ask *lower attainers* to order containers according to estimated capacity.

Plenary
Discuss the practical activities. Focus on comparisons of capacity. Discuss the copymaster questions. Ask pupils to explain in their own words what they did to solve any problems you set.

Summer Term

Lesson 3

Introduction
Recap on units and fractions of a litre. Ask quick fire questions – 'How many ml in $\frac{1}{2}$ l?' 'If I have 3 cans each holding 300 ml, how much is that altogether?'

Activities
Whole class
Discuss and demonstrate how to do calculations involving capacity. Recap on addition and subtraction methods if needed. Demonstrate how to subtract and the need to change litres to ml. Review appropriate subtraction methods
Demonstrate ways of writing capacity using mixed units.
Individual/pair
Appropriate examples. These could be word puzzles of the type similar to the quick questions in the introduction or could be based on the measuring cylinder problems on Copymaster 45. If pupils have been able to do practical work in lesson 2 it is suggested that the associated copymaster be kept for this lesson.

Differentiation
Lower ability pupils may have difficulty coping with subtraction and should be offered additional support.

Plenary
Write a problem on the board and ask pupils to offer ways of approaching the calculation. Discuss the copymaster if used in this lesson.

Lesson 4

Introduction
Review previous work done on measuring mass. Ask quick fire questions relating to mass and capacity, such as 'How many ml in $\frac{1}{4}$ l?'

Activities
Whole class
Ask for examples where you need to measure capacity and weight. Establish that these are both useful in cooking. Give an example of a recipe – this could be a recipe for making a particular drink or one needing other liquid measures, *e.g. making a sauce*. Identify appropriate questions to ask about this. Discuss how much of the various ingredients you would need to make twice the quantity etc.

Individual/pair
Provide examples of various measuring problems including recipes. Include some straightforward addition and subtraction examples.

Differentiation
Ask a variety of questions to provide work at appropriate levels for all pupils.

Plenary
Discuss examples in detail and ask pupils to describe their methods and working.

Lesson 5

Introduction
Quick fire questions relating to weights and capacity.

Activities
Whole class
Ask pupils to set similar questions for each other. Establish that if someone asks a question they must be able to provide the answer themselves. Questions should be written down and not shown to other people. Each pupil should think of at least three questions, although they could think of more. Divide the class into two groups. Pupils take it in turns to ask a question to a member of the other group. A correct answer gains a point for the team. If that person is unable to answer, the questioner's team gains a point provided that the questioner can give the correct answer, otherwise his or her team loses a point.

Individual/pair
Copymaster 46 – problems involving capacity.

Differentiation
Provide additional support for *lower attainers*.

Plenary
Discuss the examples on the copymaster. Ask pupils to explain their methods and working.

Theme 4 — Reflection and angles

Objectives
- Sketch reflection of a simple shape in a mirror
- Read and begin to write the vocabulary of movement
- Make and describe patterns involving translation
- Begin to measure angles in degrees
- Know: whole turn, 360°, 4 right angles; quarter turn, 90°, 1 right angle; half turn, 180°, 2 right angles; 30°, 60°
- Recognise 45° as half a right angle
- Identify position with reference to a square grid

Vocabulary
shape, pattern, flat, line, curved, straight, round, hollow, solid, corner, point, pointed, face, side, edge, end, sort, make, build, construct, draw, sketch, centre, radius, diameter, net, surface, angle, right-angled, base, square-based, vertex, vertices, layer, diagram, regular, irregular, concave, convex, open, closed, 3D, 2D, three-dimensional, two-dimensional, cube, cuboid, pyramid, sphere, hemisphere, spherical, cone, cylinder, cylindrical, prism, tetrahedron, polyhedron, circle, circular, semicircle, triangle, triangular, equilateral, isosceles, square, rectangle, rectangular, oblong, pentagon, pentagonal, hexagon, hexagonal, polygon, quadrilateral, heptagon, octagon, symmetry, symmetrical, turn, rotate, whole turn, half turn, quarter turn, right angle, straight line, degree, ruler, angle measurer, set square, vertical, horizontal

Resources
Copymasters 7, 8, 47 and 48, Homework copymaster 24, set of shapes to draw round, mirrors

Assessment
At the end of this theme is the pupil able to:
- Sketch a simple shape or pattern in a mirror;
- Identify mirror lines on various shapes;
- Make patterns by translating a shape;
- Understand that a translation is a movement in a plane;
- Describe a translation;
- Understand units of measurement for angles and measure simple angles to 90°?

Lesson 1

Introduction
Discuss the general use of mirrors; look for the word *reflection*. Review previous work on line symmetry.

Activities
Whole class
Explain that it is possible to show a mirror image by drawing. Draw a simple pattern on the board and indicate a mirror line. Demonstrate how to set about drawing the image. Focus on the fact that points on the image are the same distance from the mirror line as points on the object.
Demonstrate that mirrors can be placed vertically, horizontally and diagonally.
Draw a pattern on the board and ask pupils how you can find a mirror line.
Introduce the words *symmetry* and *symmetrical*. Investigate mirror lines for regular polygons.

Individual/pair
Use Copymasters 7 and/or 8. Give pupils copies and ask them to draw in the mirror line or lines.

Differentiation
Low attainers should be given the opportunity to use mirrors to help establish where to draw the mirror line. They should only be asked to show one mirror line.
High attainers should be given the opportunity to draw patterns on squared paper and to draw the reflections. They may like to draw patterns for their partners.

Plenary
Discuss how mirror images are different from the object. Discuss ways in which the image changes if you move the position of the mirror. Establish that the mirror line is the position at which both sides are identical and the object and image together form the whole pattern. Were there any shapes which did not have a mirror line?

Lesson 2

Introduction
Draw a grid on the board. Label the horizontal axis A,B,C etc. and the vertical axis 1, 2, 3 etc. Indicate squares on the grid and ask pupils to identify squares by giving a grid reference, *e.g.* C4. Introduce the vocabulary *vertical axis, horizontal axis*.

Activities
Whole class
Draw a new grid with numbering in conventional notation. Note that the numbers now refer to the points on the grid rather than the squares. Ensure that pupils are secure with the convention that the horizontal co-ordinate is given first. Demonstrate how coordinate pairs are written.
Ask pupils to give coordinates of points you indicate on the board.

Individual/pair
Provide pupils with pre-drawn grids with letters of the alphabet on random grid points. Provide coded messages, as coordinate pairs, for them to decode. They could then be asked to code messages in the same way and pass them to friends to decode. Further activities could be to join points to form pictures.

Differentiation
Higher attainers could be asked to draw pictures of their own and give co-ordinates to a partner. Check that *lower attainers* are secure with the concept of two numbers as a co-ordinate and the order of the co-ordinates.

Plenary
Review any new vocabulary introduced. Ask pupils to describe how they used their knowledge of coordinates to solve the coded messages.

Summer Term

Lesson 3

Introduction
Explain to pupils that we can move shapes around according to fixed rules on a grid. Introduce the term *translation*. Explain that shapes can move horizontally and vertically but cannot turn or flip over.

Activities
Whole class
The lesson is devoted to practical work, drawing and investigating tessellation patterns. Demonstrate some simple patterns using rectangles.

Individual/pair
Provide each group of pupils with a variety of shapes to draw round and ask them to investigate various ways of making patterns.

Differentiation
Higher attainers may like to investigate shapes which will tessellate when they are translated.

Plenary
Ask pupils to think of ways to describe their patterns and the techniques they used to construct them, *e.g. 'The shape moves to the right/left/up/down...'*

Lesson 4

Introduction
Recap on previous work on angles. Draw a circle on the board. Put a dot in the middle. Ask how many degrees you would turn if you stood on the dot and turned all the way round. Ask how many degrees you would turn if you made a half turn or a quarter turn. Ask pupils to identify a right angle in the classroom. How many degrees are there in a right angle?

Activities
Whole class
Use a clock face to make turns of 90°, 60° and 30°. Establish that moving the hour hand from 12 o'clock to 3 o'clock is a turn through 90° and thus calculate the turn from 12 o'clock to 1 o'clock and 12 o'clock to 2 o'clock.
Draw clock faces on the board with hands at appropriate times, *e.g. 6.15,* and ask pupils to identify the angle between the hands.

Individual/pair
Copymaster 47 – identify all the right angles.

Differentiation
Higher attaining pupils could be asked to identify similar angles around the room, or use a set of shapes and identify 90°, 45°, 60° and 30° angles.

Plenary
Ensure that pupils are secure with the related vocabulary. Ask pupils to describe various turns in angles. Discuss the final open-ended task. What constraints are there in drawing shapes involving right angles, *e.g. 'Can you draw a triangle with two right angles? Why not?'*

Lesson 5

Introduction
Recap on work on measuring in degrees. Use the clock face as demonstrated in the previous lesson and ask pupils to estimate turns of the hands.

Activities
Whole class
The lesson is a practical activity measuring angles accurately. Pupils will need to be introduced to the use of an angle measurer.

Individual/pair
Copymaster 48 – measuring angles.

Differentiation
Low attainers are likely to need considerable support in the practical activity. The three angles at the top of the sheet could be cut off for *high attainers*. *Lower attainers* could cut these out and use them to check the angle sizes if using an angle measurer is too difficult.

Plenary
Review the pupils' approaches to using an angle measurer. Ask selected pupils to explain the use of the angle measurer to the rest of the class.

Theme 5 — Multiples

Objectives
- Recognise multiples of 2, 3, 4, 5, 10 up to 10th multiple
- Solve number problems and puzzles
- Explain methods and reasoning orally and in writing

Vocabulary
lots of, groups of, times, product, multiply, multiplied by, multiple of, once, twice, three times, four times...ten times, times as (big, long, wide and so on), repeated, addition, array, row, column, double, halve, share, share equally, one each, two each, three each..., group in pairs, threes... tens, equal groups of, divide, divided by, divided into, divisible by, remainder, factor, quotient, inverse

Resources
Copymasters 33, 49 and 50, Homework copymaster 25, tables squares, 100 squares

Assessment
At the end of this theme is the pupil able to:
- Recognise the term multiple and explain it;
- Find multiples of a given number;
- Understand that a number can be a multiple of more than one digit?

Lesson 1

Introduction
Use a large tables square. Ask pupils to tell you numbers which appear in the 3× table. Introduce the word *multiple*. Show pupils that the multiples of 3 appear in a row on the tables square and in a column.

Activities
Whole class
Ask pupils to tell you multiples of 4. Ask if anyone can tell you another row in the tables square where these numbers appear. Deduce that all multiples of 4 are also multiples of 2.

Individual/pair
Pupils work on small 100 squares to produce patterns of multiples. Look for the patterns produced by shading multiples of a single number. Ask pupils to shade in squares to show multiples of two numbers, *e.g. 2 and 3 or 3 and 4*. Look for patterns and for numbers which appear in both tables. Shade in different colours. Copymaster 33 has an example of a part-completed tables square which could be used in this lesson.

Differentiation
Check multiplication facts are secure for *lower attainers*. *Higher attaining* pupils should be asked to describe their multiple patterns in words. They could be asked to consider numbers which continue these patterns beyond the number square.

Plenary
Discuss the patterns identified by the pupils. Encourage pupils to use appropriate vocabulary when discussing their work. Ask pupils to describe the methods they used to identify numbers which would fit their patterns. Consider numbers which are multiples of more than one other number. Look for links between common multiples.

Lesson 2

Introduction
Quick fire multiplication questions based on known tables. Ask pupils to tell you a multiple of a given number.

Activities
Whole class
Write a set of three multiples on the board. These need not necessarily be in sequence. Ask pupils to tell you which table these multiples come from. Repeat until pupils are able to identify the table quickly.

Individual/pair
Copymaster 49.

Differentiation
Lower ability pupils could be helped to identify which part of the tables square is illustrated by covering parts of the square with card rectangles.

Plenary
Ask pupils to explain how they decide which table a multiple comes from. Review the activities on the copymaster. Ask pupils to explain their methods and reasoning for solving the puzzles.

Summer Term

Lesson 3

Introduction
Quick fire multiplication questions. Review the fact that multiplication is commutative. Review the words *multiple* and *product*.

Activities
Whole class
Write three digits on the board and ask pupils to calculate the answer if they are multiplied together. Establish that multiplication is associative. Repeat until pupils are secure in multiplying three digits.
Individual/pair
Copymaster 50.

Differentiation
The initial activity can be quite challenging. You will need to focus on the use of brackets to force the order of operations. Expect more from the *higher attaining* pupils. *Lower attainers* should be able to produce some of the required answers. *Higher attainers* might like to investigate which numbers they can form with four threes.

Plenary
Discuss the problems on the copymaster. Ask pupils to explain how they worked out the answers. Encourage them to use appropriate vocabulary. Discuss any puzzles made up by the pupils and ask others to explain how they would go about solving these.

Lesson 4

Introduction
Explain that the lesson is an investigation into number patterns. Look at previous work done on number sequences and link this to the work on multiples.

Activities
Whole class
Ask pupils to make up number puzzles – give target numbers. Review work on number patterns and ask pupils to make up similar. Provide blank sequence strips or number squares if required.
Individual/pair
Pupils should work in pairs for this activity. When they have completed a given number of puzzles, these should be passed on to another pair.

Differentiation
Lower attaining pupils may find this task difficult. Prepare some very structured tasks for these pupils.
Higher attaining pupils could be encouraged to consider a wide variety of puzzles in any of the forms they have met before.

Plenary
Ask pupils to comment on the way in which they worked out their puzzles. Those pupils who had the opportunity to solve another pair's puzzles could be asked to explain how they solved these.

Lesson 5

Introduction
Ask simple word sums, using all four rules as appropriate, e.g. 'If I buy 4 biscuits each costing 10p, how much will I spend?' 'There are 24 people in class. Half of them go swimming. How many are left in class?' Ask pupils to tell you the sum you need to do.

Activities
Whole class
Write a series of sums on the board and ask pupils to make up word puzzles to go with the sums. This can be done orally and the answers can be calculated, or not, as required.

Individual/pair
Provide a sheet of word puzzles for pupils to solve. Further examples similar to those on the two copymasters could be used.

Differentiation
Ensure that the resources provided for the individual work cover a range suitable for all ability levels.

Plenary
Ask pupils how they identified the sum to solve a word problem. Discuss examples from the individual work and ask pupils to explain their methods and reasoning.

Theme 6 — Multiplication and division

Objectives
- Understand distributive law
- Round up or down after division
- Use relation between × and ÷
- Use known facts to multiply and divide
- Develop and refine written methods for TU ÷ U

Vocabulary
lots of, groups of, times, product, multiply, multiplied by, multiple of, once, twice, three times, four times…ten times, times as (big, long, wide and so on), repeated, addition, array, row, column, double, halve, share, share equally, one each, two each, three each…, group in pairs, threes… tens, equal groups of, divide, divided by, divided into, divisible by, remainder, factor, quotient, inverse

Resources
Copymasters 51 and 52, Homework copymaster 26

Assessment
At the end of this theme is the pupil able to:
- Multiply and divide TU choosing appropriate strategies;
- Solve problems which require multiplication or division;
- Understand the link between multiplication and division?

Mental maths starter 6

Lesson 1

Introduction
Review partition of 2-digit numbers into tens and units. Write a 2-digit number on the board and ask 'How many tens are there in this number? How many units?'

Activities
Whole class
Oral questions — multiples of 10 multiplied by 2, 3, 4, 5. Write a 2-digit number on the board. Partition the number and ask how you would go about multiplying this number by 2, 3, 4, or 5. Demonstrate multiplication of the partitioned number. Repeat until pupils are secure with this process. Relate to previous work on this topic.

Individual/pair
Provide appropriate examples for practice.

Differentiation
Lower attainers may need support with this activity.
Higher attainers could be asked to multiply by 6,7,8 or 9 as appropriate.

Plenary
Ask pupils to describe the methods they use to do these sums. Were there any parts of the process they found particularly difficult?

Lesson 2

Introduction
Quick fire division questions phrased in a variety of ways — 'Share 12 between 2', 'How many 10s are there in 40?', 'Is 18 a multiple of 3?'

Activities
Whole class
Review previous work on division. Encourage pupils to estimate answers.

Individual/pair
Provide appropriate examples for practice.

Differentiation
Lower attainers are likely to need considerable support with this activity.
Higher attainers could be asked to develop appropriate checking methods.

Plenary
While pupils are working individually, identify any areas of difficulty and focus on these. Discuss the methods pupils use to work on the examples.

Summer Term

Lesson 3

Introduction
Establish that division is not commutative. Write sums with missing operators on the board. Ask pupils which symbol would make the sum correct. Write a part sum e.g. 5 ☐ 6 = or 9 ☐ 3 = 'What sum could this be?' 'Why do you think this?'

Activities
Whole class
Review work on remainders. Write a sum on the board, e.g. 24 ÷ 5. Relate to known tables facts. What is the nearest multiple of 5? = 20. How many lots of 5 make 20? = 4. If we take 20 away from 24, what's left? Identify limits for the division sum based on known multiples. Discuss the meaning of a remainder with reference to real life situations, e.g. 'If I share 10 sweets between 3 people...' What are the implications of this? Do not allow fractional answers.
If you are putting things in boxes, what do you do with left overs?

Individual/pair
Copymaster 51.

Differentiation
Low attaining pupils are likely to need support with the final activity when they are required to identify the starting number. *Higher attainers* could be provided with further problems of the type on the sheet.

Plenary
Focus on the copymaster activities. Ask pupils to explain their methods and reasoning. Discuss inverse operations in relation to the final activity on the copymaster.

Lesson 4

Introduction
Quick fire questions on the relationship between multiplication and division, e.g. 'If 15 × 5 is 75, what is 75 divided by 15?'

Activities
Whole class
Review approaches to division as used in the previous lesson. Write some simple division sums on the board and ask pupils to identify which two multiples are relevant. Calculate the answer and remainder. When pupils are secure with this, move to 2-digit numbers greater than known multiples. Ask pupils to identify the highest multiple they know, i.e. 10 × .... Take this away from the original number and repeat the process with the remainder.
Record your working and reasoning.
Encourage pupils to provide an estimate of the answer.
Repeat the process until pupils are secure.

Individual/pair
Set appropriate examples for pupils to practise.

Differentiation
Ensure that examples are set at levels appropriate for the ability range.

Plenary
While pupils are working, observe any areas of particular difficulty and focus on these. Ask pupils to explain their methods and working. Ask if there are any strategies they could employ to check their answers.

Lesson 5

Introduction
Quick fire questions – Divide multiples of 100 by 10 or 100.

Activities
Whole class
Write a division sum, of the type practised in the introduction, on the board and ask pupils to identify whether the number has been divided by 10 or 100, e.g. 5000 ÷ ☐ = 500: 'What did I divide by?' Review the work done in the previous lesson. Ask pupils to suggest ways of writing the sum and working which would standardise the class approach. Demonstrate the standard written method and discuss the advantages of setting out the sum like this.
Review what happens when it becomes necessary to cross the tens boundary.

Individual/pair
Copymaster 52.

Differentiation
Lower attaining pupils frequently find division more difficult because of poor recall of tables facts. If necessary provide tables squares. *Low attainers* may also have difficulty with calculations which involve crossing the 10s boundary. Consider limiting examples for these pupils.

Plenary
Focus on the pupils' approaches to the standard division questions. Ask pupils to explain their methods step by step. Did they estimate the answer? Did they find a way to check their answers?

Theme 7 — Solving problems

Objectives
- Choose appropriate operations and calculation methods to solve money and real life word problems with one or more steps
- Explain working
- Check results by approximating

Vocabulary
seconds, minutes, hours, big, bigger, small, smaller, weight, heavy/light, heavier/lighter, heaviest/lightest, weigh, weighs, kilogram, half-kilogram, gram, length, width, height, long, short, tall, high, low, wide, narrow, deep, shallow, thick, thin, longer, shorter, taller, higher, longest, shortest, tallest, highest, edge, kilometre, metre, centimetre, millimetre, ruler, measure, measuring, estimate, penny, pence, pound, price, cost, buy, bought, sell, sold, spent, spend, pay, change, costs more, costs less, cheaper, less/least expensive, how much? how many? total, amount, value

Resources
Copymasters 53 and 54, Homework copymaster 27, appropriate resources for lesson 5 – holiday brochures, modified versions of price lists and timetables

Assessment
At the end of this theme is the pupil able to:
- Choose appropriate operations to solve real life problems;
- Calculate using mental or pencil and paper methods as appropriate;
- Demonstrate secure use of a variety of units for measurement?

Lesson 1

Introduction
Review units of measurement. Ask pupils how many cm = 1m etc. Establish which units would be appropriate for measuring items in the classroom, the length or breadth of a room, distances between towns etc. Quick fire questions on any of these involving simple calculation.

Activities
Whole class
Write a problem on the board. Choose measures which may need pencil and paper calculation. Ask pupils to explain the process needed to approach the problem. Ask pupils to identify the sum needed. Ask a pupil to demonstrate and do the sum, explaining the method used. Repeat with a variety of problems until pupils can easily identify the appropriate operation and method.

Individual/pair
Identify and list several items around the classroom. Add some longer distances which may be familiar to the pupils. Ask pupils to copy the list into a table and to write in their estimate of the lengths involved. For all appropriate measurements, pupils should then measure the real length and write this in their table.

Differentiation
Set additional written problems for *higher attainers*.

Plenary
Compare the table of results. Ask who got close in their estimates. Compare estimates of longer distances.

Lesson 2

Introduction
Review work done on money. Check pupils can tell you how many pence in a pound etc. Give simple calculation problems relating to change – How many of these can I buy with £1? etc. Quick fire questions involving simple calculation of money using all four rules.

Activities
Whole class
Write a money problem on the board. Base this on any of the types of sum covered in the introduction. Ask pupils to explain the process needed to approach the problem. Ask pupils to identify the sum needed. Ask a pupil to demonstrate and do the sum, explaining the method used. Repeat with a variety of problems until pupils can easily identify the appropriate operation and method.

Individual/pair
Copymaster 53 – real life problems.

Differentiation
Set additional problems for *higher attainers*.

Plenary
Discuss the problems on the copymaster. Encourage pupils to explain their reasoning and methods.

Summer Term

Lesson 3

Introduction
Ask pupils to identify units used to measure mass. How many grams = 1 kg, $\frac{1}{2}$ kg? Ask 'This box weighs ..., the smaller one weighs half. How much does the small one weigh?' Total weights in both grams and kilograms. Quick fire questions on mass involving simple calculation.

Activities
Whole class
Draw a set of weights on the board. Ask pupils to tell you the total weight. Write a shopping list on the board. Ask pupils to tell you appropriate weights for the various items.

Individual/pair
Set written problems involving all four rules. Refer to the shopping lists: I buy 4 tins of beans and 2 tins of sausages etc.

Differentiation
Set more challenging problems for *higher attainers*.

Plenary
Ask pupils to explain their methods and working with reference to the problems set.

Lesson 4

Introduction
Review vocabulary related to time. Check pupils' understanding of the calendar.
Draw clock faces on the board. Ask 'What is the time now? What time will it be in 10 minutes?' etc. Check understanding of both analogue and digital clock faces.

Activities
Whole class
Ask questions involving adding or subtracting time: 'My journey to the supermarket took 20 minutes each way. I spent 30 minutes in the supermarket. How long did my shopping take?' 'John arrived home at 4.15. School finished at 3.30. How long did it take him to get home?' Review using a timetable. Draw a timetable on the board and ask appropriate questions relating to journey times.

Individual/pair
Copymaster 54.

Differentiation
Provide additional examples for *higher attainers*.

Plenary
Discuss the problems on the worksheet. Ask pupils to demonstrate their approach to the problems. Ask them to explain their reasoning and methods.

Lesson 5

Introduction
Explain that the lesson is about going on holiday. Pupils will have to choose appropriate dates for their holidays, find out the cost for a family and look at plane, train or coach timetables.

Activities
Whole class
You should prepare appropriate details for three different holidays: a holiday abroad involving air travel; a coach tour; and a seaside holiday travelling by train. Provide information on dates, holiday cost for a family with children and appropriate timetables. Base these on the tables in holiday brochures but ensure that they are accessible to all pupils. You could also provide real holiday brochures for discussion if required.

Individual/pair
Pupils should choose a holiday from the list; decide when they want to go and work out the total cost for their family; write a timetable for the day they travel, including the time of leaving home, travel times and arrival time. This information should be presented for display.
Note: This lesson could last for two lessons if required and could replace the previous lesson on time.

Differentiation
Allow *lower attaining* pupils to work in pairs.
Higher attainers should work alone.

Plenary
Discuss the various holidays planned by pupils. Ask them how they worked out costs etc.

Theme 8 — Fractions and decimals

Objectives
- Begin to use ideas of simple proportion
- Recognise the equivalence of decimal and fraction forms of one half, one quarter and tenths

Vocabulary
part, equal parts, fraction, one, whole, half, quarter, eighth, third, sixth, fifth, tenth, twentieth, proportion, in every, for every, decimal, decimal fraction, decimal point, decimal place

Resources
Copymasters 37, 55 and 56, Homework copymaster 28

Assessment
At the end of this theme is the pupil able to:
- Identify fraction–decimal equivalents;
- Order decimals;
- Compare objects of different size and describe in terms of a fraction?

Lesson 1

Introduction
Draw a simple repeating pattern on the board, *e.g. 3 white squares followed by one coloured*. Ask pupils to describe the pattern in words. Look for '…every 4th one is coloured, 3 out of 4 are white' etc.

Activities
Whole class
Show pictures of everyday items in different sizes, *e.g. a metre rule and a 50 cm rule, a piece of A4 paper and a piece of A5 paper*, and ask 'What fraction of the longer/larger is the shorter/smaller of these?' Ask 'What fraction of a £ is 50p?' 'How much is $\frac{1}{10}$ of £1.00?' Recap on fractions of a whole number, *e.g. 'What is $\frac{1}{4}$ of 40? What is $\frac{3}{4}$ of 40?'*

Individual/pair
Copymaster 55.

Differentiation
Higher attainers should be provided with further work on comparison of size and expressing an amount as a fraction of a bigger amount.

Plenary
Review the examples on the copymaster. Ask pupils to explain their methods of working. Focus on any areas of difficulty.

Lesson 2

Introduction
Recap on relative sizes of fractions. Ask 'Which is bigger: $\frac{1}{2}$ or $\frac{1}{4}$?' 'Which is smaller: $\frac{3}{5}$ or $\frac{4}{5}$?' Write sets of fractions on the board and ask pupils to arrange these in order of size. Discuss any difficulties in making decisions about size.

Activities
Whole class
Review work on finding fractions of metres, £ etc. covered in the previous lesson. Ask pupils questions about tenths of numbers, *e.g. 'What is $\frac{1}{10}$ of 20?'* Write these on the board and look for patterns. Ask pupils to identify $\frac{1}{100}$ of £1.00 and $\frac{1}{100}$ of a metre.
Review previous work on mixed numbers.

Individual/pair
Copymaster 56.

Differentiation
Provide further examples for *higher attainers*.

Plenary
Discuss the work on the sheet. Ask pupils to explain how they worked out $\frac{1}{10}$. Are there any patterns to this that they could use to check future answers?

Summer Term

Lesson 3

Introduction
Review previous work on decimals. Quick fire questions – Write 0.1 on the board and ask 'What fraction is the same as this decimal?' Establish all the fraction–decimal equivalents.

Activities
Whole class
Ask pupils to write down several sums of money, *e.g. two pounds twenty five pence, four pounds fifty pence*. Ask how many whole pounds there are. Ask how many pennies. Ask if anyone can recall what fraction of £1 one penny is. Pupils should be able to say that 1p is $\frac{1}{100}$. Focus on the notation and relate to normal decimal notation. Ask how you could write 50p as a decimal of £1.00. Focus on the use of the zero.

Individual/pair
Ask pupils to work out how many pennies in $\frac{1}{2}$ of £1.00, $\frac{1}{4}$ of £1.00, $\frac{3}{4}$ of £1.00 and express these as decimals. Set out the results in a chart or table.

Differentiation
Extension work for *higher attainers*: set division sums involving sums of money in £ or m, *e.g. 'half of ... $\frac{1}{5}$ of'* and ask pupils to write these as decimals.

Plenary
Review and discuss the relationship between decimal fractions of £1.00 and decimal fractions in general. Link fraction–decimal equivalents for $\frac{1}{4}$ and $\frac{3}{4}$. Review the use of the zero when writing pence with a pound sign. Link this to the work on mixed numbers.

Lesson 4

Introduction
Quick fire questions on decimals – 'Which is bigger: 0.3 or 0.4? Can you explain why?'

Activities
Whole class
Draw a number line with ten divisions. Start with zero and end with one. Write a decimal number on the board and ask where on the line it should go.

Individual/pair
Prepare a page of number lines in advance, with various starting points, *e.g. lines from 0 to 2, from 3 to 5*. Give each pupil a page. Write appropriate sets of decimals on the board and ask pupils to write these in order onto the number lines.

Differentiation
Ensure that the number lines and sets of decimals give a range appropriate to all abilities.

Plenary
Discuss how you identify where the decimal should go on the number line. Where would you put the decimal equivalents of $\frac{1}{4}$ and $\frac{3}{4}$?

Lesson 5

Introduction
Quick fire questions on one place decimals – 'What is the whole number part of...?' 'What is the decimal part of...?' 'Tell me a decimal between...'

Activities
Whole class
If $\frac{1}{10}$ can be written as 0.1, how would we write $\frac{2}{10}$, $\frac{3}{10}$ etc? Establish the decimal equivalent of $\frac{1}{2}$.

Individual/pair
Copymaster 56. The fraction wall on Copymaster 37 could be used to enable pupils to investigate decimal/fraction equivalents.

Differentiation
Lower attaining pupils could be asked to draw more diagrams, based on those on the copymaster, to illustrate other decimal and mixed numbers.
Higher attaining pupils could be asked to investigate decimal fraction equivalents for other appropriate fractions. Avoid $\frac{1}{3}$ and $\frac{1}{6}$.

Plenary
Review the examples on the sheets. Ask pupils to describe relationships between fractions and decimals in their own words.

Theme 9 — Time problems

Objectives
- Consolidate understanding of addition and subtraction
- Add/subtract mentally any pair of 2-digit whole numbers
- Refine column addition and subtraction
- Read timetables and use this year's calendar
- Solve problems involving time

Vocabulary
time, Monday, Tuesday…, January, February…, spring, summer, autumn, winter, day, week, fortnight, month, year, leap year, century, millennium, weekend, birthday, holiday, calendar, date, date of birth, morning, afternoon, evening, night, am, pm, noon, midnight, today, yesterday, tomorrow, before, after, next, last, now, soon, early, late, earliest, latest, quick, quicker, quickest, quickly, fast, faster, fastest, slow, slower, slowest, slowly, old, older, oldest, new, newer, newest, takes longer, takes less time, how long ago? how long will it be? how long will it take to? timetable, arrive, depart, hour, minute, second, o'clock, half past, quarter to, quarter past, clock, watch, hands, digital/analogue clock, timer, how often? always, never, sometimes, usually

Resources
Copymasters 57 and 58, Homework copymaster 29, display-size copy of calendar page for the current month

Assessment
At the end of this theme is the pupil able to:
- Read a timetable and answer questions based on it;
- Answer questions about the calendar;
- Solve problems involving time?

Lesson 1

Introduction
Quick fire questions on all four rules with particular emphasis on addition and subtraction. Ask pupils to stand up. Ask questions round the class. If a pupil answers incorrectly or cannot answer within a specified time they sit down. Continue questioning those standing until five remain. Then set a more complex question on the board and allow pupils to work it out on paper if necessary. The winner is the first to give the correct answer.

Activities
Whole class
Review adding using pencil and paper methods. Ask pupils to demonstrate techniques to the rest of the class. Write several sums on the board and set a time limit for their completion.
Review subtraction using pencil and paper methods. Ask pupils to demonstrate their working methods and discuss any problem areas involved in the subtraction process. Write several sums on the board and set a time limit for their completion.

Individual/pair
Write two appropriate sets of numbers on the board and ask pupils to use numbers from these sets to make as many different addition and subtraction sums as possible. Pupils should then do the sums. Ask them to give estimates of their answers.

Differentiation
Encourage *higher attainers* to form more complex sums including addition of 3 numbers.

Plenary
Review the methods used by pupils to do their sums. Ensure that all pupils are able to give an account of the methods they use.

Lesson 2

Introduction
Review working with time. Quick fire questions – 'How long between two given times?' 'If I start at a given time and do something for half an hour, what time will I finish?'

Activities
Whole class
Write a list of the day's plan on the board, e.g. Assembly, Literacy Hour…
Ask pupils to suggest a period of time appropriate for each activity. Write these times beside the activities.
Using these times, plan out a timetable for the school day. Ask pupils to give you starting and finishing times for the day. Establish how long lessons, playtimes and lunch time should be.

Individual/pair
Draw a weekly timetable on the board, or provide a copy for each pair, and set questions on reading information from the timetable, e.g. 'How many hours a week do we spend doing maths?'

Differentiation
Higher ability pupils could be asked to draw up a timetable for a day, or week, on holiday.

Plenary
Discuss the sort of information which can be displayed on a timetable. What makes a timetable easy to read? Ask pupils to explain how they did any calculations involved, e.g. 'Do you have a maths lesson each day? Is it always the same length of time? What sort of sums did you do to work out total times?'

Summer Term

Lesson 3

Introduction
Ask pupils to give examples of timetables other than the daily timetable discussed in the previous lesson. Try to establish that we use timetables for most forms of travel, especially bus and train. TV programme listings might be considered. Ask 'Why do we need timetables?'

Activities
Whole class
Draw a simple example of a bus timetable on the board. Ask pupils questions based on this timetable.

Individual/pair
Copymaster 57 – reading and understanding a timetable.

Differentiation
Lower attaining pupils may have problems working out how long between stops. Check their ability to do calculations based on time.

Plenary
Watch for any pupils who are experiencing difficulties with this work. Focus on any areas of difficulty. Review the questions on the copymaster and ask pupils to explain how they approached the tasks.

Lesson 4

Introduction
Review vocabulary connected with the calendar. How many days in a week? In a year? What is a leap year?

Activities
Whole class
Have a prepared large copy of the calendar for the month in which you are working. Ask questions based on the calendar page, e.g. 'How many Tuesdays are there?' 'What is the date today?' 'What will the date be in a week's time?' Identify any birthdays during the months.

Individual/pair
Provide each pair with a year's calendar and a set of similar questions which they can answer by referring to this.

Differentiation
Lower attainers could be provided with part of a calendar, 3 or 4 months, and similar questions set at an appropriate level for their ability.
Higher attainers could be asked to produce a set of similar questions of their own and ask these of a partner.

Plenary
Ask pupils to explain how they set about solving the problems with reference to the calendar.

Lesson 5

Introduction
Review names for longer periods of time – millennium, century. Discuss events which happen weekly, monthly and annually.

Activities
Whole class
Produce a time line to record significant events of the past year. Discuss how this could be extended to show events over a much longer period of time. Choose a period appropriate to the pupils' experiences.

Individual/pair
Copymaster 58. Review the number of days in each month – perhaps with reference to the rhyme '30 days has September...' Note that the months shown on the copymaster have 30, 31, 31 days respectively. Examine the year calendar to identify which months these are likely to be.

Differentiation
If *lower attaining* pupils have difficulty working out the times, they could either put this information onto a time line or could draw digital clock faces as an aid.
Ask *higher attaining* pupils to make up a timetable of their own relating to the local area.

Plenary
Ask pupils to explain their approaches to the problems. How did they decide which months were shown? Was there another set of possibilities? How did they work out the times for the bus timetable?

65

Theme 10 Handling data

Objectives
- Solve a given problem by collecting, classifying, representing and interpreting data in Venn and Carroll Diagrams: two criteria
- Use a computer and a branching tree program to sort shapes or numbers

Vocabulary
count, tally, sort, vote, survey, questionnaire, data graph, block graph, pictogram, represent, group, set, list, chart, bar chart, tally chart, table, frequency table, Carroll Diagram, Venn Diagram, label, title, axis, axes, diagram, most popular, most common, least popular, least common

Resources
Copymasters 7, 8, 59 and 60, Homework copymaster 30, sets of shapes

Assessment
At the end of this theme is the pupil able to:
- Draw a Venn or Carroll Diagram and put information into the correct regions;
- Classify information into sets according to given criteria;
- Understand and use a tree diagram;
- Collect and classify data?

Lesson 1

Introduction
Quick fire questions on number properties, e.g. *'Tell me a multiple of 4, 8, 20, 15, 37 – Which of these are odd numbers?', 'If you add two odd numbers together, what type of number do you get?'*

Activities
Whole class
Draw a circle on the board and write a set of numbers in the circle. Ask pupils to tell you a common property, using the vocabulary above. Repeat this activity using a variety of criteria. Draw a circle with even numbers to 20. Ask pupils to identify the common property. Establish that they are all multiples of 2. Ask if there is another property which applies to some of them. Establish that they are multiples of 4. Repeat with multiples of 5 and establish that some are also multiples of 10.
Write individual numbers on the board and ask pupils to identify sets the numbers could belong to.
Use these numbers to form several sets and demonstrate how you could use two overlapping circles to show how these go together. Introduce the term *Venn Diagram*.

Individual/pair
Copymaster 59.

Differentiation
Provide further examples for *high attainers*.

Plenary
Discuss examples from the copymaster. Ask pupils to explain how they organised the data. How did they decide on the common property for a set of numbers?

Lesson 2

Introduction
Ask pupils to explain methods previously employed for collecting data. They should be able to identify a *tally chart*. Draw a tally chart on the board for numbers 1 to 6. Go round the class asking pupils to give you a number in this range and tally their responses.

Activities
Whole class
Ask pupils to give you a list of their six favourite activities. List these activities on the board and then draw a tally chart. Go round the class and ask pupils to tell you their two favourites from the list. Tally the responses. Discuss how this information could be displayed. Look for awareness of pictograms or bar charts.

Individual/pair
Ask pairs to produce a list of six favourite animals. The animals identified by the pair may contain a different selection. Pairs should then ask other pupils to name their favourite two from the list. Results should be shown on a tally chart and finally each pair should produce a frequency table.

Differentiation
Higher attaining pupils could be asked to draw a bar chart showing the information gathered.

Plenary
Ask pupils to report on their findings and collect all the information into one frequency table. Discuss how the information might have altered if people had been asked to give two points for their favourite and one point for their second.

Summer Term

Lesson 3

Introduction
Quick fire questions relating to shapes and their properties, *e.g. 'What is the name we give to a shape with 5 sides?' 'Tell me a shape which has 4 right angles.'*

Activities
Whole class
Draw several shapes on the board and ask pupils to tell you as many facts as they can about each one. Classify the shapes into groups using some of the criteria suggested by the pupils. Relate the process to the work done in lesson 1 on classifying numbers.
Explain that there is an alternative diagram which can be used to classify. Demonstrate a *Carroll Diagram* and introduce the term. Choose appropriate sets and classify some of the shapes by putting them into the right place on the diagram.

Individual/pair
Use Copymasters 7 and 8 and ask pupils to classify the shapes according to two criteria, *e.g. regular shapes and quadrilaterals*. Pupils should then put the shapes into the correct place on a Carroll Diagram.

Differentiation
Higher attaining pupils should be asked to identify other possible criteria and to draw Carroll Diagrams to demonstrate these.

Plenary
Discuss how pupils decided where to put each shape. Discuss other criteria which might have been used. Ask what an empty region shows.

Lesson 4

Introduction
Review the two types of diagram used. Ensure that pupils are familiar with the terms. Discuss the similarities between the two. Review the vocabulary associated with classifying data.

Activities
Whole class
Draw either a Venn Diagram or a Carroll Diagram on the board. Relate this to possible journeys to work, *e.g. people could go to work by car or by train.* Discuss what each of the various regions shows.

Individual/pair
Prepare a copymaster similar to Copymaster 59. Ask pupils to describe marked regions in words. Give a diagram with sets of numbers in the regions and ask pupils to identify the regions by name and give a pair of sorting criteria.

Differentiation

Plenary
Discuss work done by the pupils. Ask them to explain how they decided what things could go in which region and how they decided on the criteria.

Lesson 5

Introduction
Draw several patterns, based on a rectangle, on the board. Patterns could include shading, spots or vertical or horizontal lines. Label diagrams a...b...c... etc. Demonstrate how these can be classified into groups according to various criteria. Ask pupils 'Which shape has three spots and vertical shading?' etc.

Activities
Whole class
Demonstrate how to devise a tree diagram with this information which will lead to a classification of all the shapes.

Individual/pair
Copymaster 60.

Differentiation
Higher attainers could attempt to draw a tree diagram to assist in the classification of appropriately selected 2D shapes.

Plenary
Ask pupils to explain the decisions they made. Review the results obtained on the copymaster. Ask pupils to draw or describe other mini-beasts which could be included in one of the categories.

Copymaster 1

Doubles – patterns and puzzles

Write in the doubles of these numbers.

8	—		32	—		86	—	
80	—		61	—		92	—	
9	—		28	—		132	—	
90	—		74	—		219	—	
24	—		35	—		352	—	

Write in a half of each of these numbers.

60	—		84	—		240	—	
40	—		62	—		180	—	
70	—		76	—		264	—	
30	—		32	—		428	—	
50	—		120	—		504	—	

I think of a number and double it. My answer is 24. What is my number?

I think of a number and double it. I add 6. My answer is 28. What is my number?

I think of a number and double it. My answer is 56. What is my number?

I think of a number and double it. I add 5. My answer is 37. What is my number?

I think of a number and double it. I add 9. My answer is 81. What is my number?

I think of a number and double it. I take away 6. My answer is 44. What is my number?

I think of a number and double it. I subtract 5. My answer is 85. What is my number?

I think of a number and halve it. My answer is 14. What is my number?

I think of a number and halve it. I add 5. My answer is 30. What is my number?

I think of a number and halve it. I take away 7. My answer is 73. What is my number?

Missing numbers

1 I did my homework and left it on the table. My baby brother threw his tea all over it. Can you help by filling in the missing numbers?

100 − 32 = ◯   100 − 89 = ◯   100 − 15 = ◯

32 + ◯ = 100   89 + ◯ = 100   15 + ◯ = 100

79 + 95 = ◯   38 + 59 = ◯   44 + 62 = ◯

174 − ◯ = 79   97 − ◯ = 59   ◯ − 44 = 62

2 Here are some sums made up with different number tiles. Write in any missing numbers to make the sums right.

Write each sum in a different way using the same number tiles but $\boxed{-}$ instead of $\boxed{+}$ or $\boxed{+}$ instead of $\boxed{-}$.

| 83 | + | ☐ | = | 100 | | 26 | + | ☐ | = | 100 | | 13 | + | 94 | = | ☐ |
| ☐ | ☐ | ☐ | = | ☐ | | ☐ | ☐ | ☐ | = | ☐ | | ☐ | ☐ | ☐ | = | ☐ |

| ☐ | − | 41 | = | 100 | | 75 | − | 58 | = | ☐ | | 67 | − | 9 | = | ☐ |
| ☐ | ☐ | ☐ | = | ☐ | | ☐ | ☐ | ☐ | = | ☐ | | ☐ | ☐ | ☐ | = | ☐ |

| 100 | − | 22 | = | ☐ | | 39 | − | 18 | = | ☐ | | ☐ | + | 41 | = | 132 |
| ☐ | ☐ | ☐ | = | ☐ | | ☐ | ☐ | ☐ | = | ☐ | | ☐ | ☐ | ☐ | = | ☐ |

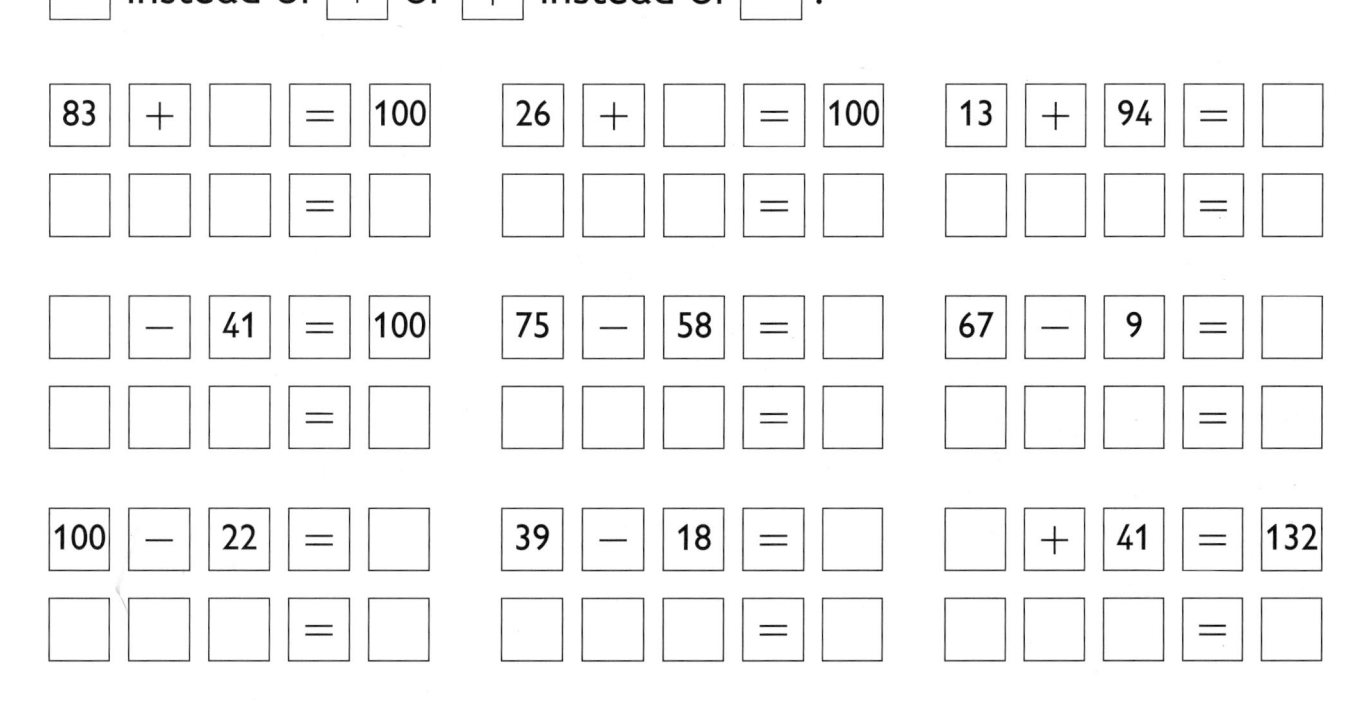

Copymaster 3

| 1p | 2p | 5p |

75p	122p	31p	107p	305p
221p	230p	27p	155p	112p
57p	17p	206p	211p	16p
125p	301p	53p	71p	170p
26p	310p	115p	255p	152p

225p	302p	35p	260p	13p
121p	32p	222p	56p	151p
80p	130p	160p	350p	62p
212p	27p	203p	65p	215p
106p	252p	72p	320p	111p

10p

20p

50p

£1.00

£2.00

Money problems

Jo had three rides on the bumper cars at the park. Each ride cost 80p. How much did he spend?
Write down the sum:

Emily bought six doughnuts. Each doughnut cost 20p. How much did she spend?
Write down the sum:

Billy went out for the day. His train fare was £18.00 and he spent £7.00 on food. How much did he spend?
Write down the sum:

Mum bought four boxes of new tiles for the kitchen. Each box cost £10.00. How much did the boxes cost altogether?
Write down the sum:

Mum bought a cake for £2.50, a packet of biscuits for £0.99 and two loaves of bread costing 60p each. How much did she spend?
Write down the sum:

Sam's mum took Sam and five friends into town on the bus. Mum's fare was £2.00. A child fare was £1.00. How much did Sam's mum have to pay?
Write down the sum:

The teacher bought some treats for her class. She bought 10 chocolate bars costing 40p each, 10 packets of sweets costing 50p each, 10 packets of crisps costing 25p per packet and 4 cereal bars costing 30p each. How much did she spend altogether?
Write down the sum:

Brian bought a computer game costing £29.99, a CD costing £9.99 and two tapes costing £4.99 each. How much did he spend?
Write down the sum:

Copymaster 5

Maps

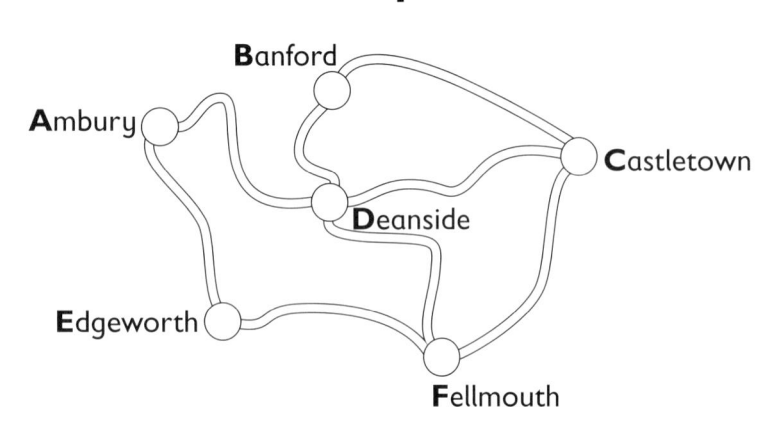

Map: Banford, Ambury, Castletown, Deanside, Edgeworth, Fellmouth

Distance (km) To

From\To	A	B	C	D	E	F
A				9	8	
B			17	5		
C		17		21		19
D	9	5	21			11
E	8					12
F			19	11	12	

1 On the map, write the distances between each of the villages.

2 My auntie came to stay and my mum took her for a drive. They went from Fellmouth to Edgeworth then to Ambury, Deanside and Castletown.
They drove straight back to Fellmouth. How far did they travel altogether?

3 Which village did they miss out?

4 This table shows the distances between some towns in miles. Use it to help you answer these questions.

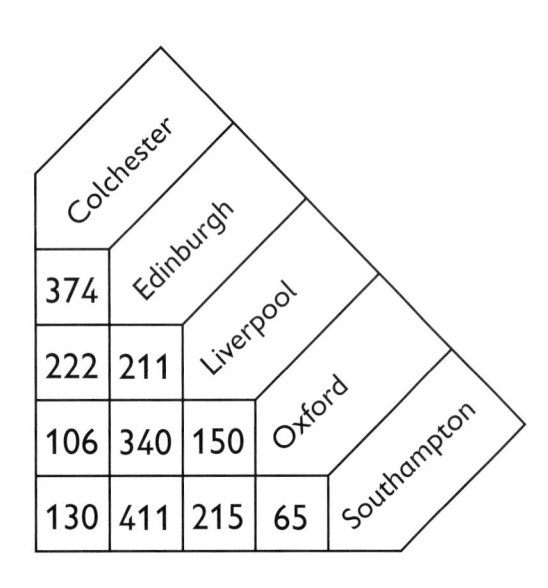

Distance table:
- Colchester
- Edinburgh: 374
- Liverpool: 222, 211
- Oxford: 106, 340, 150
- Southampton: 130, 411, 215, 65

a How far is it from Southampton to Edinburgh?
b How far is it from Colchester to Liverpool?
c Which journey would be the longest?
d What would the shortest journey be?

5 Use these distance tables to make up some problems of your own. Give them to a friend to do.

Real life measuring

1) Tony, Bill and Giles went to the fair. On one of the rides there was a minimum height of 1 m 30 cm. Tony is $1\frac{1}{4}$ m tall. Bill is $1\frac{1}{2}$ m tall and Giles is 135 cm tall.
Which of the boys could go on the ride?

2) Mum wants new bedroom curtains. The windows are 120 cm long and 200 cm wide. You can buy curtains in lengths of 1 m, $1\frac{1}{2}$ m and 2 m. Which length would be best for our windows?

3) Mrs. Brown wanted to build some new bookshelves. She wanted 4 shelves each 80 cm long. The wood comes in lengths of 1 m. How much wood was wasted for each shelf? If you put all the shelves in one long line how long would the line be?

4) Dad wants to paint the ceiling. He can reach up to $2\frac{1}{4}$ m. The ceiling is 2 m 20 cm from the floor. Will dad be able to reach?

5) Our new hall carpet is 6 m long. The hall is 5 m 60 cm long. How much carpet will we have to cut off?

6) The teacher wanted to take a group photograph. She wanted two rows. The tallest people had to stand at the back.
Ellie is 1 m 20 cm tall, Sarah is 115 cm tall, Leo is $1\frac{1}{4}$ m tall, Laura is 142 cm tall, Sam is 1 m 17 cm tall and Joseph is 138 cm tall.
Which three people stood in the back row?

7) For another photo the group had to stand in order of height, starting with the shortest. Write their names in the order they had to stand.

8) I had to pack the baby's bricks into their box. Each brick is 5 cm thick. The box will hold three layers. How deep is the box.

9) Tony was using centimetre cubes in the lesson. He made a row of the cubes. There were 283 cubes altogether. How long was his row?

A puzzle

Dad wants to chop back the creeper on our house. The creeper grows up to 4 m on the wall. We have a ladder 2 m long. How high up the wall do you think Dad can reach?

Copymaster 7

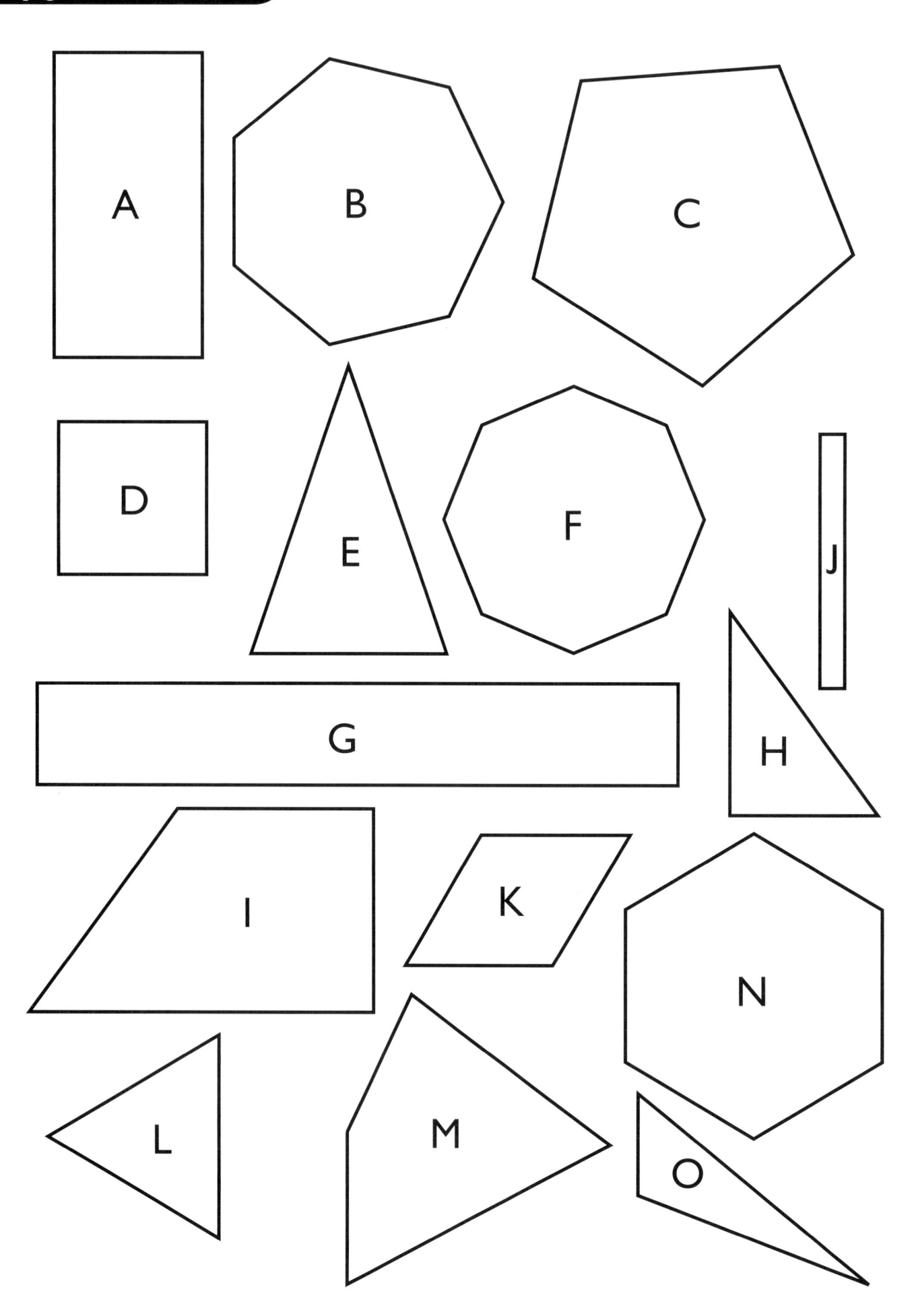

Copymaster 8

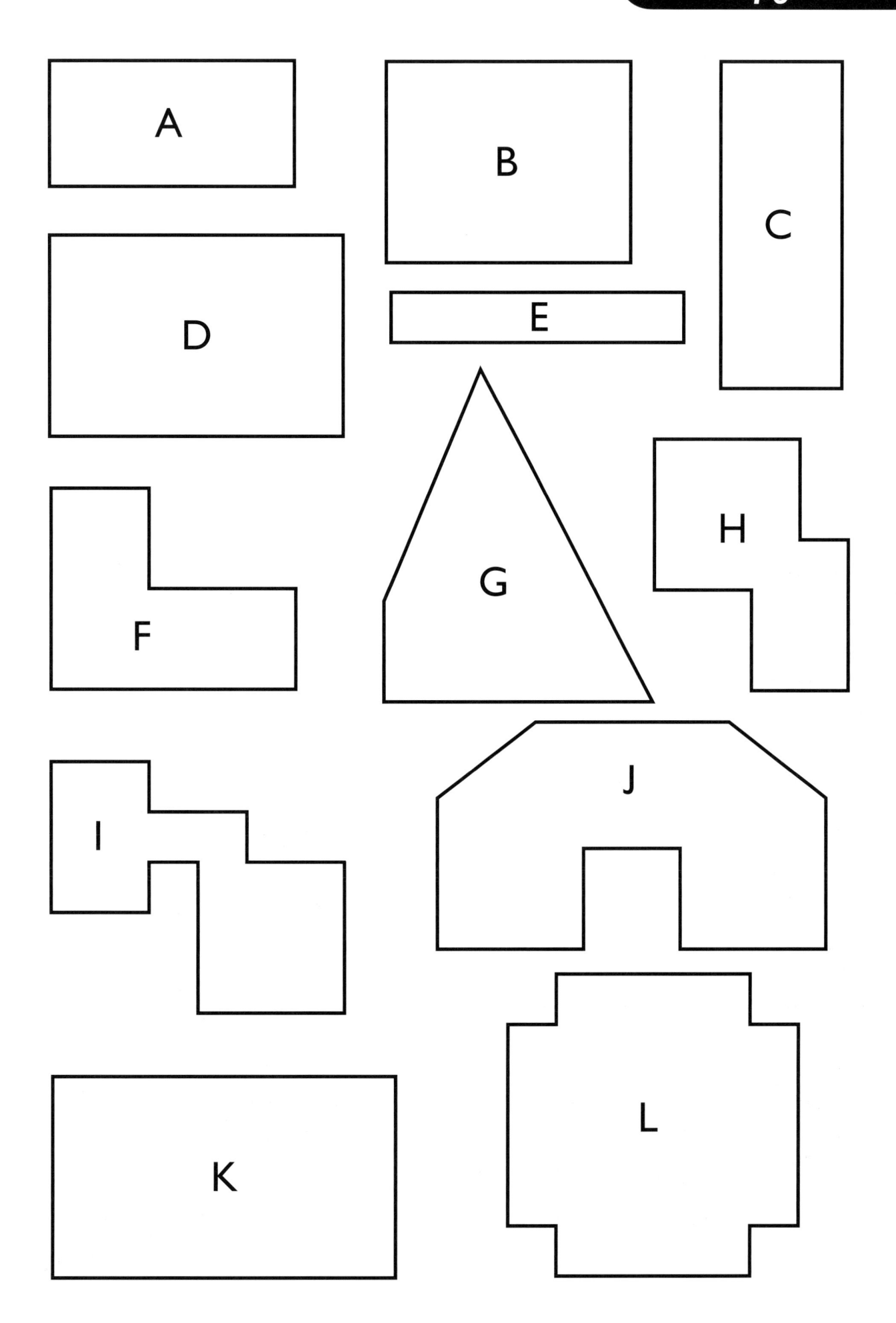

A
B
C
D
E
F
G
H
I
J
K
L

Copymaster 9

Here are some objects that you might find at home or at school. Write the name of the shape or solid the object is most like.

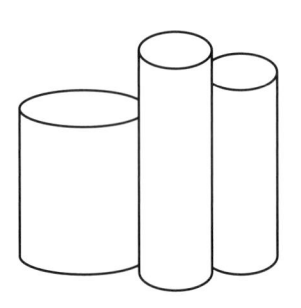

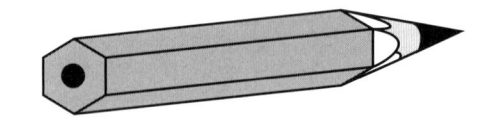

This pencil is a _____

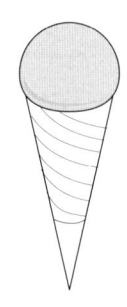

This pencil holder is 3 _____

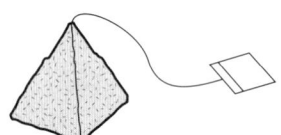

This ice-cream is a _____
and a _____

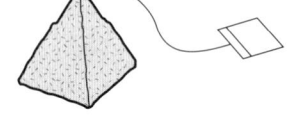

This tea bag is a _____

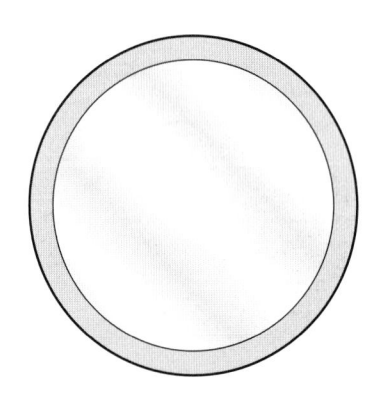

This book is a _____

This mirror is a _____

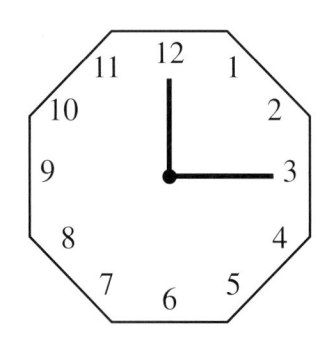

One kitchen tile is a _____

Together they make a _____

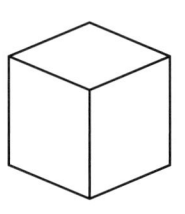

This clock face is an _____

This building block is a _____

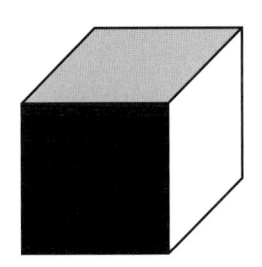

Copymaster 10

This solid is a _____
Each face is a _____

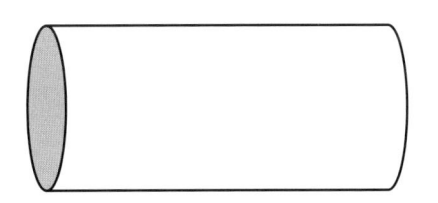

This solid is a _____
The grey face is a _____

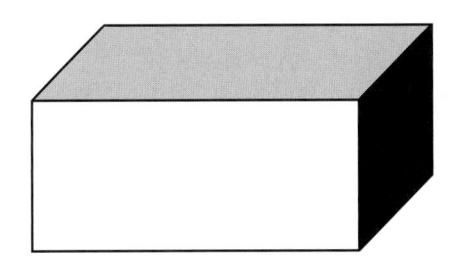

This solid is a _____
The white face is a _____

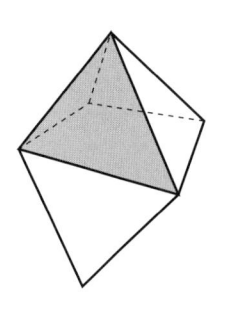

This solid is a _____
The grey face is a _____

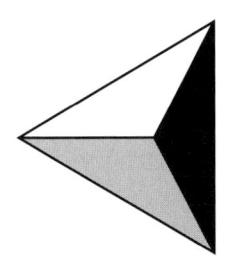

This solid is a _____
Each face is a _____

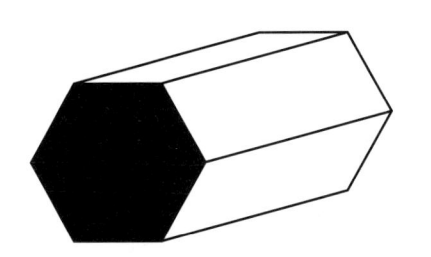

This solid is a _____
The black face is a _____

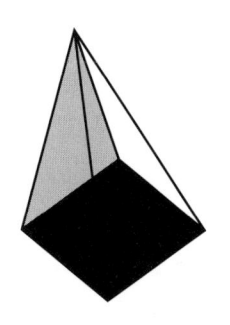

This solid is a _____
The black face is a _____

This solid is a _____
The white face is a _____

77

Copymaster 11

Number snakes

Work out the number pattern and fill in the missing numbers on the snakes.

13, 23, 33, ..., ..., 63, ..., ..., ...

To finish the pattern I had to
_____
_____

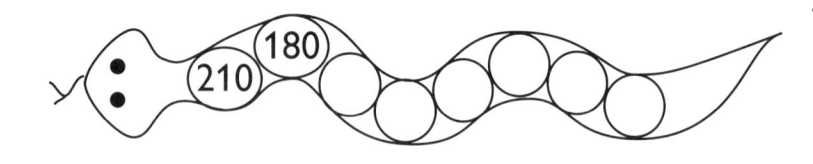

210, 180, ..., ..., ..., ..., ..., ...

To finish the pattern I had to
_____
_____

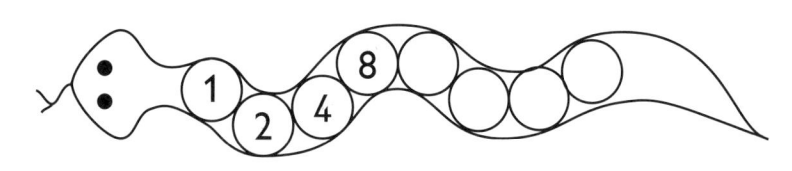

1, 2, 4, 8, ..., ..., ..., ...

To finish the pattern I had to
_____
_____

18, 27, 36, ..., ..., 63, ..., ..., ..., ...

To finish the pattern I had to
_____
_____

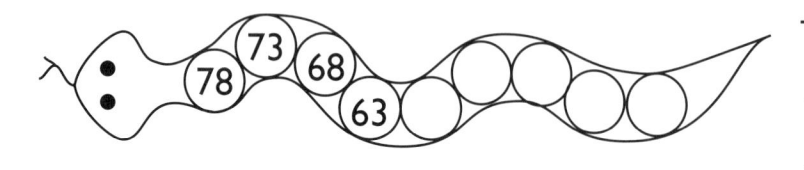

78, 73, 68, 63, ..., ..., ..., ...

To finish the pattern I had to
_____
_____

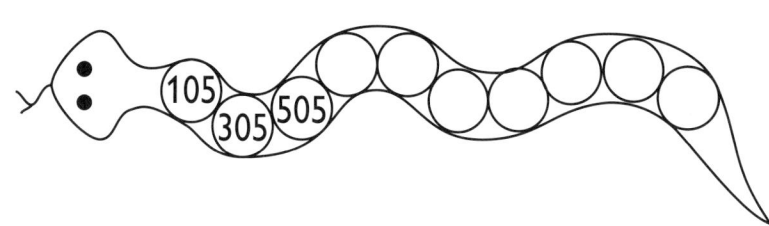

105, 305, 505, ..., ..., ..., ..., ...

To finish the pattern I had to
_____
_____

78

Copymaster 12

Number puzzles

Fill in the missing numbers for each of these number squares.
In each square the rows, columns and diagonals must add up to the same number (*magic number*).

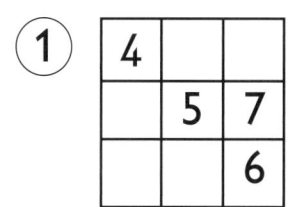

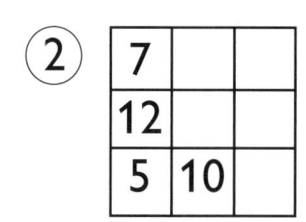

1)
4		
	5	7
		6

2)
7		
12		
5	10	

3)
11	12	7
		14
13		

In square 1 the magic number is _____

The numbers used in the square are _____

I could find these number sequences in the square _____

_____

In square 2 the magic number is _____

The numbers used in the square are _____

I could find these number sequences in the square _____

_____

In square 3 the magic number is _____

The numbers used in the square are _____

I could find these number sequences in the square _____

_____

24

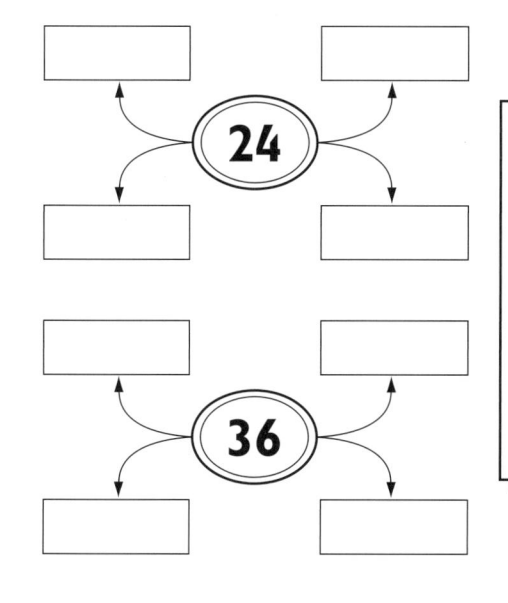

36

Target Numbers

How many different sums can you find for each target number?

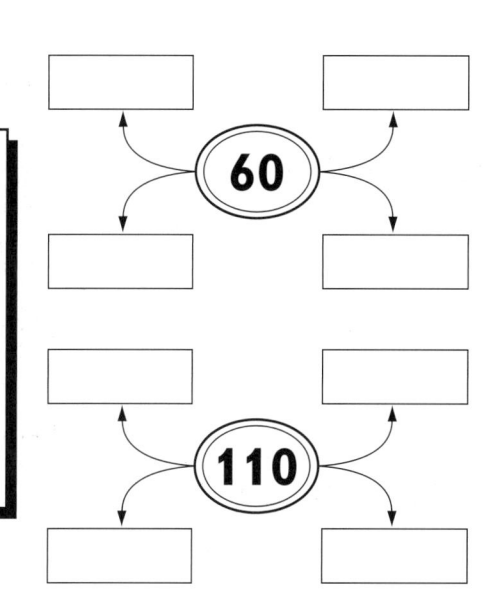

60

110

79

Copymaster 13

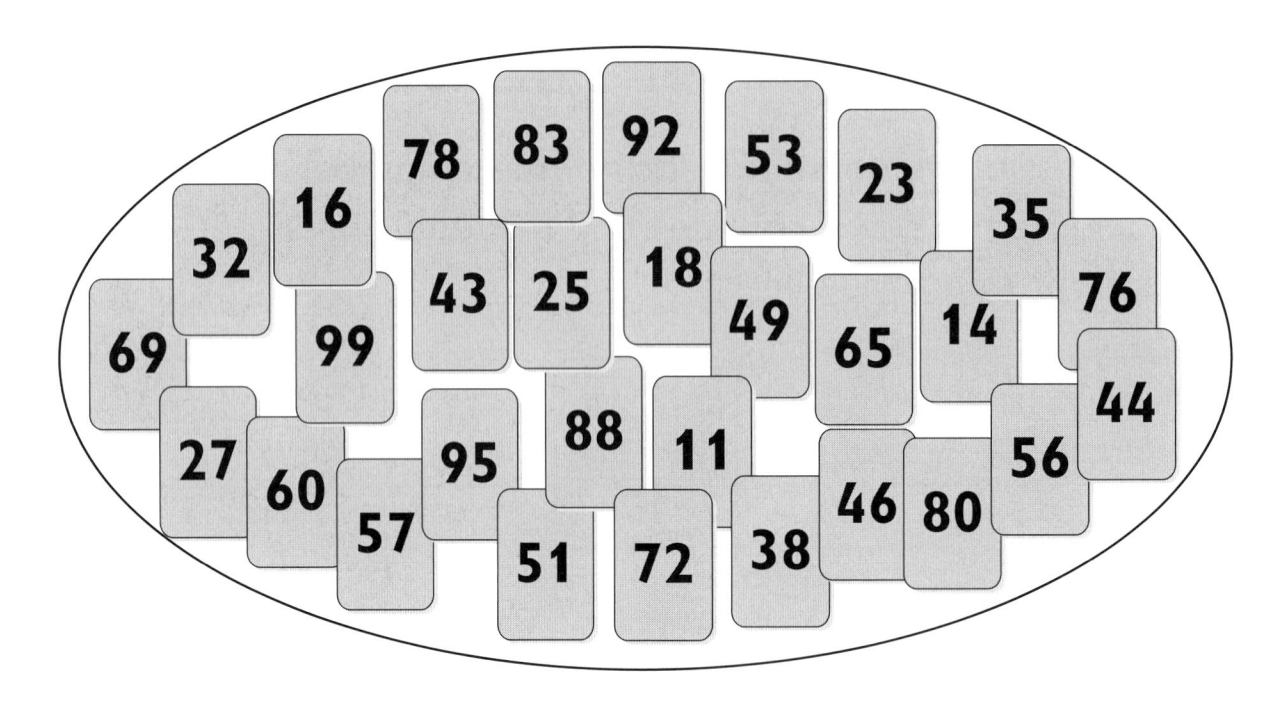

[Oval containing scattered number cards: 78, 83, 92, 53, 23, 16, 32, 35, 43, 25, 18, 76, 69, 99, 49, 65, 14, 44, 27, 60, 95, 88, 11, 56, 57, 46, 80, 51, 72, 38]

1. Find 3 numbers with a 2 in the units column.
   Write the numbers in the boxes and do the sums.

   ☐☐ × 3 = _____   ☐☐ × 3 = _____

   ☐☐ × 3 = _____

2. Find 4 numbers with a 4 in the tens column.
   Write the numbers in the boxes and do the sums.

   ☐☐ × 2 = _____   ☐☐ × 2 = _____

   ☐☐ × 2 = _____   ☐☐ × 2 = _____

3. Find 4 numbers with a 1 in the tens column.
   Write the numbers in the boxes and do the sums.

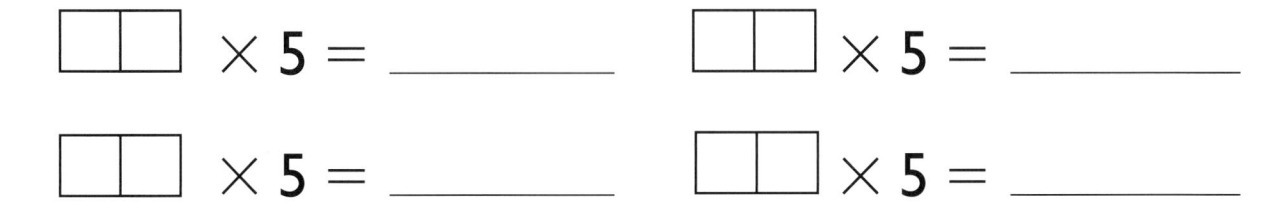

   ☐☐ × 5 = _____   ☐☐ × 5 = _____

   ☐☐ × 5 = _____   ☐☐ × 5 = _____

Copymaster 14

Here are some sums made up with number tiles. Write in any missing numbers to make the sums right.

Write each sum in a different way using the same number tiles but $\div$ instead of $\times$ or $\times$ instead of $\div$.

| 6 × 3 = ☐ | 7 × 2 = ☐ | 5 × ☐ = 35 |
| ☐ ÷ 3 = ☐ | ☐ ÷ 7 = ☐ | 35 ÷ ☐ = ☐ |

| 10 × 2 = ☐ | ☐ × 4 = 32 | 5 × 6 = ☐ |
| ☐ ÷ 2 = ☐ | 32 ÷ ☐ = ☐ | ☐ ÷ ☐ = 6 |

| 4 × ☐ = ☐ | ☐ × ☐ = 12 | 10 × ☐ = ☐ |
| ☐ ÷ 4 = ☐ | 12 ÷ ☐ = ☐ | ☐ ÷ 10 = ☐ |

Do these sums:

$28 \div 5 =$ $30 \div 5 =$ $11 \div 2 =$

$17 \div 4 =$ $9 \div 4 =$ $27 \div 5 =$

$30 \div 4 =$ $30 \div 3 =$ $31 \div 10 =$

$25 \div 3 =$ $21 \div 2 =$ $24 \div 4 =$

$39 \div 5 =$ $43 \div 4 =$ $32 \div 4 =$

81

Copymaster 15

Each of these diagrams has a shaded part. What fraction of the whole diagram is the shaded part? Write your answer in the box.

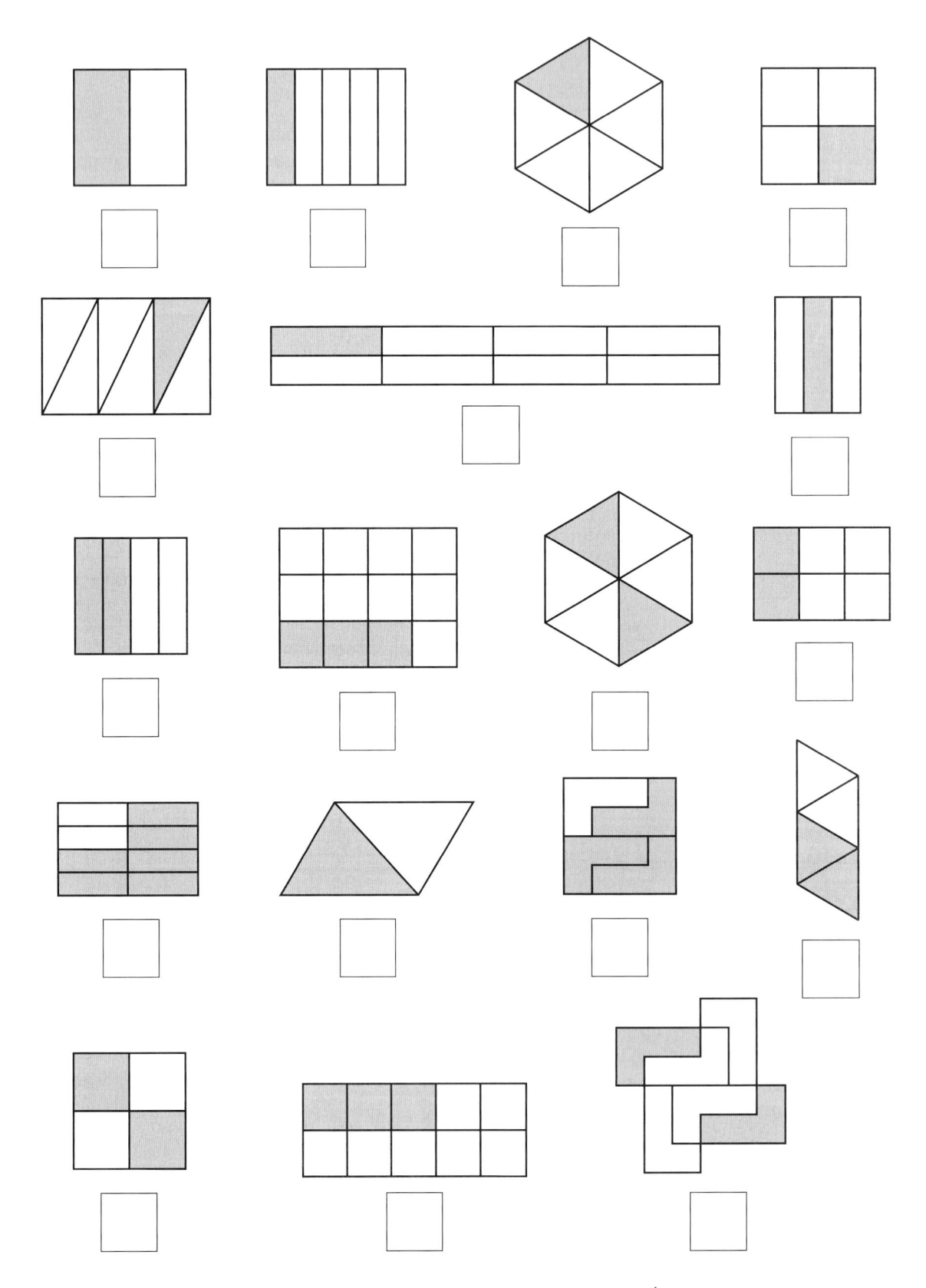

Draw a circle round each diagram which has $\frac{1}{2}$ shaded.

Fractions

Work out the answers to these fraction sums.

$\frac{1}{2}$ of 18 $\frac{1}{4}$ of 36 $\frac{1}{10}$ of 80

$\frac{1}{5}$ of 45 $\frac{1}{3}$ of 21 $\frac{1}{8}$ of 64

$\frac{1}{4}$ of 100 $\frac{1}{6}$ of 60 $\frac{1}{3}$ of 33

$\frac{1}{4}$ of 40 $\frac{3}{4}$ of 40

$\frac{1}{10}$ of 50 $\frac{3}{10}$ of 50 $\frac{7}{10}$ of 50

$\frac{1}{3}$ of 27 $\frac{2}{3}$ of 27

$\frac{1}{6}$ of 24 $\frac{2}{6}$ of 24 $\frac{5}{6}$ of 24

A jar holds 40 sweets. How many sweets are there if the jar is half full?

There are 224 pupils in my school. Half the pupils go on a trip to the wildlife park. A quarter go to the sea-life centre and the rest go to the country park. How many go to each place?

My writing book has 32 pages. I have written on 4 of them. What fraction of my book have I used?

Ajit collected 18 beetles and kept them in a jar. One third of them escaped. How many escaped?

Lucy drew a line 12 cm long. She put a mark $\frac{1}{6}$ of the way from the start. How many centimetres did she have left to measure?

Mum made a chocolate cake and cut it into 18 pieces. Simon ate three pieces. What fraction did he eat?

Copymaster 17

What time is shown by each of these clocks?
Write your answer in words.

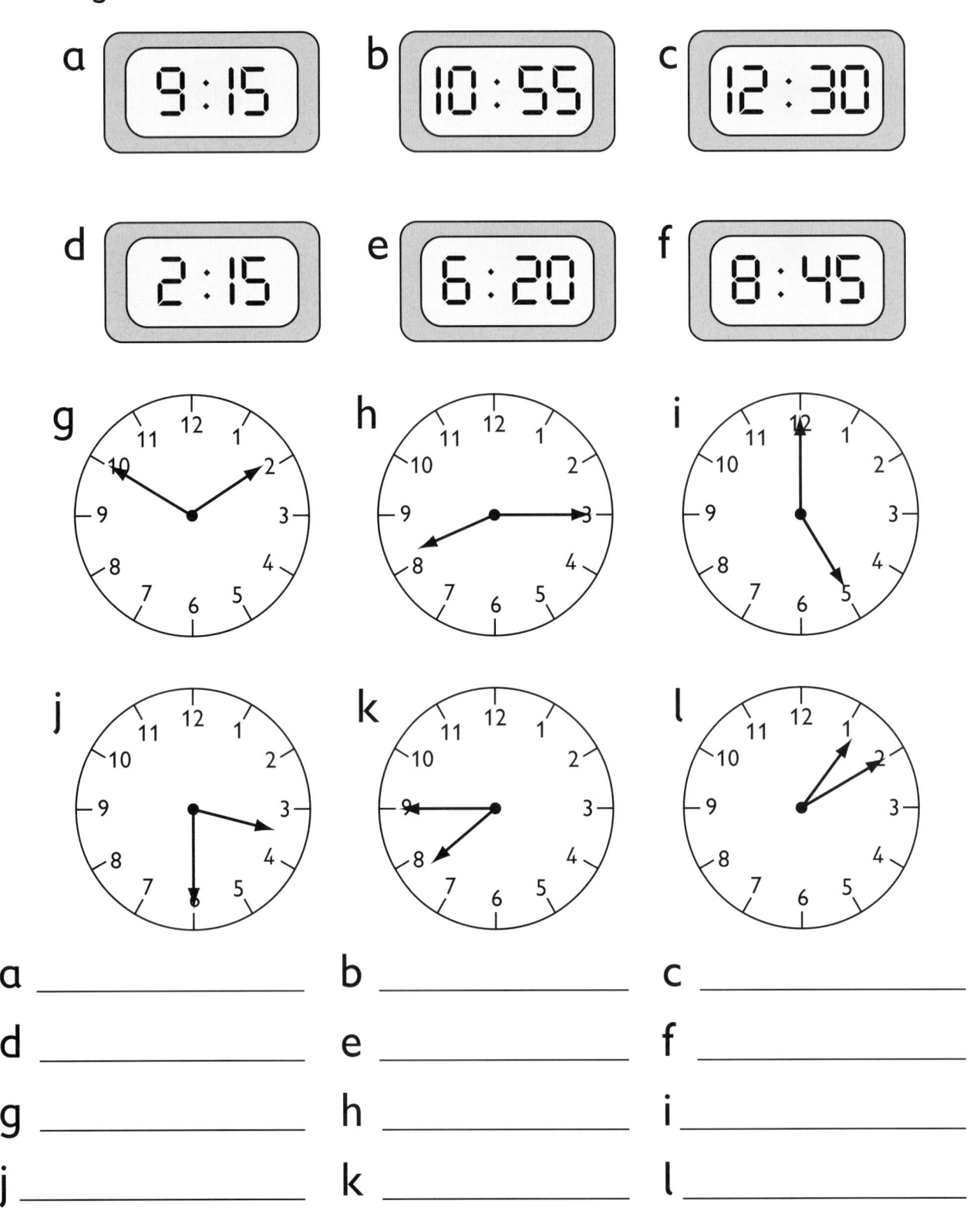

a 9:15   b 10:55   c 12:30

d 2:15   e 6:20   f 8:45

g   h   i

j   k   l

a _____   b _____   c _____

d _____   e _____   f _____

g _____   h _____   i _____

j _____   k _____   l _____

All the times shown on clocks g–l are between 8 am and 8 pm. Write the letters of the clock faces in order of the times – starting with the closest to 8 am.

84

Copymaster 18

Time puzzles

Brian had to get up at half past seven. He woke up 30 minutes early. What time was it when he woke up?

Gilly was going to meet friends at four o'clock. She knew it would take fifteen minutes to walk to their house. What time did she have to leave?

Lessons start at 9.20 am. We have two lessons of 50 minutes and then it's playtime. What time is playtime?

I watched the television from 4.30 pm until 6.00 pm and then from 6.20 pm until 7.00 pm. How long did I watch altogether?

Leesa played a chess match with her friend. They started at ten past three and the match lasted for 40 minutes. What time did they finish?

When mum goes shopping the bus journey takes 20 minutes. She leaves the house ten minutes before the bus comes. If she left the house at a quarter past ten what time would she get to the shop?

Harry wanted to make a cake. He spent 35 minutes in preparation time. The cake needed 2 hours 40 minutes to cook. He started cooking at a quarter past two. What time was the cake ready to be taken out of the oven?

Sarah and Billy went to watch a football match. The match started at 2.30. It was an hour and a half long with a break of 20 minutes at half time. What time did the match finish?

William went to watch a tennis match. The match started at eleven o'clock and lasted for four hours twenty minutes. What time did the match end?

Ellie went to a birthday party. The party started at 5 o'clock and she was picked up by her dad at 6.45 pm. How long was she at the party?

Copymaster 19

40 children were asked their favourite activity.
The results are shown in this pictogram.

Reading	♀♀♀♀♀♀♀♀♀♀♀♀♀
Computer	♀♀♀♀♀♀♀
Swimming	♀♀
Watching TV	♀♀♀♀
Playing with friends	♀♀♀♀♀♀♀♀♀♀

How many people said they liked **reading** best? _____

How many people said they liked **playing** best? _____

How many people said they liked **watching TV** best? _____

How many people said they liked **swimming** best? _____

Some pupils in a school were asked to name their favourite lessons. Here are the results.

☺ is two people.

How many people does this symbol ☺ show?

Maths	☺☺☺☺☺☺☺☺☺☺☺☺
English	☺☺☺☺☺☺☺☺☺☺☺
Technology	☺☺☺☺☺☺☺☺
Geography	☺☺☺☺
History	☺☺
PE	☺☺☺☺☺☺☺☺☺☺☺☺☺

How many people said they liked **Maths** best? _____

How many people said they liked **English** best? _____

How many people said they liked **Technology** best? _____

How many people said they liked **History** best? _____

How many people said they liked **PE** best? _____

Copymaster 20

Everyone in Simon's class did a traffic survey. They each had to count in a different place. At the end of the survey Simon's group put their results together. These are the tally charts from Simon's group.

Simon	Megan	Carl
cars ⊬⊬ \\	cars ⊬⊬ ⊬⊬	cars ⊬⊬ ⊬⊬ \\
vans \\\	vans \	vans ⊬⊬ \\
lorries \	lorries \\	lorries \\\\
bicycles \\	bikes \	bicycles
	motorbikes \\\	tanker \

Jo	Leesa
cars \\\\	cars ⊬⊬ \\\\
vans \\	vans ⊬⊬ \
lorries	lorries \\\
bicycles	bikes
tractors \	horses \

Who had the busiest stretch of road? _____

Draw a tally chart and put all five sets of marks onto your new chart.

Draw a frequency table from the new tally chart.

Draw a pictogram to show the results from Simon's group.

Here is a frequency table that Simon's class did from their traffic surveys for a week.

cars	200
vans	95
lorries	75
bicycles	30
motorbikes	65
tractors	1
horses	3
tankers	5

Choose a symbol which shows five units to display this information on a pictogram.

How can you show 1 using your symbol?

How can you show 3 using your symbol?

87

Copymaster 21

You have this set of number cards.
You must pick three cards at a time.

You can only use each card once.

Write down all the different sums you can make.

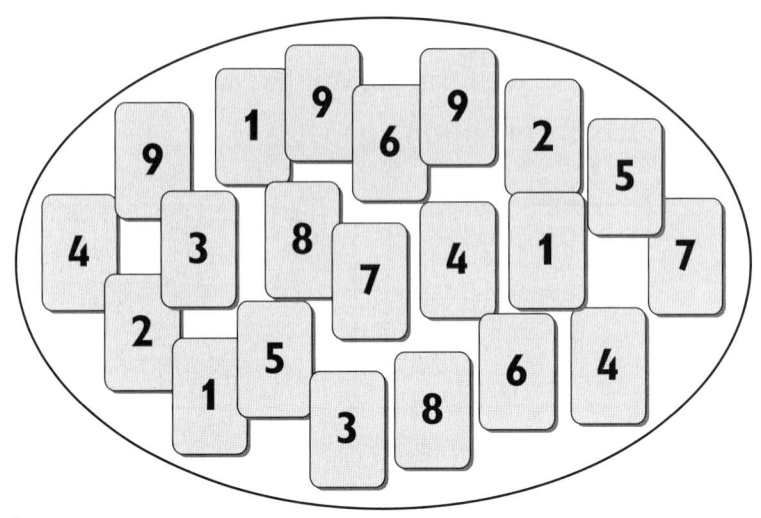

These are the sums I can make:

_____   _____

_____   _____

_____   _____

_____   _____

Write down all the pairs of numbers which total 10.

_____   _____

_____   _____

_____   _____

Do these sums by looking for pairs of numbers which total 10.

8 + 7 + 2 = _____   6 + 2 + 3 + 4 = _____

1 + 9 + 3 = _____   8 + 4 + 2 + 1 = _____

5 + 3 + 2 + 7 = _____   2 + 1 + 6 + 9 + 8 = _____

4 + 1 + 6 + 9 = _____   7 + 3 + 3 + 5 + 5 = _____

3 + 2 + 1 + 8 = _____   5 + 4 + 3 + 6 + 7 = _____

Copymaster 22

You have this set of number cards.

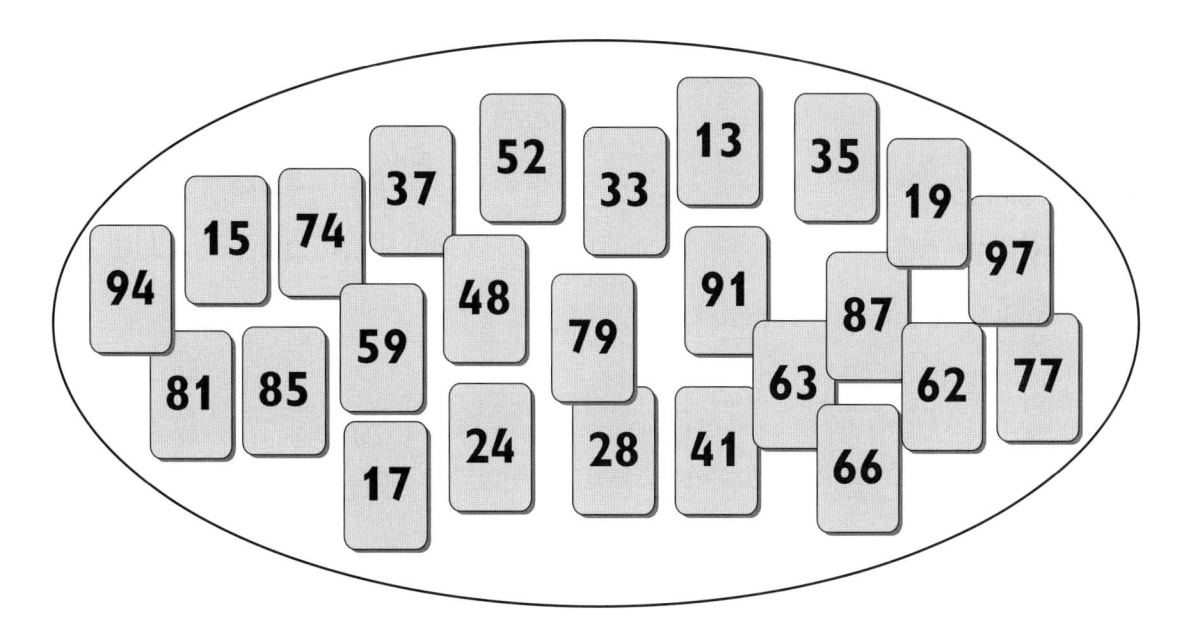

Numbers in the set: 94, 15, 74, 37, 52, 33, 13, 35, 19, 48, 91, 87, 97, 59, 79, 63, 62, 77, 81, 85, 17, 24, 28, 41, 66

Write down all the numbers which will split into 80 + another single digit.
_____

Write down all the numbers which have a 2 in the tens column.
_____

Find 10 pairs of numbers which you can add to give an answer with 0 in the units column.
_____

Write down a pair of numbers which total 100.
_____

Write down all the numbers between 35 and 55, in order.
_____

Write down all the numbers which will split into 60 + another single digit.
_____

Write down 3 numbers which make a sequence which increases in 3s.
_____

Write down 3 numbers which make a sequence which decreases in 2s.
_____

Copymaster 23

5p + 8p = 9p + 7p + 1p =
13p + 4p = 4p + 8p + 6p =
9p + 16p = 45p + 3p + 7p =
20p + 9p = 90p + 30p =
38p + 6p = 80p + 50p + 20p =

£ p	£ p	£ p	£ p	£ p
0.41	0.57	0.72	0.59	0.62
0.59 +	0.28 +	0.19 +	0.25 +	0.34 +

£ p	£ p	£ p	£ p	£ p
2.30	4.50	3.57	8.15	21.39
1.40 +	5.20 +	2.70 +	6.72 +	10.84 +

80p − 30p = £1.00 − 80p = £1.20 − 15p =
45p − 13p = £1.00 − 35p = £1.80 − 90p =
69p − 27p = £1.00 − 72p = £2.00 − £1.50 =

£ p	£ p	£ p	£ p	£ p
5.50	8.74	6.92	10.41	12.96
1.30 −	3.50 −	5.61 −	7.31 −	8.75 −

£ p	£ p	£ p	£ p	£ p
7.50	3.80	6.49	9.39	7.00
2.45 −	1.25 −	3.70 −	5.75 −	2.99 −

Copymaster 24

1. Lee May wanted a bar of chocolate which cost 35p, a packet of crisps costing 28p and a packet of chewing gum costing 24p.

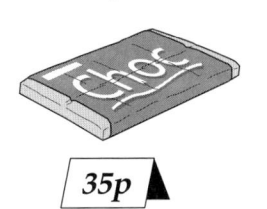

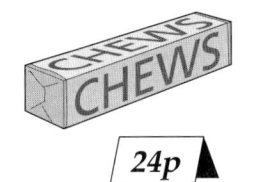

   35p   28p   24p

   She had these coins:

   50, 20, 10, 10, 5, 2, 1, 1

   Which coins did she use to pay? _____
   Did she get any change? _____

2. Gary went shopping with mum. She bought these things:

   58p   46p   89p   £1.09

   How much did they cost altogether? _____
   She paid with a £5.00 note. How much change did she get? _____

3. Sam and his mum went to the café.
   Sam wanted a fizzy drink and a cream cake.
   His mum wanted a cup of tea and a scone.
   How much did his mum have to pay? _____

   If you wanted something to eat and a drink, what could you choose if you had £2.00 to spend?

   What could you choose if you had £3.00 to spend?

   _____

   CAFÉ CRÈME
   tea   45p
   coffee   80p
   fizzy drinks 90p
   cream cakes   75p
   scones   45p
   sandwiches   £1.30
   baked potato £2.30

Copymaster 25

1 What weight does each of these scales show?

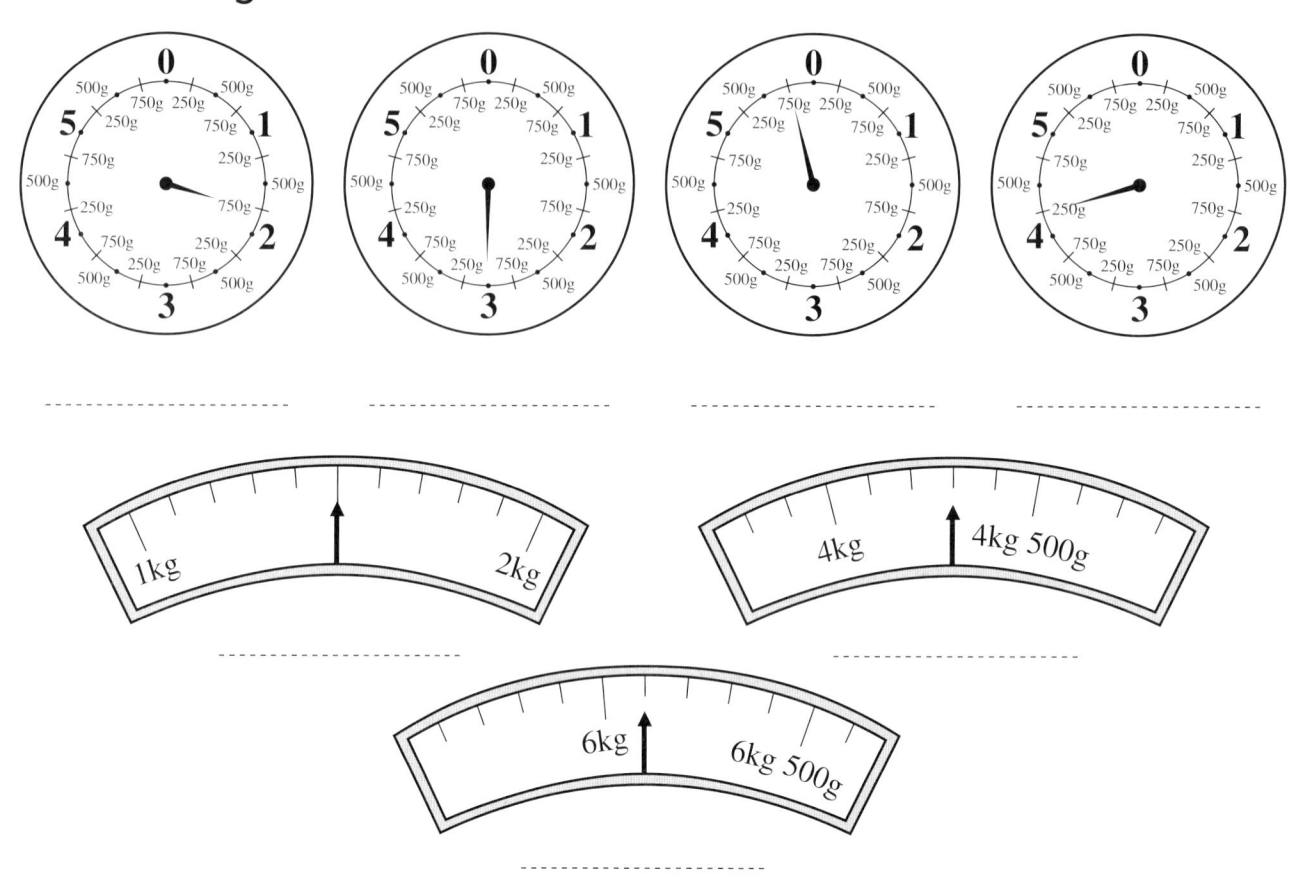

_____   _____   _____   _____

_____   _____

_____

2 What mass would make each of these sets of scales balance? Write your answers in grams.

_____   _____   _____

3 Draw the pointer on each of these scales to show the mass written below.

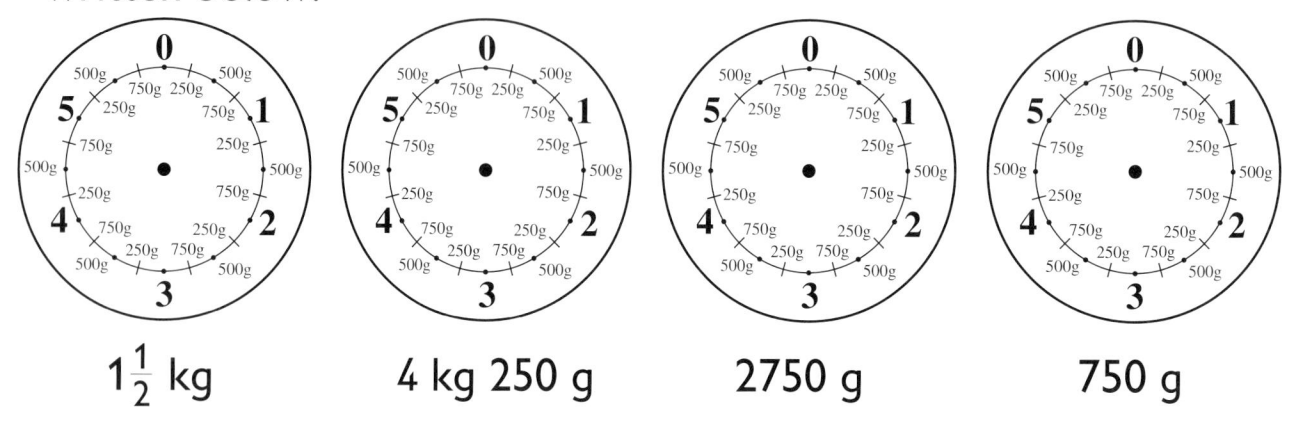

$1\frac{1}{2}$ kg   4 kg 250 g   2750 g   750 g

92

Copymaster 26

1. Mum goes to the supermarket to buy cheese.
   She wants 200 g. This piece weighs 400 g.
   Where should it be cut?

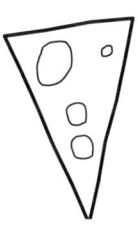

   _____

2. At a fete, one of the stalls is 'Guess the Weight of the Cake'.
   This slice weighs about 100 g.

   What is your estimate of the weight of the whole cake?

3. The contents of a packet of crisps weigh 25 g.
   You want to find the weight of the packet.
   How could you do it?

4. Philly wants to find the weight
   of his goldfish.
   How could he do it?

5. Sita wants to weigh her cat. The cat jumps off the scales.
   How could she do it?

6. A man buys a sack of potatoes to share equally with his 2 friends. The sack weighs
   24 kg. He has these weights:

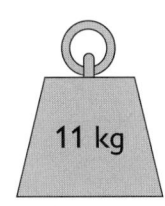

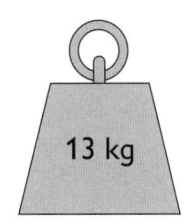

   5 kg   11 kg   13 kg

   Can you work out how he could do this using a pair of balance scales?

Copymaster 27

Work out the area of each of these shapes by cutting them into rectangles.

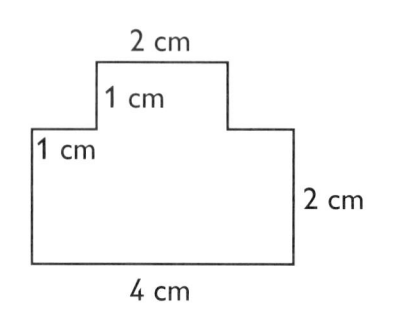

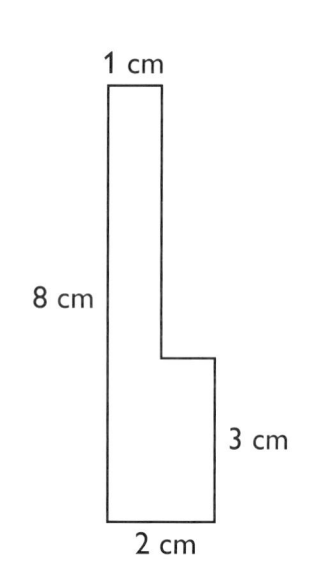

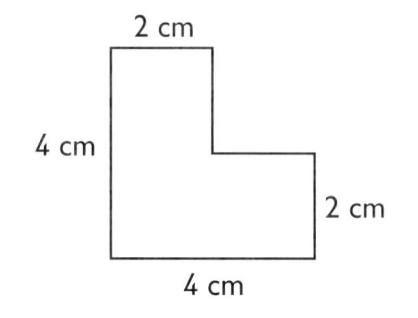

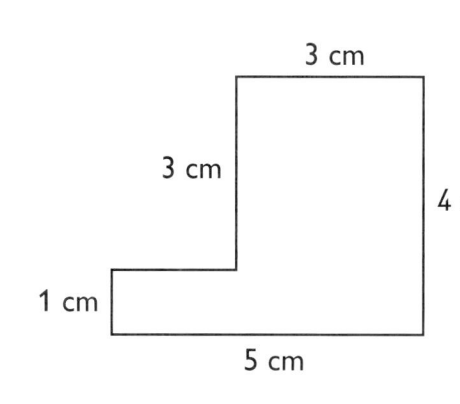

Shape 1: 2 cm (top), 4 cm (left), 2 cm (right), 4 cm (bottom)

Area = ... cm² + ... cm²
    = ... cm²

Shape 2: 2 cm (top), 1 cm, 1 cm, 2 cm (right), 4 cm (bottom)

Area = ... cm² + ... cm²
    = ... cm²

Shape 3: 1 cm (top), 8 cm (left), 3 cm (right), 2 cm (bottom)

Area = ... cm² + ... cm²
    = ... cm²

Shape 4: 3 cm (top), 3 cm, 4 cm (right), 1 cm, 5 cm (bottom)

Area = ... cm² + ... cm²
    = ... cm²

Shape 5: 6 cm, 6 cm, 4 cm, 2 cm, 2 cm, 2 cm, 8 cm

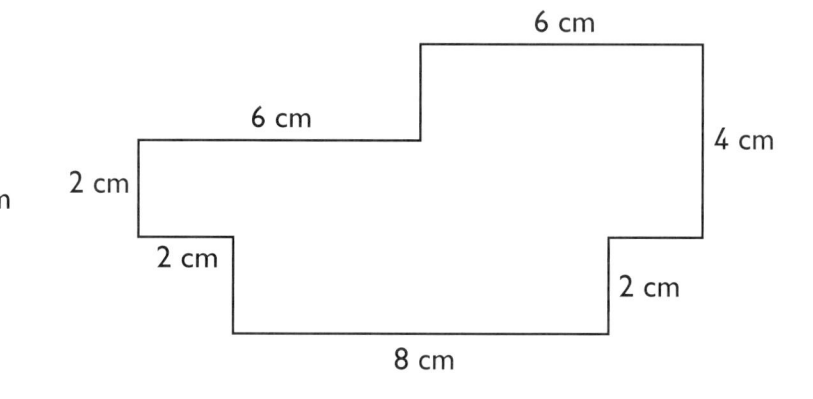

Area = ... cm² + ... cm² + ... cm²
    = ... cm²

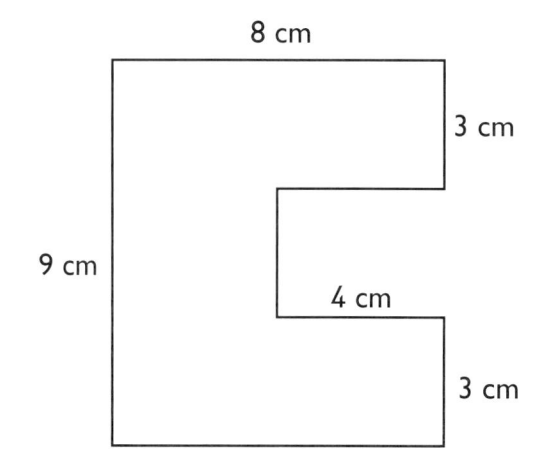

Shape 6: 8 cm (top), 3 cm, 9 cm (left), 4 cm, 3 cm

Area = ... cm² + ... cm² + ... cm²
    = ... cm²

94

Copymaster 28

This is a plan of my garden.

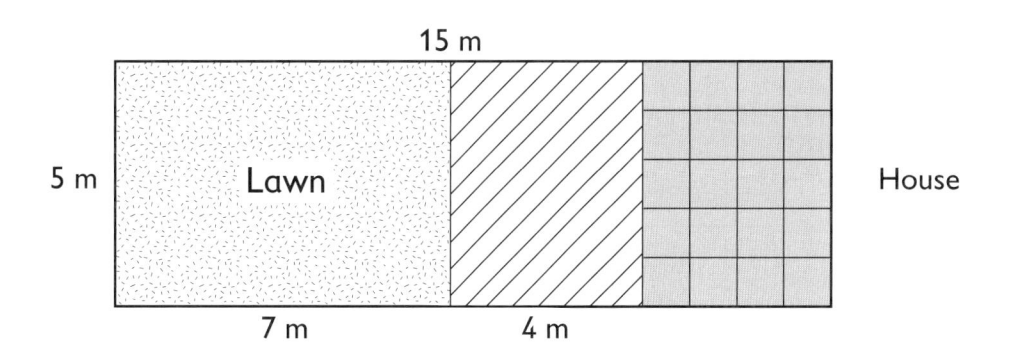

The grey area is the patio. How many square metres is this? _____

I want to make the shaded area into a patio too. How many squares is this? _____ How many paving slabs will I need for the new patio? _____

What is the area of the lawn? _____

My children think this will be boring and say they want something different.

Use these two plans to try some other designs.

I want the area of the lawn to stay the same but I don't mind what shape it is.

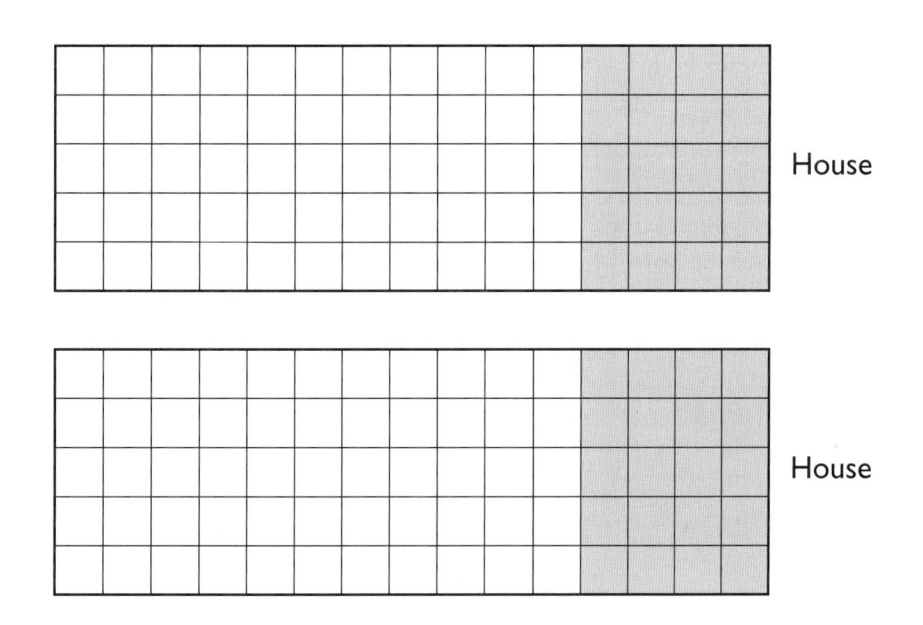

Copymaster 29

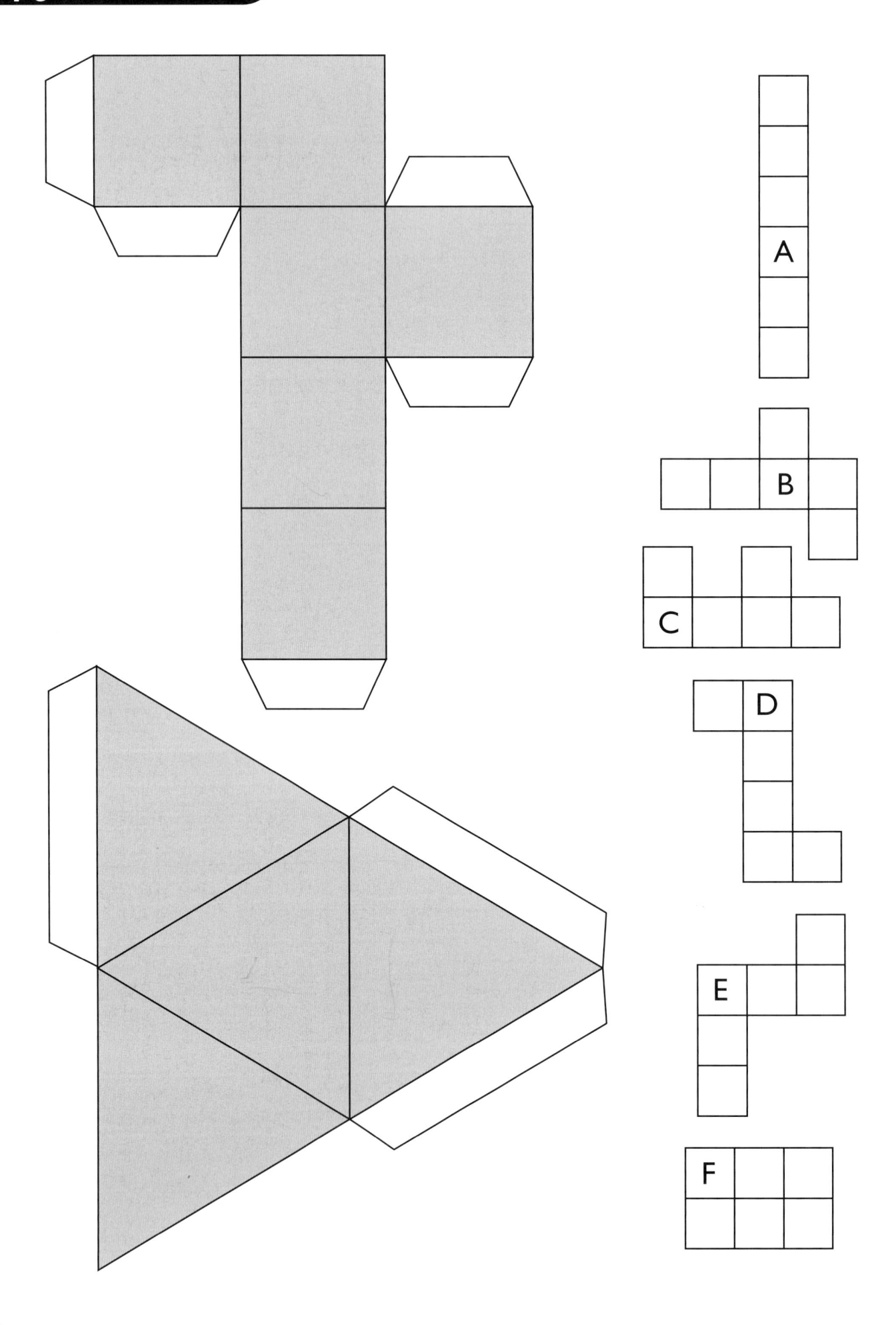

96

Copymaster 30

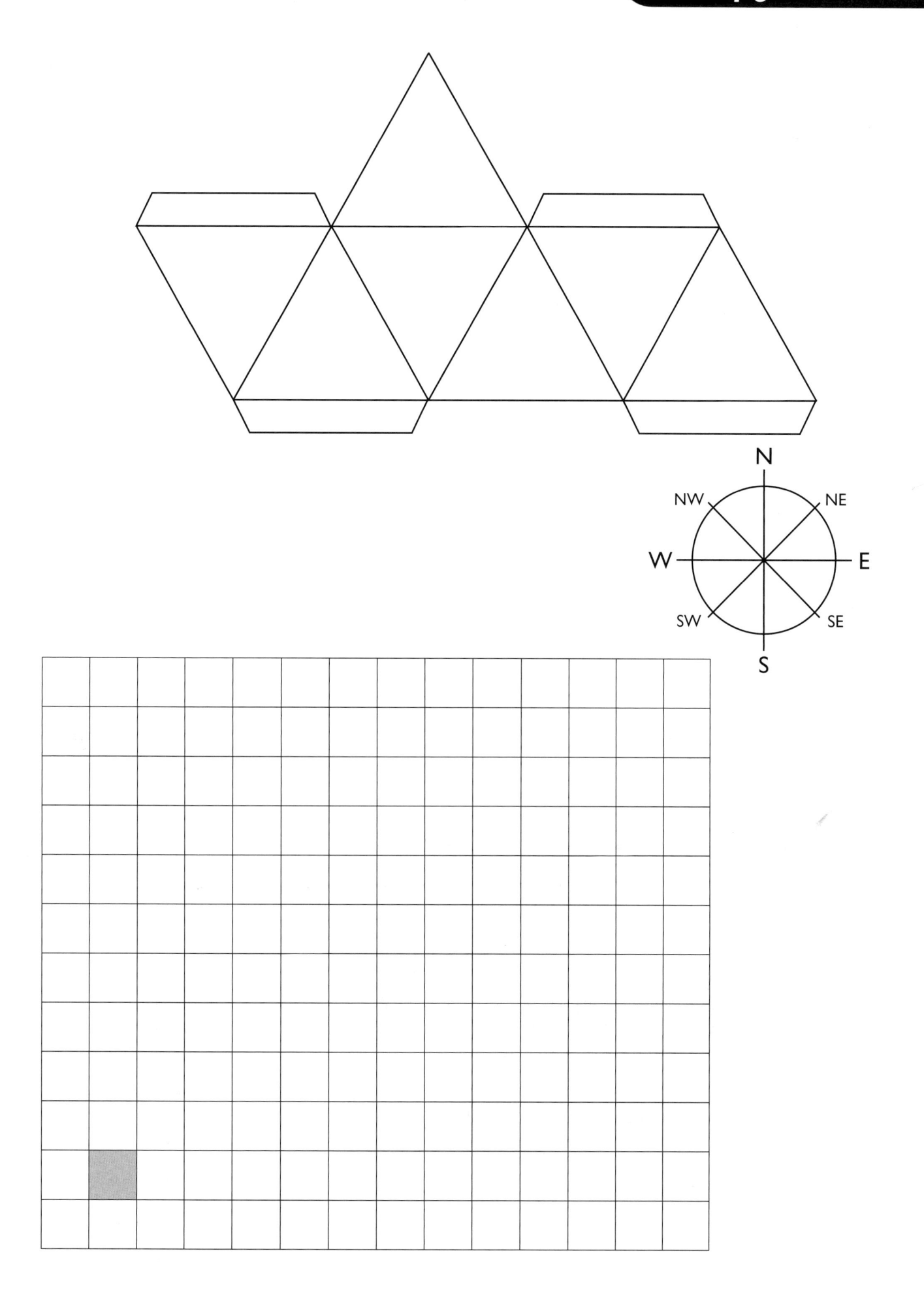

Copymaster 31

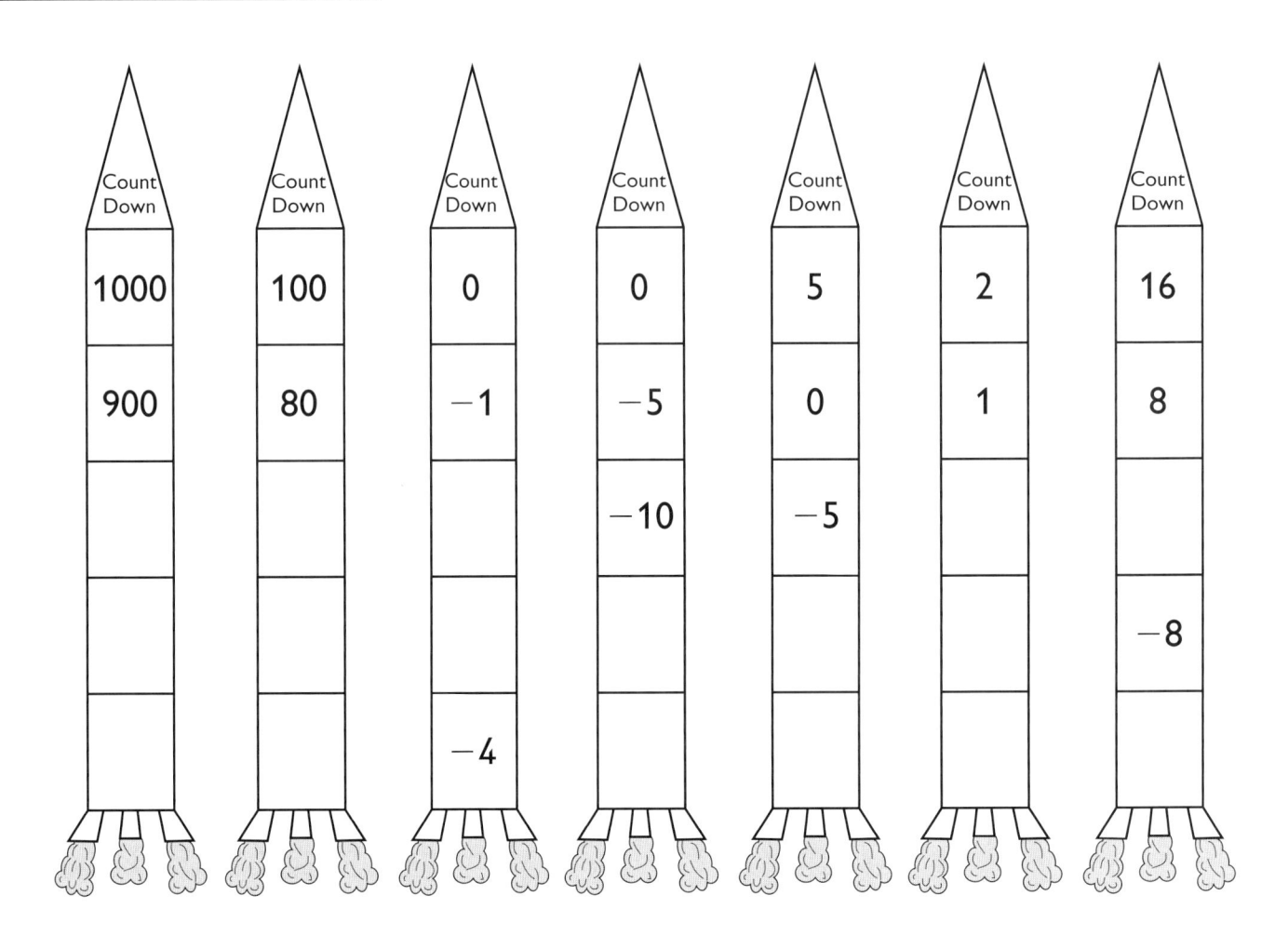

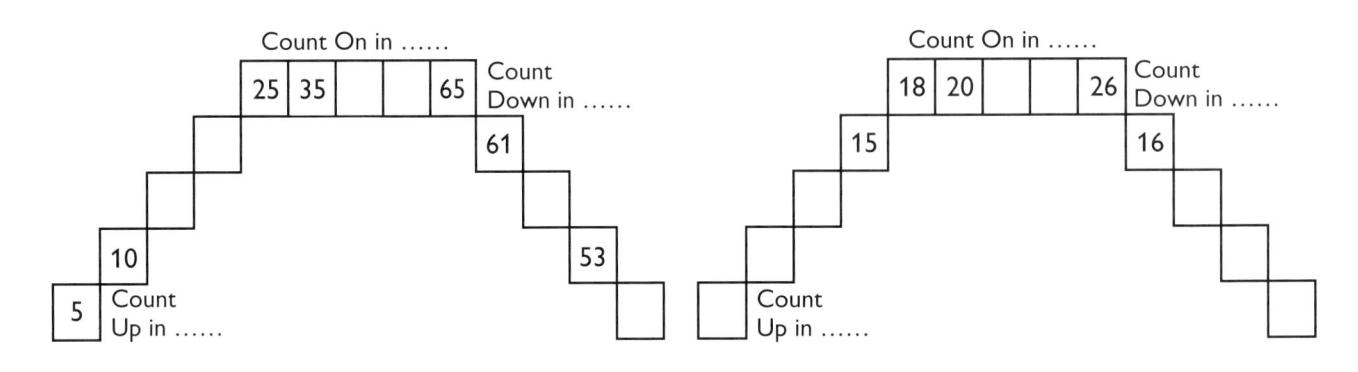

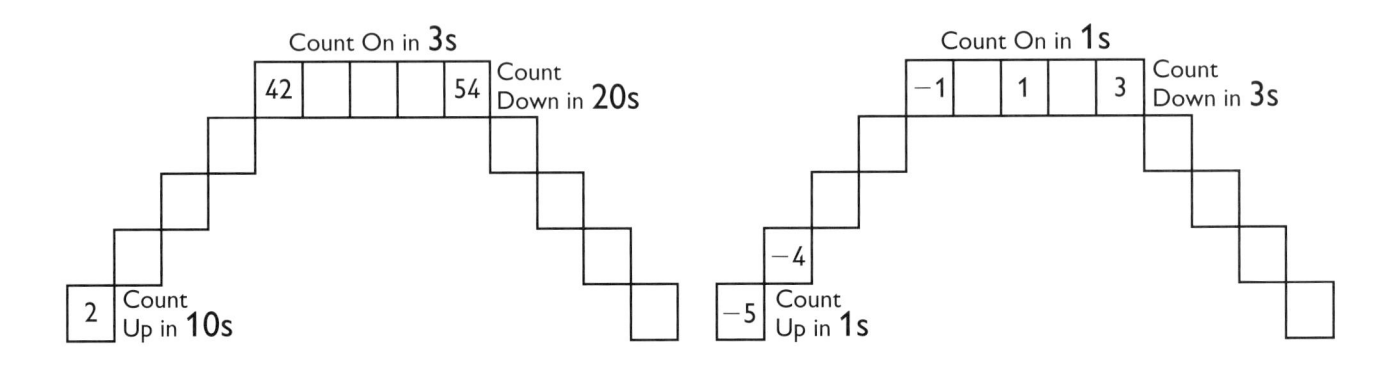

Rocket 1 (Count Down): 1000, 900, _, _, _

Rocket 2 (Count Down): 100, 80, _, _, _

Rocket 3 (Count Down): 0, −1, _, _, −4

Rocket 4 (Count Down): 0, −5, −10, _, _

Rocket 5 (Count Down): 5, 0, −5, _, _

Rocket 6 (Count Down): 2, 1, _, _, _

Rocket 7 (Count Down): 16, 8, _, −8, _

Arch 1:
Count On in …… / Count Down in ……/ Count Up in ……
Top row: 25, 35, _, _, 65
Right side down: 61, _, 53, _
Left side up from: 5, 10, _

Arch 2:
Count On in …… / Count Down in …… / Count Up in ……
Top row: 18, 20, _, _, 26
Left side up: _, 15
Right side down: 16, _

Arch 3:
Count On in 3s / Count Down in 20s / Count Up in 10s
Top row: 42, _, _, 54
Left side up from: 2

Arch 4:
Count On in 1s / Count Down in 3s / Count Up in 1s
Top row: −1, 1, _, 3
Left side up: −5, −4

98

Copymaster 32

Starting number ... 25
Rule ... add 6

Starting number ... 5
Rule ... take away 2

Starting number ... 4
Rule ... the four times table

Starting number ... 92
Rule ... take away 5

Starting number ... 1
Rule ... double

Starting number ... 50
Rule ... take away 10

Starting number ... 3
Rule ... minus 1

Starting number ... 67
Rule ... take away 12

Starting number ... 33
Rule ... add 11

Starting number ... 0
Rule ... add 9

Copymaster 33

1. Here is a tables square. Fill in all the blank spaces.
   You shouldn't need to do all the sums.
   Just remember that 8 × 2 = 2 × 8 and 4 × 6 = 6 × 4.

	1	2	3	4	5	6	7	8	9	10
2										
3										
4										
5										
6						36	42	48	54	
7							49	56	63	
8								64	72	
9									81	
10										100

2. You are playing a game where you have to pick 3 cards and multiply the numbers together. Look for the easiest sum you can make for each one.
   Write down the sum and work out the answer.

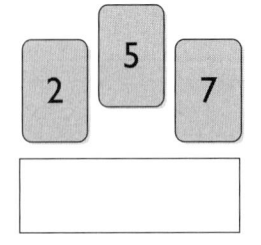

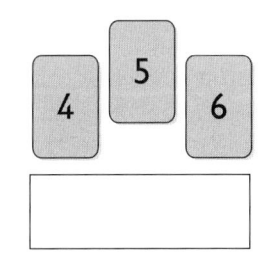

   Cards: 2, 5, 7

   Cards: 9, 2, 2

   Cards: 4, 5, 6

   Cards: 8, 2, 3

Copymaster 34

Do these sums by ×10 then adding or taking away.

24 × 9 | 24 × 10 =
           | − 24 |

41 × 11 | 41 × 10 =
           | + 41 |

83 × 9

73 × 11

54 × 9

86 × 11

37 × 9

58 × 11

66 × 9

92 × 11

| 5 | 1 | × 5 = [ ][ ] × 5
            + [ ] × 5
          =

| 7 | 3 | × 3 = [ ][ ] × 3
            + [ ] × 3
          =

| 3 | 2 | × 4 = [ ][ ] × 4
            + [ ] × 4
          =

| 6 | 5 | × 3 = [ ][ ] × 3
            + [ ] × 3
          =

Do these sums the same way.

39 × 2   16 × 5   18 × 4

25 × 3   53 × 4   29 × 5

Copymaster 35

1 How many 10s are there in each of these numbers?

39 _____   55 _____   92 _____   103 _____   76 _____

2 Double each of these numbers.

39 _____   55 _____   92 _____   103 _____   76 _____

3 Do these sums as quickly as you can.

$8 \times 2 =$ _____ $9 \times 3 =$ _____

$6 \times 4 =$ _____ $5 \times 3 =$ _____

$4 \times 9 =$ _____ $4 \times 6 =$ _____

$6 \times 7 =$ _____ $3 \times 8 =$ _____

4 Do these sums.

22×3 61×4

71×4 39×3

62×3 94×3

17×5 68×5

68×2 57×2

Write the sum for each of these problems.

How much will 10 stamps cost if they are 38p each?

I buy 4 chocolate bars costing 50p each. How much do I spend?

3 cans of drink cost 75p. How much does 1 cost?

Tony bought 3 ices. One cost 99p and the other 2 cost £1.20 each. How much did he spend?

The bus journey to school costs 45p for a single ticket. How much do I spend each day?

5 packets of crisps cost £1.90. How much does 1 packet cost?

I have £5.00 to spend. I want to buy as many sweets as I can. How many of each of these can I buy?

Dark Chocolate 80p   CHOCOLATE £1.50   Choca £2.80   Chews 75p   Mini-bars £2.30 (10)

Kenny went to the fair. He took £4.50. All rides cost 50p. He went on two. Then he bought a hot-dog costing £1.30. Next he bought a can of drink for 85p and some candy floss costing £1.00. He wanted another ride before he went home. Did he have enough money left?

Sara was invited to a birthday party. She bought a present for £8.70 and needed a card. She had £10.00 to spend altogether. Which of these cards could she buy?

75p   £1.20   £1.80   HAPPY BIRTHDAY! £1.35

If she bought this one how much change would she have?

Copymaster 37

What fraction is shaded in each of these shapes?

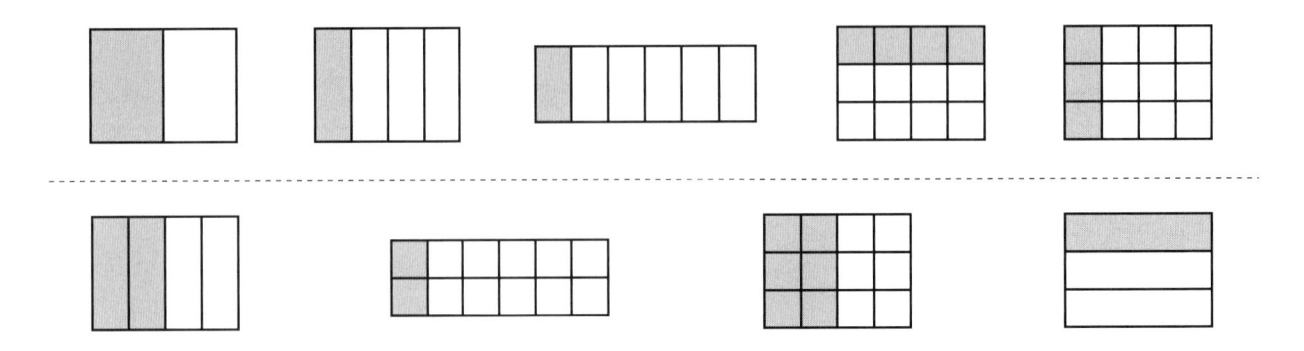

Write all the fractions you know which are equivalent to $\frac{1}{2}$.

$\frac{1}{2} =$

How many fractions can you write down which are equivalent to $\frac{1}{4}$?

$\frac{1}{4} =$

Can you write any fractions equivalent to $\frac{1}{3}$?

$\frac{1}{3} =$

Write the fraction for each shaded part of this fraction wall.

This fraction strip shows $\frac{1}{10}$.

Can you shade in equivalents of $\frac{1}{2}, \frac{1}{4}$ and $\frac{3}{4}$? Use the fraction wall to help.

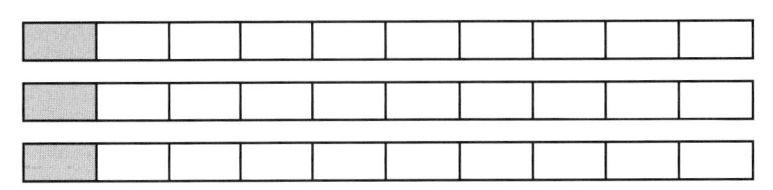

Copymaster 38

Fill in the missing numbers in these sentences.

100p = £1.00 so 1p = £0._____

100 cm = 1 m so 1 cm = 0._____ m

You have these amounts of money in your pocket. What decimal fraction of a pound do you have?

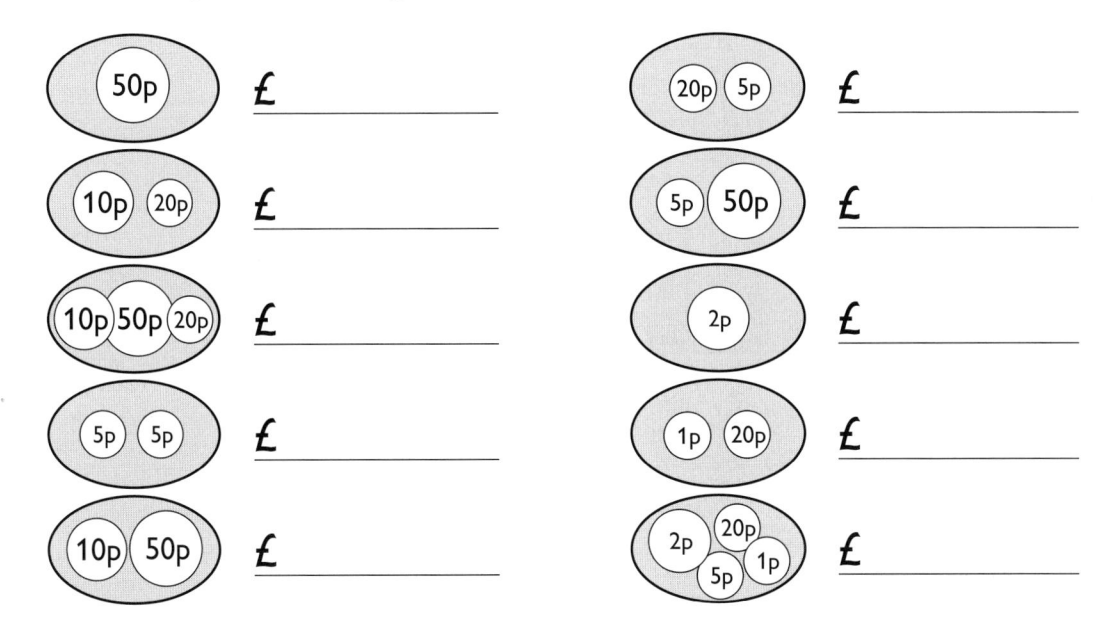

(50p) £ _____   (20p)(5p) £ _____

(10p)(20p) £ _____   (5p)(50p) £ _____

(10p)(50p)(20p) £ _____   (2p) £ _____

(5p)(5p) £ _____   (1p)(20p) £ _____

(10p)(50p) £ _____   (2p)(20p)(5p)(1p) £ _____

What decimal fraction of a metre is shown on each of these?

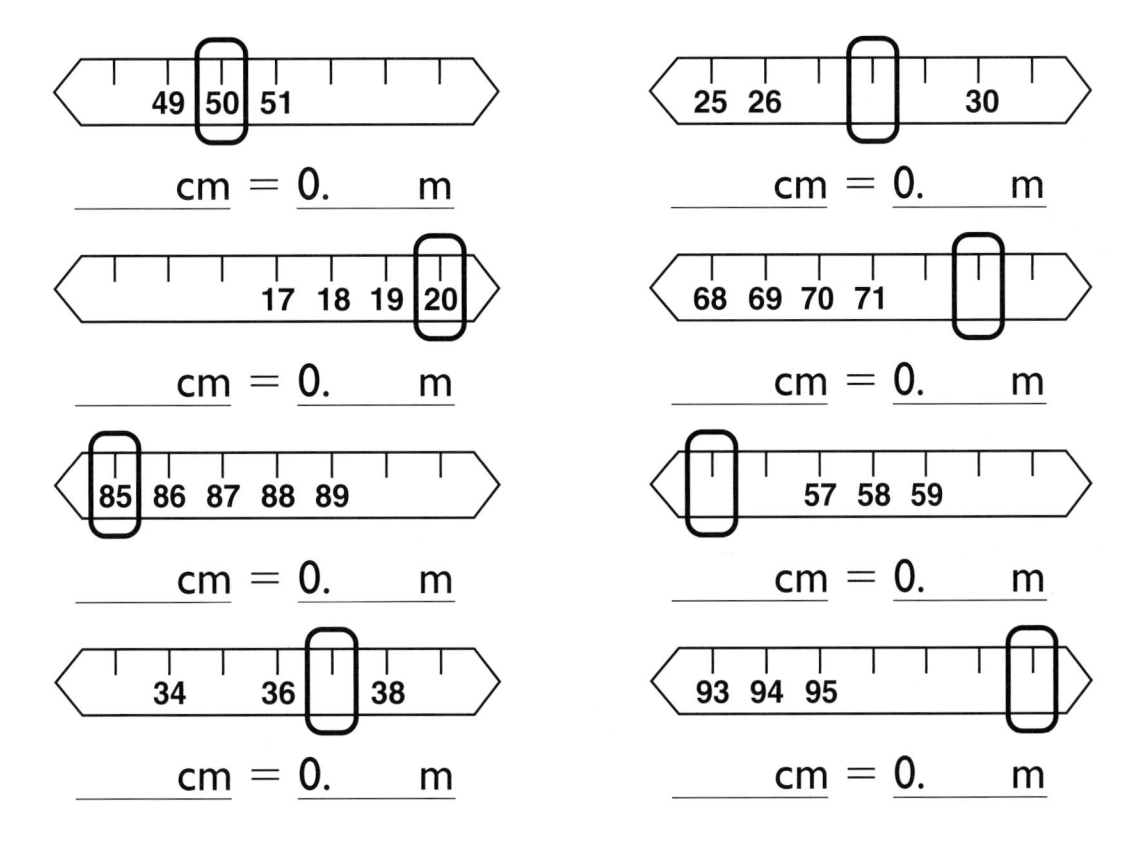

49 |50| 51   25 26 | | 30
____ cm = 0.____ m   ____ cm = 0.____ m

17 18 19 |20| 68 69 70 71 | |
____ cm = 0.____ m   ____ cm = 0.____ m

|85| 86 87 88 89 | | 57 58 59
____ cm = 0.____ m   ____ cm = 0.____ m

34   36 | | 38   93 94 95 | |
____ cm = 0.____ m   ____ cm = 0.____ m

105

Copymaster 39

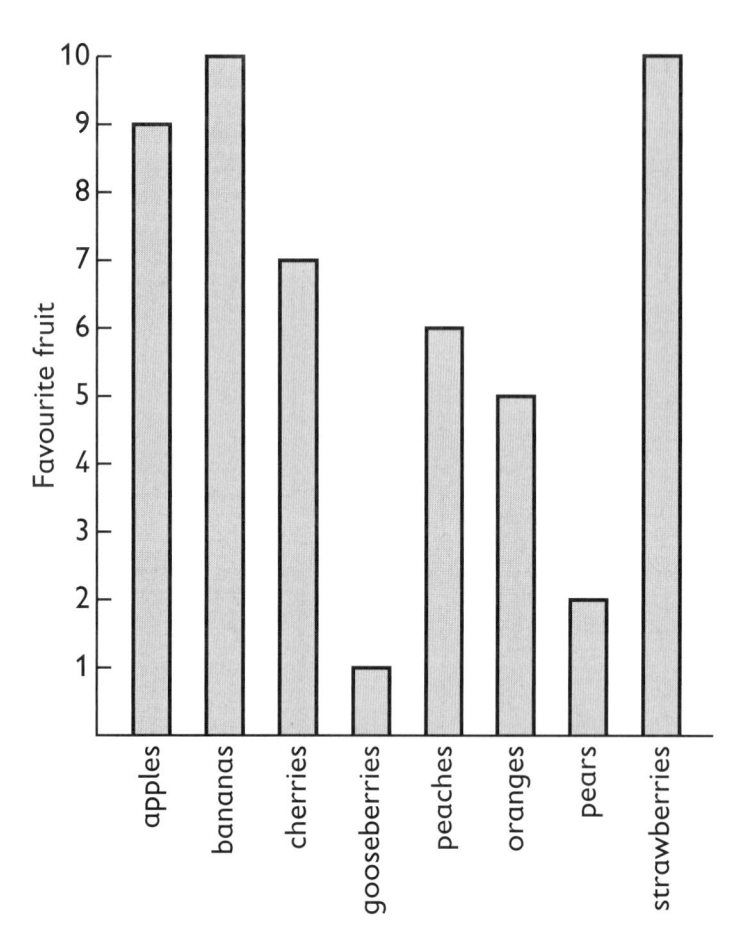

Draw a frequency table to show this information.

Which fruit was the favourite?

How many people were asked about their favourite fruit?

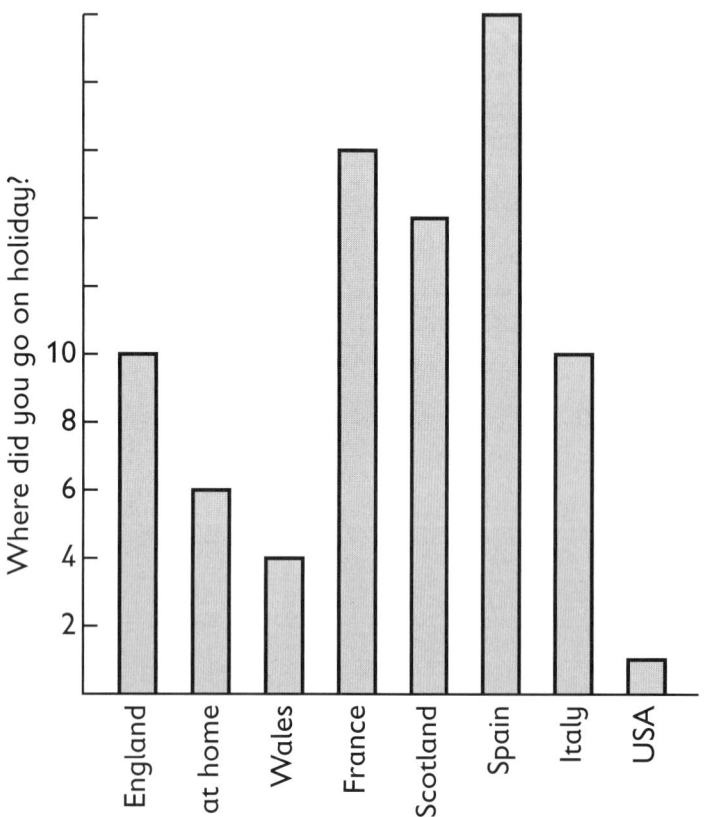

Draw a frequency table to show this information.

How many people were asked about their holidays?

Copymaster 40

How much TV do you watch in a day?

	Sunday	Monday	Tuesday	Wednesday	Thursday	Friday	Saturday
None	0	1	1	1	1	0	0
up to 1 hour	0	2	1	2	1	1	0
1–2 hours	5	6	3	4	2	2	0
2–3 hours	7	11	9	13	10	6	0
3–4 hours	10	7	16	12	14	12	13
4–5 hours	8	4	2	0	3	6	15
over 5 hours	2	1	0	0	1	5	4

Every day for a week Mr Jones gave the class a spelling test of their maths words. This table shows how many people got the words wrong each day.

	Monday	Tuesday	Wednesday	Thursday	Friday
bar chart	0	1	1	0	0
tally	0	0	0	0	0
diagram	1	2	1	1	0
frequency	5	6	7	4	3
pictogram	2	1	2	1	1
axis	3	1	2	1	1
data	1	0	0	1	0
table	4	2	3	2	2
vertical	6	3	5	4	2
horizontal	8	5	6	4	3

Copymaster 41

Do these sums as quickly as you can.

18 − 7 =   16 − 12 =   20 − 13 =

15 − 3 =   19 − 15 =   20 − 9 =

19 − 8 =   11 − 8 =   20 − 11 =

11 − 3 =   13 − 8 =   20 − 14 =

12 − 9 =   15 − 9 =   20 − 7 =

Now try these sums.

37 − 19 =   72 − 9 =

58 − 21 =   33 − 17 =

49 − 39 =   82 − 49 =

60 − 31 =   74 − 57 =

62 − 27 =   90 − 78 =

Copymaster 42

You have these sets of number cards.

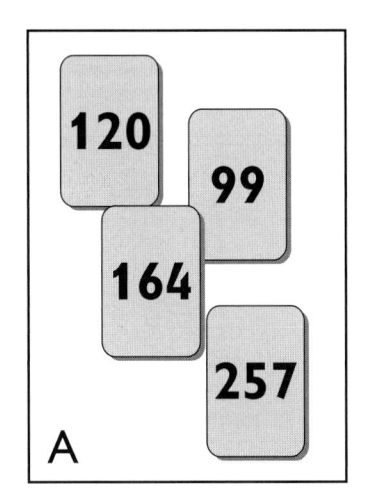

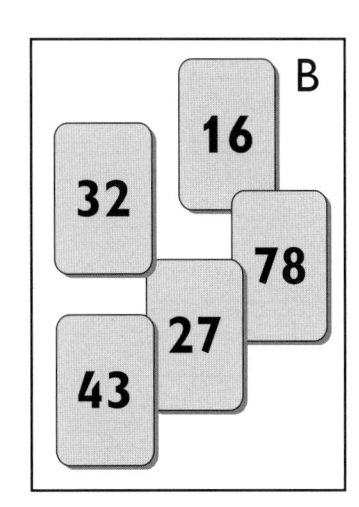

Set A: 120, 99, 164, 257

Set B: 16, 32, 78, 27, 43

Choose 1 number from set A and 1 number from set B.
How many adding sums can you make?
Write out the sums and do them. Try to find at least 5 different ones.

You have these sets of number cards.

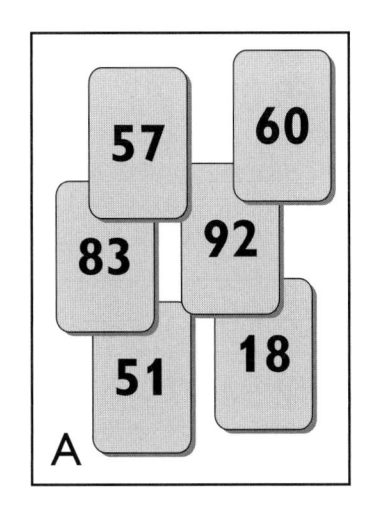

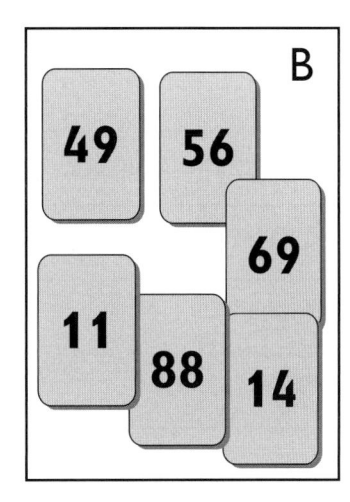

Set A: 57, 60, 83, 92, 51, 18

Set B: 49, 56, 69, 11, 88, 14

Choose 1 number from set A and 1 number from set B.
How many subtraction sums can you make?
Write out the sums and do them. Try to find at least 6 different ones.

109

Copymaster 43

If I have these coins how much will I have for each row?

£2.00	£1.00	50p	20p	10p	5p	2p	1p	Total
1		2	4				6	
2		1		5		8		
		3			6	10	12	
1	5		2			3	5	
3	2			3				
5	3	2						

Do these sums.

```
  £  p         £  p         £  p         £  p         £   p
  5.30         2.54         4.07         5.75        28.69
  1.90 +       3.73 +       3.70 +       6.78 +       6.34 +
  ____         ____         ____         ____         ____
```

How much change will I get?

I have	I spend	Change
£1.00	40p	
£2.00	£1.25	
£10.00	£6.99	
£5.20	£3.20	
£3.65	75p	

How much did I spend?

I have	I spend	Change
£8.00		£5.01
90p		24p
£3.30		80p
£5.00		£1.33
£2.54		96p

Do these sums.

```
  £  p         £  p         £  p         £  p         £   p
  7.39         6.60         6.00         9.00        17.00
  5.25 −       3.48 −       1.70 −       8.08 −       9.99 −
  ____         ____         ____         ____         ____
```

Copymaster 44

I can buy a multi-pack of 10 chocolate bars for £1.30. How much would one bar cost?

In one week mum spends £8.25 on Monday, £6.44 on Tuesday and £85.39 on Friday. How much does she spend altogether.

Mrs. Smith earns £5.00 an hour in her part time job. She works for 24 hours a week. How much does she earn in a week.

My mum bought 6 tins of beans. Each tin cost 28p. How much did she spend?

Rob bought 35 chews costing 4p each. How much did he spend?

Angie spent £3.73. She paid it with 6 coins. What coins did she use?

Pete is saving up to buy Christmas presents. He saves £1.30 a week. It is 10 weeks till Christmas. How much will he have saved up by then?

He really needs £26.00. How much should he save each week?

The bus fare to town is 90p for a child and £2.10 for an adult. Mrs. Jones wants to take her 3 children. What will the trip cost them?

Ali is saving for his holidays. It is 5 weeks until he goes away. He saves £2.00 for 2 weeks, £3.00 for 2 weeks and has £15.00 to go with. How much did he save in the last week?

Copymaster 45

Mark the measuring cylinder to show where each container would fill to.

[Cola 300 ml] [Vinegar 250 ml] [Milk ½ L]

[Cough Medicine 150 ml] [Perfume 50 ml] [Cooking Oil 1 litre]

If you filled a one litre measuring cylinder from each of these, how much would be left? Draw a line to show this.

[Bath Foam 1½ L] [Milk 4 L] [Squash 2L]

112

Copymaster 46

At Christmas I was given 3 bottles of bath foam. One contained 250 ml, one contained 500 ml and one contained 1 l. How much bath foam did I get altogether?

I bought 3 one litre bottles of lemonade for my party. Three bottles will fill 20 mugs. How much lemonade does a mug hold?

Dad filled the car with petrol. It needed 18 l to fill it. If it was half full when he started, how many litres does the petrol tank hold?

A bottle of cough mixture holds 40 ml. The dose is 5 ml. How many doses can you get from the whole bottle?

We drink a 4 l container of milk in 2 days. How much milk do we drink each day?

Dad bought a 5 l container of paint. Mum painted the kitchen and used half of it. How much paint was left?

I needed $\frac{1}{2}$ l of liquid for my cooking. I had 350 ml. How much more liquid did I need?

In the fridge we had 1 l of orange juice, 250 ml of grapefruit juice and $\frac{1}{2}$ l of pineapple juice. I mixed these together with a litre bottle of lemonade. How much drink did I have altogether?

The baby's bath contained 15 l of water. When he had finished his bath there was 12 l 800 ml left. How much water did he tip out of the bath?

I drink 1 can of orange every day and my brother drinks 2 cans of lime a day. A can holds 330 ml. How much do we drink in a day?

Copymaster 47

How many right angles can you find in each of these patterns?
Write the number in the box.

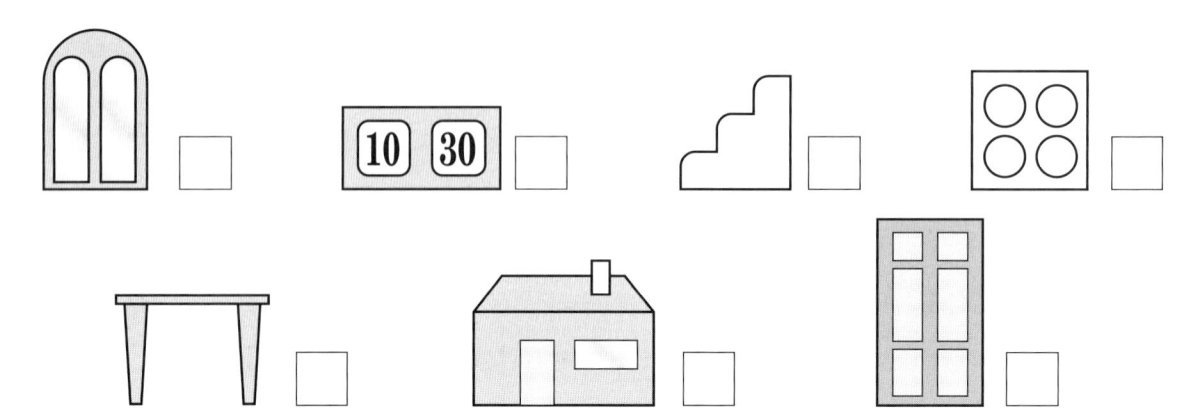

What is the angle between the hands on each of these clock faces?

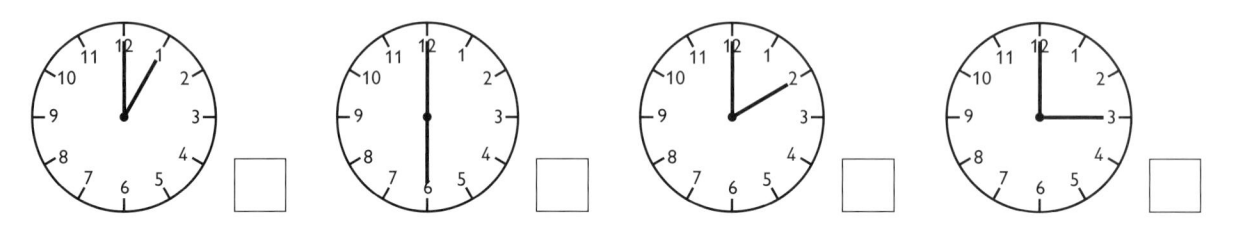

Look at this pattern. Start from the thick line.

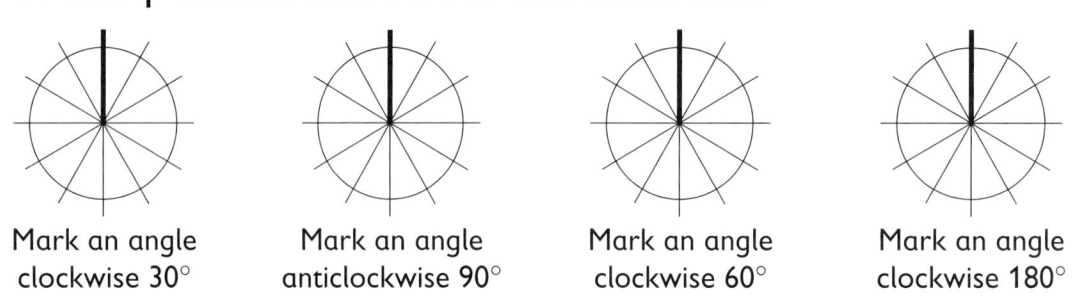

Mark an angle clockwise 30°   Mark an angle anticlockwise 90°   Mark an angle clockwise 60°   Mark an angle clockwise 180°

Draw:

a triangle with 1 right angle.
a quadrilateral with 2 right angles.
a hexagon with 1 right angle.

Can you draw a quadrilateral with only 3 right angles?

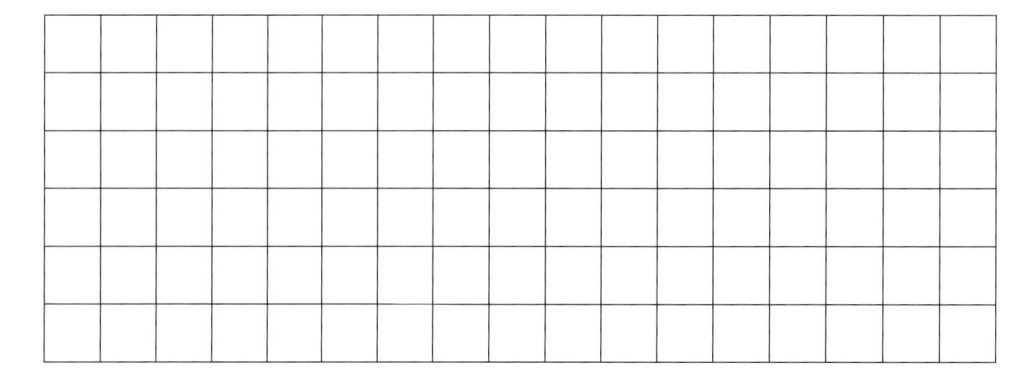

114

Copymaster 48

This angle is 60°

This angle is 30°

This angle is 90°

Copymaster 49

1 Put a ring round the multiples of 2:

   14   20   17   11   8   2   3   7

2 Put a ring round the multiples of 5:

   6   20   45   24   30   50   35   27

3 Put a ring round the multiples of 10:

   15   44   20   80   12   100   32   50

4 Put a ring round the multiples of 2 and a box round the multiples of 5:

   18   15   9   16   20   50   35   28

5 Which numbers are multiples of 2 and 5? _____ and _____

6 Here are some rows and columns from the tables square. What multiples do they show?

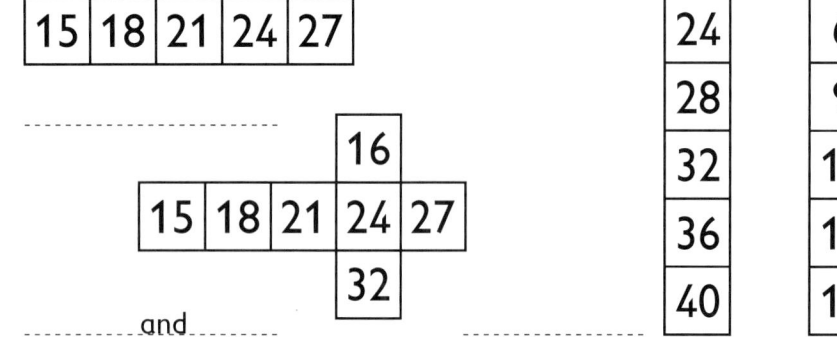

Copymaster 50

Four 4s [4]   You can use four 4s and make any of these sums.

[4] [4]   [+] [−] [×] [÷]
 [4]

Put the fours together – can you make the answers ① and ② ?

I can: (4 + 4) [÷] (4 + 4) = ①   Can you find other ways of making these answers?

(4 × 4) [÷] (4 + 4) = ②   How many more numbers can you make using four 4s?

1 **Find a pair of numbers for each of these:**

Added they make 7, times they make 12   The numbers are _____
Their sum is 8, their product is 15   The numbers are _____
2 consecutive numbers, added they make 35   The numbers are _____
Added they make 16, times they make 60   The numbers are _____

2 **Use these numbers:**

| 2 3 4 5 10 |

Make up some puzzles like these.

Using these numbers, what is the biggest total you can make with any two digits? _____

Using these numbers, what is the biggest product you can make with any two digits? _____

3 Match the problem with the right sum.

| Chloe shared 24 sweets with her friend. How many did they each get? |

| Brian had 20 cards and gave away 7. How many did he have left? |

| 20 − 7 = |

| Gary had 14 pairs of socks. Mum bought him 3 more pairs. How many pairs did he have? |

| 5 × 6 = |

| 14 + 3 = |

| 24 ÷ 2 = |

| Mum's cake tin had 5 rows and 6 columns. How many buns did it make? |

117

Copymaster 51

1. The baker sells:

    - bread rolls
    - cream cakes
    - doughnuts
    - scones
    - iced buns

    He has different sized boxes for each thing:

    - bread rolls go in boxes of 10
    - cream cakes go in boxes of 2
    - doughnuts go in boxes of 5
    - scones go in boxes of 4
    - iced buns go in boxes of 3

    One morning he has to sell 9 boxes of scones. How many scones is that? _____

    He has 30 boxes of cream cakes. How many cream cakes are there? _____

    He has 50 doughnuts. How many boxes will he need? _____

    He has 26 iced buns. How many boxes will he need? _____

2. Ali, Bora and Catherine are investigating division.
   They are dividing by 3.
   Sometimes their numbers will divide exactly. Sometimes there is a remainder.

   They have 45 counters.
   Draw the counters in their circles to show how they would divide.

   Ali ◯   Bora ◯   Catherine ◯

   They investigate lots of numbers and draw a table to show their results.
   Can you fill in the missing numbers?

We started with	We each had	We had a remainder of
29		
48		
16		
	30	0
	16	0
	7	2
33		
69		

Copymaster 52

1 Fill in the missing numbers in each of these strips from the tables square.

| 6 | 12 | | | 36 | | | |

| 7 | | | | 42 | | 63 |

| 8 | | | | | 56 | 64 | |

| 9 | | | | | | 72 | 81 |

2 Do these sums as quickly as you can.

$24 \div 6 =$ $20 \div 5 =$ $24 \div 8 =$ $42 \div 7 =$

$42 \div 6 =$ $27 \div 3 =$ $18 \div 9 =$ $70 \div 7 =$

$45 \div 9 =$ $72 \div 8 =$

3 Do these sums as quickly as you can.

$5\overline{)85}$ $6\overline{)78}$ $6\overline{)91}$

$4\overline{)96}$ $7\overline{)94}$ $4\overline{)77}$

$3\overline{)81}$ $7\overline{)82}$ $9\overline{)94}$

$8\overline{)96}$

4 We had to put our books on the shelves.
   We had 6 shelves and 84 books.
   How many books went on each shelf?

5 At lunch time we have 8 tables.
   We need 6 glasses for a table.
   We have 42 glasses.
   Do we have enough?

6 Gilly's mum buys 75 tins of cat food.
   The cat eats 7 tins a week.
   How long will the cat food last?

Copymaster 53

1. Mum wants some new shelves for the kitchen.

   a She wants 3 shelves.
      What length of wood will she need altogether? 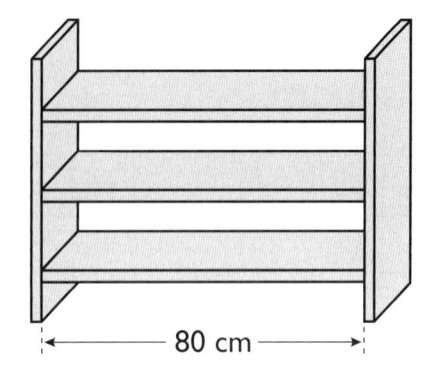

   b You can only buy wood in 1 m lengths.
      How much wood will she waste on each shelf?
      How much is that altogether?

   c The wood costs £2.25 a metre. How much will the shelves cost?

2. We had a competition to see who could build the biggest tower.
   Each building block was 8 cm thick.
   Phil used 20 blocks. Janie used 23 blocks. David used 30 blocks. Fran used 15 blocks.
   How tall was each tower?

   Phil _____
   Janie _____
   David _____
   Fran _____

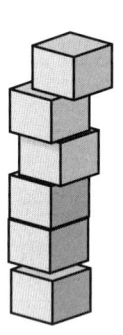

3. Dad bought new curtains for the bedrooms. His bedroom needed curtains 2 m in length. My curtains were 150 cm. My brother's were 150 cm. The curtains cost £24.00 a pair for 2 m length and £16.80 for $1\frac{1}{2}$ m length. How much did all the curtains cost?

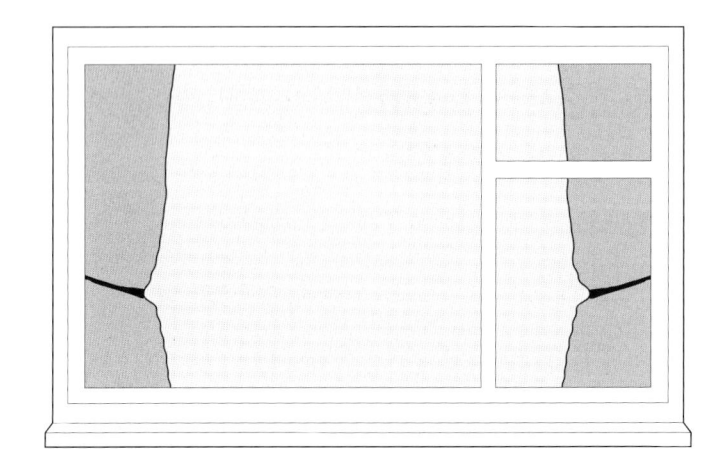

Copymaster 54

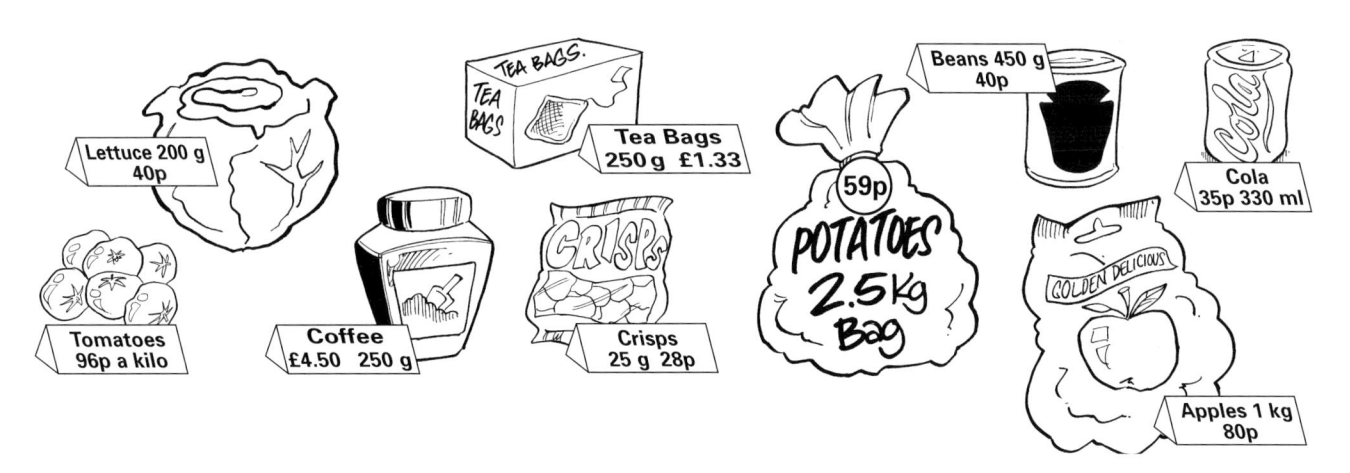

Lettuce 200 g 40p
Tea Bags 250 g £1.33
Beans 450 g 40p
Cola 35p 330 ml
Tomatoes 96p a kilo
Coffee £4.50 250 g
Crisps 25 g 28p
Potatoes 2.5 kg Bag 59p
Apples 1 kg 80p

1 Here are my shopping lists:

Monday
Jar of coffee
Packet of tea

Wednesday
4 tins of baked beans
6 cans cola
8 packets of crisps

Friday
bag of potatoes
bag of apples
1 lettuce
$\frac{1}{2}$ kg of tomatoes.

Work out how much I have to pay each day.

Monday: _____

Wednesday: _____

Friday: _____

Work out the weight of my shopping each day.

Monday: _____

Wednesday: _____

Friday: _____

How much does my shopping cost altogether? _____

How much does my shopping weigh altogether? _____

2 Claire left school at 2.50 pm. She went to the park with a friend and stayed for $\frac{3}{4}$ of an hour. Then she went home. It took 5 minutes to walk to the park and 10 minutes to walk home. What time did she get home?

_____

3 Charlie needs to leave school at 11.45 to go to the dentist.
She looks at the clock.
How long is it until she needs to leave?

_____

Copymaster 55

1 Look at these big and small containers.
   What fraction of the larger one is the smaller one?

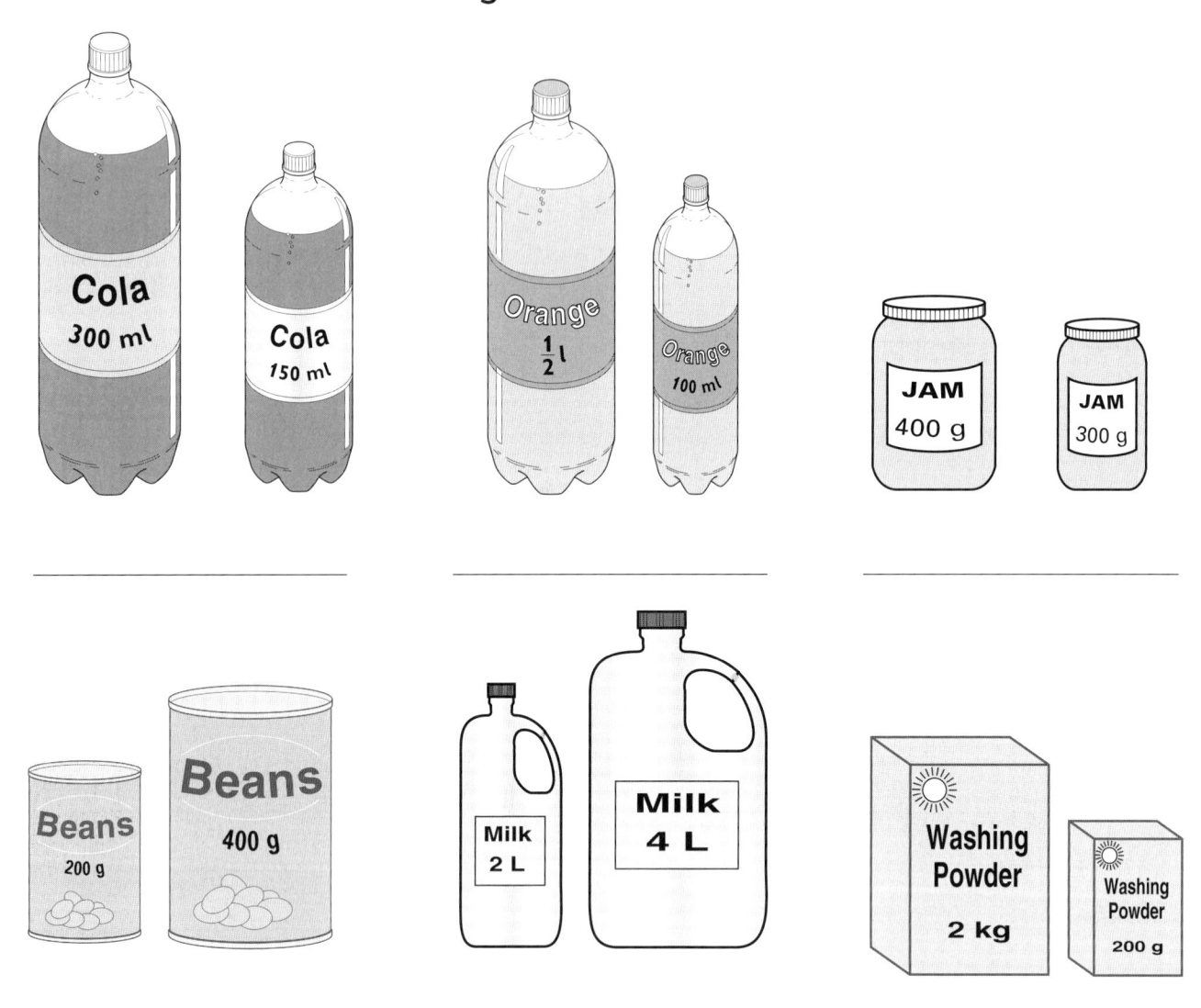

   Cola 300 ml / Cola 150 ml

   Orange ½ l / Orange 100 ml

   JAM 400 g / JAM 300 g

   Beans 200 g / Beans 400 g

   Milk 2 L / Milk 4 L

   Washing Powder 2 kg / Washing Powder 200 g

2 Shade in these fractions on the rulers.

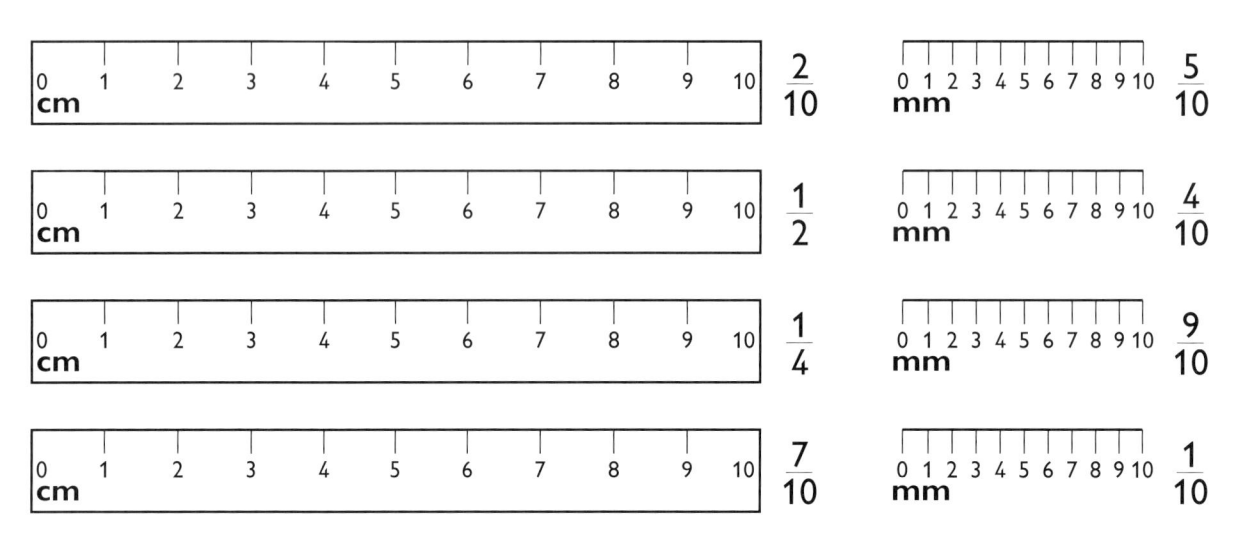

   0–10 cm ruler — $\dfrac{2}{10}$

   0–10 mm ruler — $\dfrac{5}{10}$

   0–10 cm ruler — $\dfrac{1}{2}$

   0–10 mm ruler — $\dfrac{4}{10}$

   0–10 cm ruler — $\dfrac{1}{4}$

   0–10 mm ruler — $\dfrac{9}{10}$

   0–10 cm ruler — $\dfrac{7}{10}$

   0–10 mm ruler — $\dfrac{1}{10}$

122

Copymaster 56

Write down $\frac{1}{10}$ of each of these numbers or amounts.

$\frac{1}{10}$ of 90 = ____ $\frac{1}{10}$ of £2.50 = ____ $\frac{1}{10}$ of 150 cm = ____

$\frac{1}{10}$ of 60 = ____ $\frac{1}{10}$ of £3.10 = ____ $\frac{1}{10}$ of 6 m = ____

$\frac{1}{10}$ of 100 = ____ $\frac{1}{10}$ of £10.00 = ____ $\frac{1}{10}$ of 600 cm = ____

$\frac{1}{10}$ of 1000 = ____ $\frac{1}{10}$ of 40p = ____ $\frac{1}{10}$ of 1 kg = ____

$\frac{1}{10}$ of £2.00 = ____ $\frac{1}{10}$ of 40 cm = ____ $\frac{1}{10}$ of 1000 g = ____

This block is a whole one.   We write this mixed number as $1\frac{5}{10}$

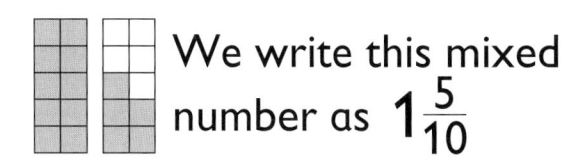

Write a mixed number or a fraction for these.

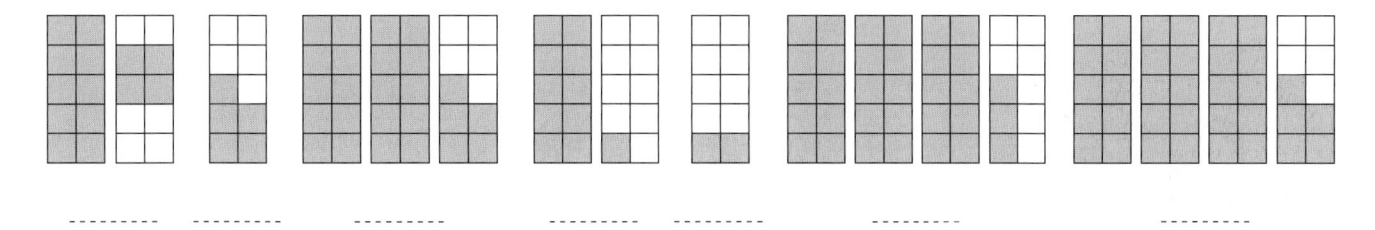

_____   _____   _____   _____   _____

Shade these to show the decimals.

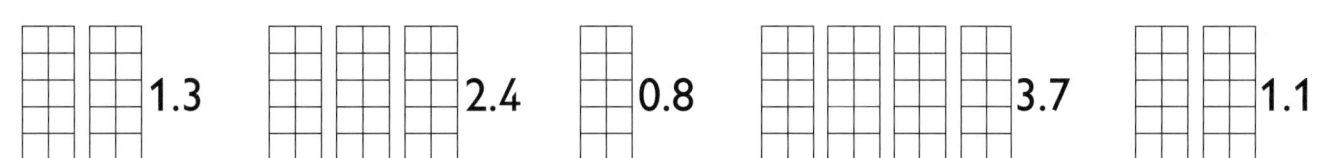

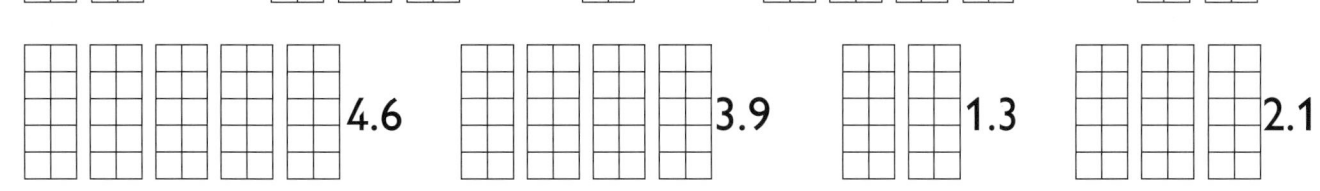

1.3   2.4   0.8   3.7   1.1

4.6   3.9   1.3   2.1

Copymaster 57

A bus leaves the High Street to go to Old Forge Lane every half an hour.
Here is part of the timetable.

Bus to:	leaves at am		
High St.	7.00	Old Forge Lane	7.35
Church Lane	7.04	New Road	7.40
Bridge St.	7.13	Bridge St.	
New Road	7.25	Church Lane	
Old Forge Lane	7.30	High St.	

This is the timetable for the first bus. Fill in the missing times for the return journey. How long does the bus wait at Old Forge Lane before it turns round? _____

Here is the timetable for later in the day.
The journeys take the same time as in the morning.
Fill in the rest of the times.

Bus to:	leaves at pm		
High St.	3.30	Old Forge Lane	
Church Lane		New Road	
Bridge St.		Bridge St.	
New Road		Church Lane	
Old Forge Lane		High St.	

The last bus leaves the High Street at 7 o'clock.
What time does it get to Old Forge Lane? _____
What time will it get back to the High Street? _____

Copymaster 58

Here are three calendar pages. They are for 3 consecutive months in the same year.
Can you work out which months they might be? _____

Su	M	T	W	Th	F	Sa
1	2	3	4	5	6	7
8	9	10	11	12	13	14
15	16	17	18	19	20	21
22	23	24	25	26	27	28
29	30					

A

Su	M	T	W	Th	F	Sa
		1	2	3	4	5
6	7	8	9	10	11	12
13	14	15	16	17	18	19
20	21	22	23	24	25	26
27	28	29	30	31		

B

Su	M	T	W	Th	F	Sa
31					1	2
3	4	5	6	7	8	9
10	11	12	13	14	15	16
17	18	19	20	21	22	23
24	25	26	27	28	29	30

C

What day of the week is the first day of month A? _____
What day of the week is the last day of month C? _____
What day of the week was the last day of the month before month A? _____
Which month has the most Wednesdays? _____

Here is part of the bus timetable.
The journey from Mill Lane to Church Street takes 35 minutes.
From Mill Lane to River Road takes 6 minutes, and from Mill Lane to Park Road takes 15 minutes.
Fill in all the times on the timetable for a bus which leaves Mill Lane at 9.55 am.

Mill Lane	
River Road	
Park Road	
Church Street	

Trains go from Castletown Junction to Fellmouth every two hours.
They start at 6.45 am and the last train is at 6.45 pm. The journey takes $1\frac{3}{4}$ hours.

How many trains run each day? _____
On Sundays there are only 5 trains. What time is the last one? _____

I need to be at Fellmouth before 2.00 pm. What time train should I catch? _____

Trains leave Fellmouth to return to Castletown Junction after a 15 minute stop.
What time does the last train leave Fellmouth?

125

Copymaster 59

1 You have these counters. (25) (29) Colour all the multiples of 10 in red.

(34) (42) (18)
(40) (30) (20) Colour all the multiples of 2 in blue.

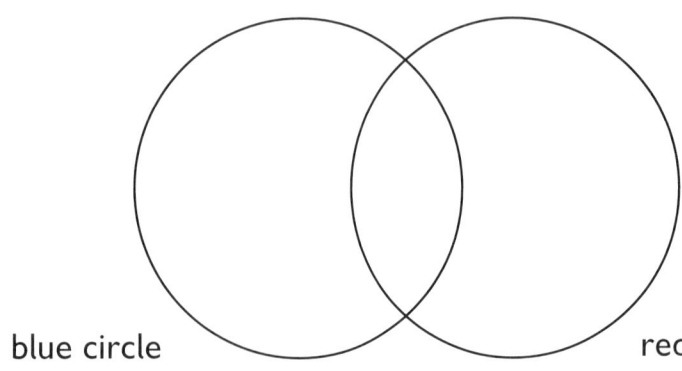

Draw lines from each counter to the right place on the diagram.

blue circle   red circle

2 You have these counters.

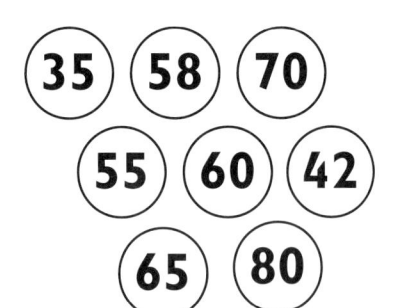

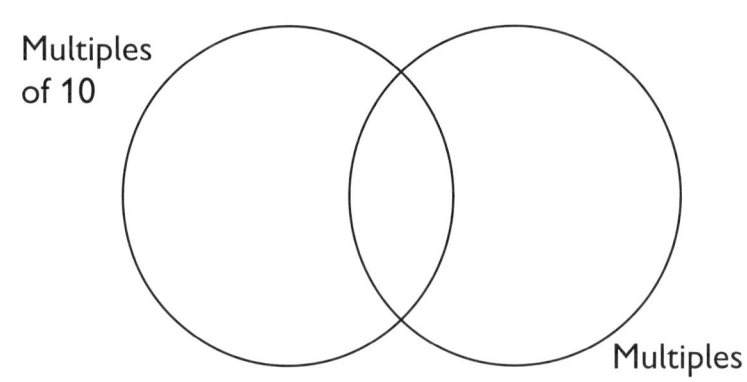

(35) (58) (70)
(55) (60) (42)
(65) (80)

Multiples of 10

Multiples of 5

Write the numbers in the right places on the diagram.

3 You have these counters.

(45)
(120) (265)
(95) (150)
(38)
(189) (80)
(27)

Odd numbers

Numbers bigger than 100

Write the numbers in the right place on the diagram.

Copymaster 60

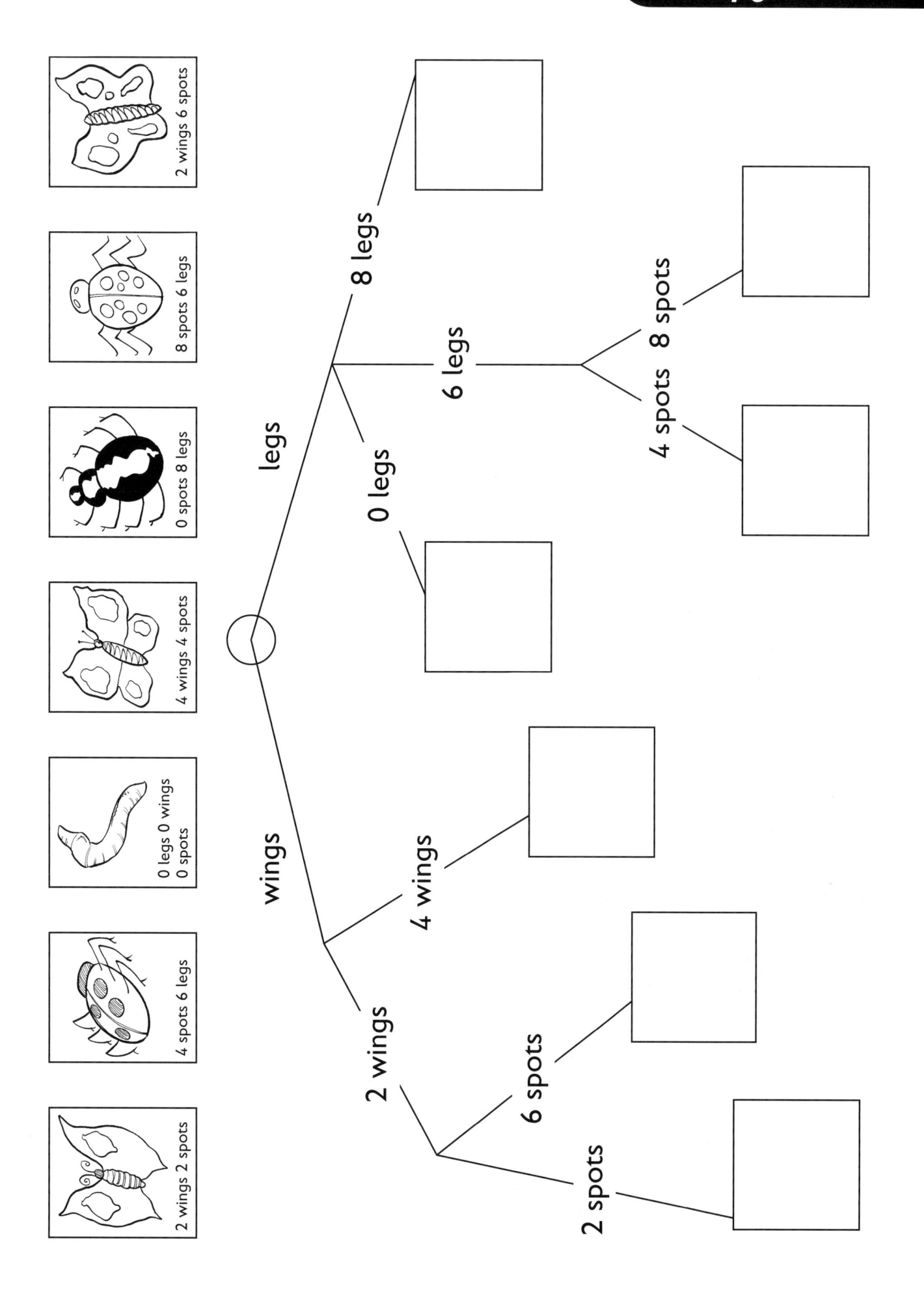

Homework copymaster 1

> This week we have been working on adding and subtracting numbers.

1 Jo had five number cards:

| 6 | 23 | 42 | 69 | 87 |

She was asked to write down 10 sums using the numbers on her cards.
She could use any pair of cards and could choose to add or take away.

Here are 3 of her sums. Do these sums.

87 − 23 = ☐   42 + 69 = ☐   23 + 87 = ☐

How many different sums do you think Jo could have made with her cards? ☐

2 You have these number cards:

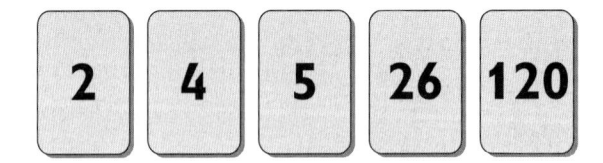

| 2 | 4 | 5 | 26 | 120 |

You can double or halve the numbers or add more than two numbers if you need to.
Can you write a sum for each of these target numbers using the numbers on the cards?

94	
14	
3	
150	
10	

Homework copymaster 2

> This week we are learning about money.

I can: change an amount in pennies and write it as pounds.
change an amount in pounds to an amount in pennies.
work out the cost of more than one thing I want to buy.
write down a sum, and do it, to work out how much I would spend on lots of things.
work out if I have enough money to buy something.
work out how much change I would get.

Fill in the gaps in this table.

Pounds	pence
£9.00	
	300p
£13.80	
	592p
	806p
£72.00	
	2059p
£28.65	

Write a sum for each of these money problems, and then do the sum.

1) John spent £3.99 on a book and £6.00 on a jigsaw puzzle. How much did he spend?

2) Mandy bought five colouring pens. Each pen cost 99p. How much did she spend?

3) Sarah bought a writing pad costing £1.80, a packet of envelopes costing £2.30 and 5 stamps costing 20p each. How much did she spend?

4) I want to buy a new game which costs £10.00. I have got £7.50. How much more do I need?

5) Lee bought six cakes costing 70p each. He had a five pound note. How much change did he get?

6) Make a list of all the coins we use.

7) You have one of each coin in your pocket. You take out five of the coins without looking at them. What might your five coins add to? Work out what different amounts you could make like this.

Homework copymaster 3

> This week we have learnt about units of measurement.

I can:
- Choose best units to use
- Estimate lengths
- Measure accurately

Write down the units we use to measure length. _____

What would be the best units to measure:
- The length of a pencil? _____
- The distance from one town to another? _____
- The width of an exercise book? _____
- The length of your fingernail? _____
- The height of a bookcase? _____
- The length of the school hall? _____
- The distance from the Earth to the Moon? _____

Measure each of these lines in centimetres.

_____

_____

_____

Draw lines measuring:
- 80 mm
- 5 mm
- $3\frac{1}{2}$ cm
- $7\frac{1}{2}$ cm
- 4 cm

This table shows measurements of some lines. Fill in the table with the measurements written in centimetres.

90 mm	cm
1 m	cm
$2\frac{1}{2}$ m	cm
100 mm	cm
25 mm	cm

$\frac{3}{4}$ m	cm
5 m	cm
1000 mm	cm
$\frac{1}{4}$ m	cm
20 m	cm

Homework copymaster 4

> This week we have been finding perimeters.

To find the perimeter of a shape you must measure _____

This rectangle has a perimeter of _____

Draw 5 more patterns using 8 squares. Write the perimeter for each one.
Each of these small squares represents a centimetre square.

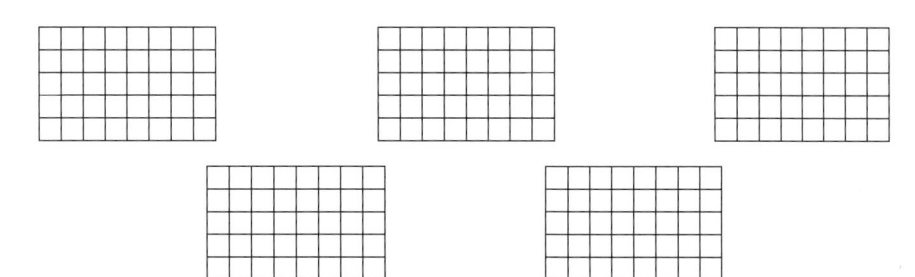

How many shapes can you draw with a perimeter of 16 cm? Each square/shape in the diagrams below represents a centimetre square.

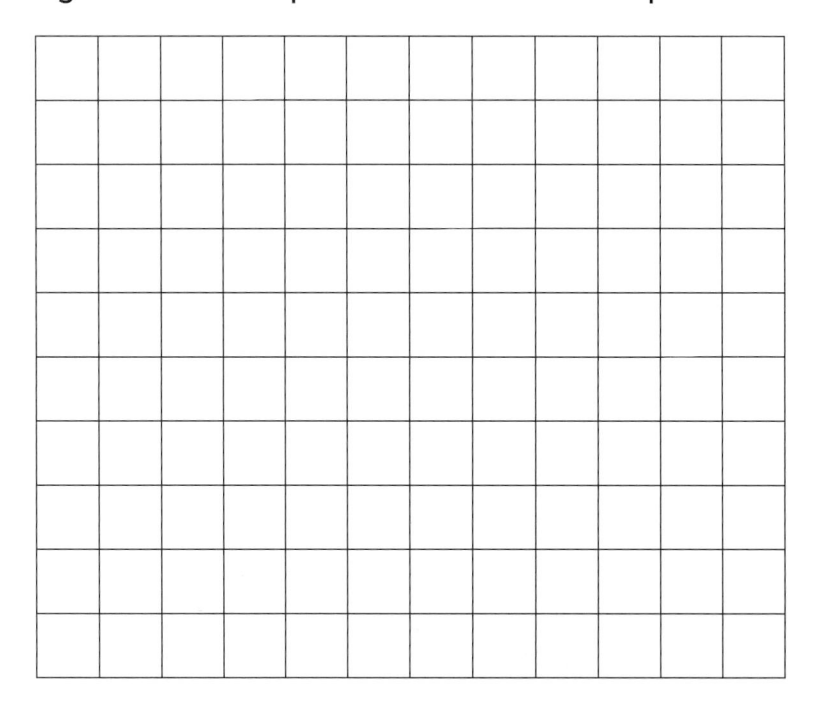

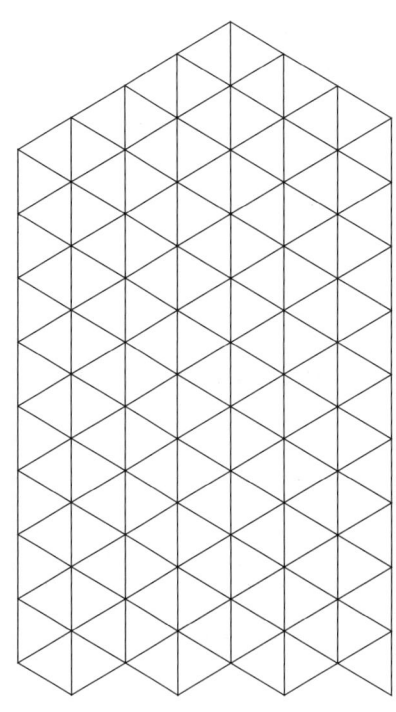

131

Homework copymaster 5

> This week we have been working on shapes.

I can:
    Write the names of the shapes.
    Explain the difference between two-dimensional and three-dimensional shapes.
    Tell you some facts about a shape if you tell me its name.

Here are some shape names.

heptagon   circle   isosceles triangle   square triangle   octagon   rectangle   quadrilateral semi-circle   equilateral triangle   hexagon

On a separate piece of paper write the name of each of these shapes.

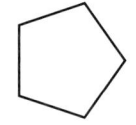

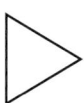

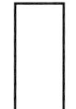

Draw the other shapes listed in the box and write their names.

Each of these shapes is made by putting 2 shapes together. Write the name of the shape used and the name of the shape you make.

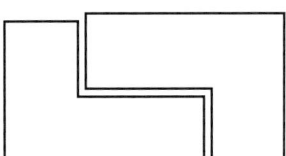

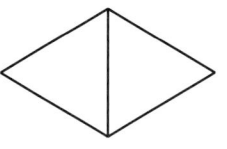

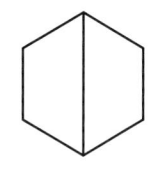

One shape is _____
Together they make _____

One shape is _____
Together they make _____

One shape is _____
Together they make _____

How many cubes are used to make each of these solids?

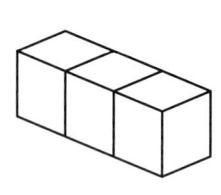

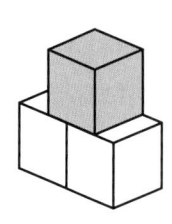

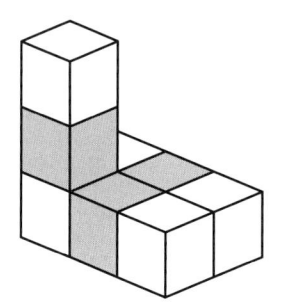

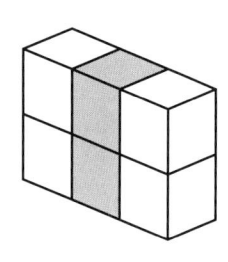

Homework copymaster 6

> This week we have learnt about number patterns.

I can:

Write a sequence of numbers from a rule.

Tell you interesting facts about odd and even numbers.

Work out number puzzles and find patterns.

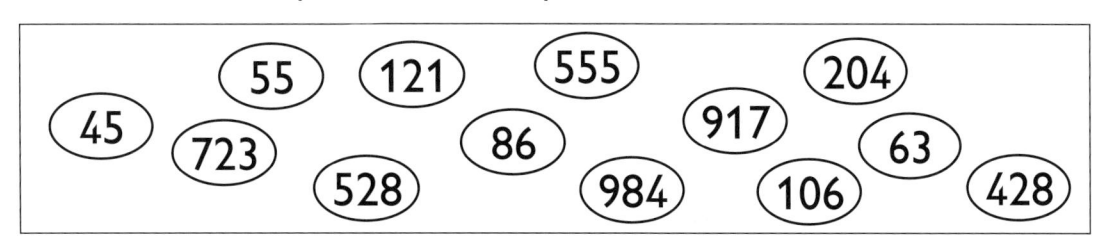

| 45 | 55 | 121 | 555 | 204 |
| 723 | 528 | 86 | 917 | 984 | 106 | 63 | 428 |

Look at the number counters in this box. Colour in the odd numbers.

Choose any two of the counters and write a number sequence which includes both counters. _____

This line is part of a tables square. What table does it show? Fill in the missing numbers.

| | 12 | | | | 36 | | |

What other times tables might include these numbers? _____

Fill in the number lines for each of these rules.

Starting number 140   Starting number 1000   Starting number 78
Count on in jumps of 100   Count back in jumps of 150   Count on in jumps of 38

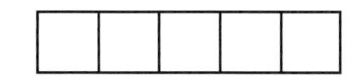

Fill in the missing numbers to make each side of this triangle add up to 18.

     8
   ○   ○
 ○   9   3

You can use any or all of the digits 1, 2, 3 and 4 and you can +, −, ×, and ÷

Which of these target numbers can you make?

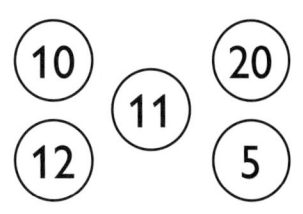

10   20
   11
12   5

Write down your sums.

133

Homework copymaster 7

This week we have worked on multiplication and division.

You have these number cards. Choose the right cards to answer the questions.

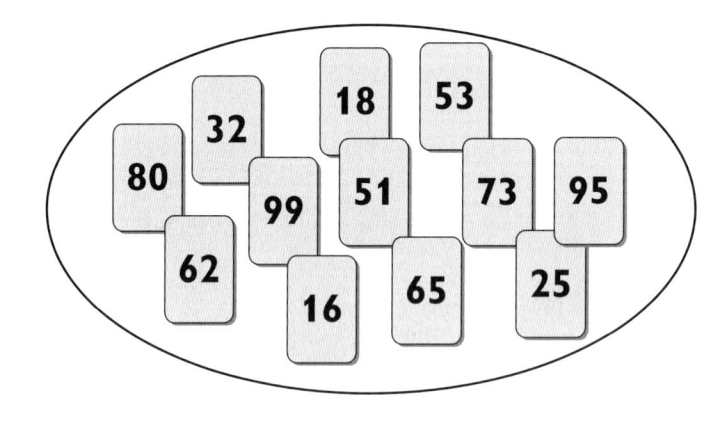

80, 32, 18, 53, 99, 51, 73, 95, 62, 16, 65, 25

1 Which number is double 20, double again?

   _____

2 If you double 2 and keep doubling, which 2 numbers would appear in the sequence?

   _____

3 Which 3 numbers could you divide by 3 and get no remainder?

   _____

4 Which number could you divide by 10 and have a remainder of 1?

   _____

5 Which 3 numbers can you divide by 5 but not by 10?

   _____

6 You have 3 cards left over. Write down the numbers in order, biggest first.

   _____

Homework copymaster 8

This week we have been working on fractions.

I can:
- Shade in a fraction on a shape.
- Write fractions as numbers.
- Work out a fraction of a number.

What fraction of each of these is shaded? Write your answer in the box.

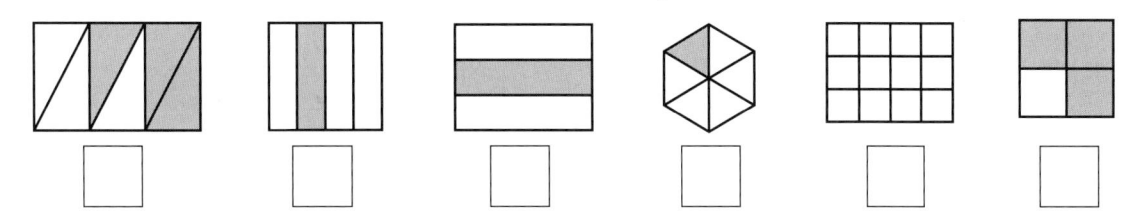

In the box under these shapes is a fraction. Shade the shape to show that fraction.

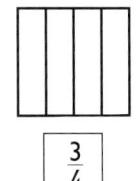

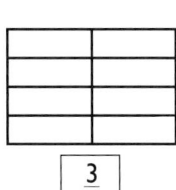

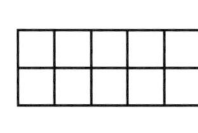

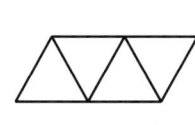

$\frac{3}{4}$ $\frac{5}{6}$ $\frac{3}{8}$ $\frac{7}{10}$ $\frac{1}{4}$

Draw a box round the fractions which are the same as a half.

$\frac{2}{3}$ $\frac{4}{8}$ $\frac{3}{6}$ $\frac{3}{4}$ $\frac{5}{10}$ $\frac{5}{8}$ $\frac{2}{4}$ $\frac{6}{12}$ $\frac{7}{12}$ $\frac{5}{6}$

Write these fractions in order of their size. Start with the smallest.

$\frac{1}{4}$ $\frac{1}{8}$ $\frac{1}{3}$ $\frac{1}{2}$ $\frac{1}{10}$ $\frac{1}{7}$

_____

Write these fractions in order of their size. Start with the biggest.

$\frac{1}{3}$ $\frac{2}{3}$ $\frac{1}{2}$ $\frac{1}{4}$

_____

How many different fractions can you show on this shape. Shade in the shape and write the fraction.

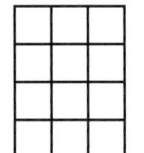

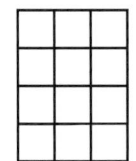

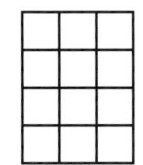

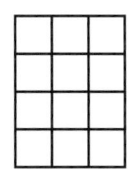

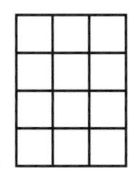

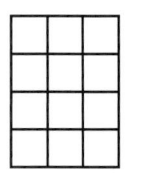

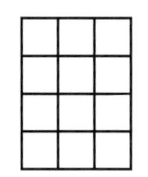

Homework copymaster 9

This week we have been learning about time.

1 Write the time shown on each of these clocks.

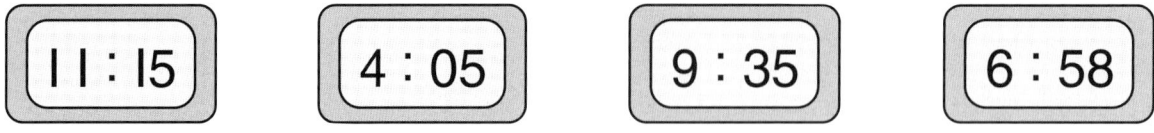

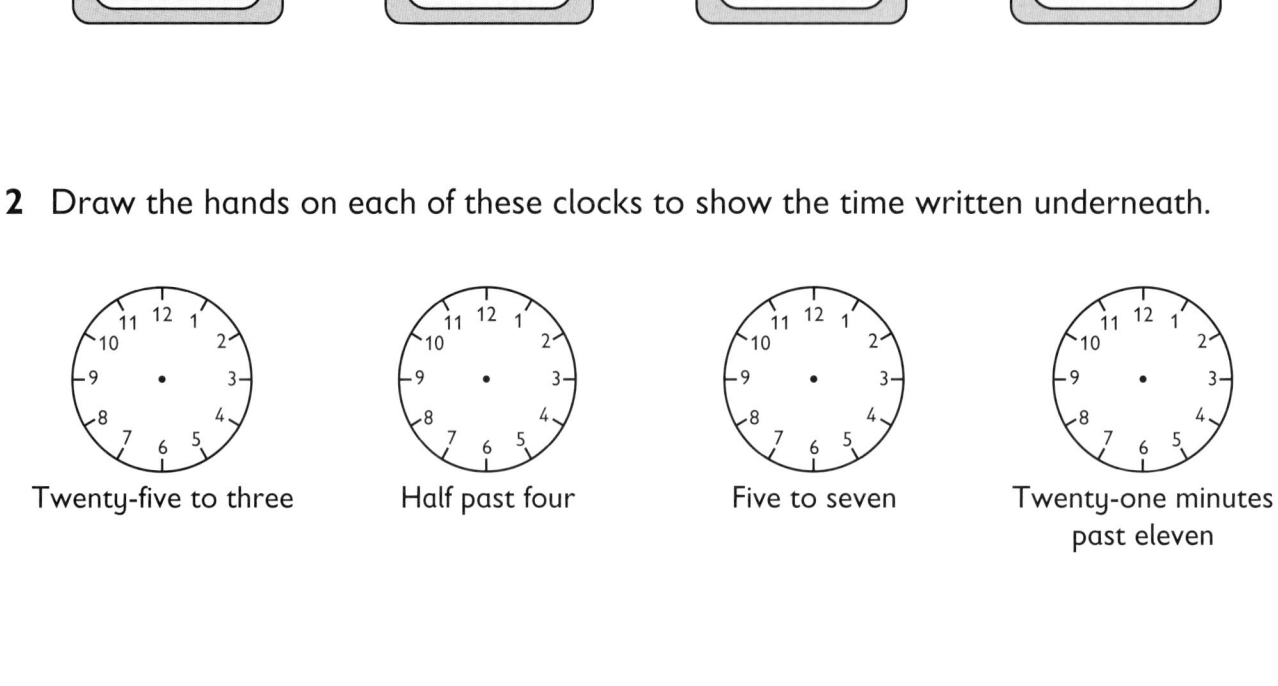

| 11:15 | 4:05 | 9:35 | 6:58 |

2 Draw the hands on each of these clocks to show the time written underneath.

Twenty-five to three   Half past four   Five to seven   Twenty-one minutes past eleven

3 How many minutes are there between the times shown on each of these pairs of clocks?

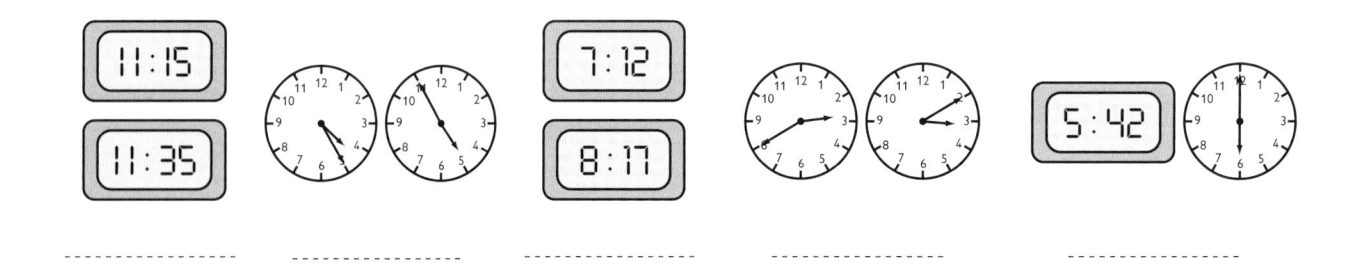

11:15
11:35

7:12
8:17

5:42

Homework copymaster 10

> This week we have learnt about data handling.

I can:

    Make a tally chart.

    Draw a frequency table from my data.

    Draw a pictogram to display my data.

    Read information from a pictogram.

Put the information from this tally chart into a frequency table.

Our Class Weather records

sunny all day	卌 ||
wet day	卌 卌 ||||
cold day	卌	
showers	卌 ||
cloudy all day	卌 卌 卌

sunny all day	
wet day	
cold day	
showers	
cloudy all day	

Put this data into a pictogram.

Choose a good symbol to show 5 days and draw it here ___

Can you show 1 day with your symbol? Draw the symbol for 1 day here ___

sunny all day	
wet day	
cold day	
showers	
cloudy all day	

Investigation:

Ask someone at home, your mum, dad, brother or sister, what activities they do in a day. Make a tally chart to collect the information. Draw a pictogram to show your results.

Homework copymaster 11

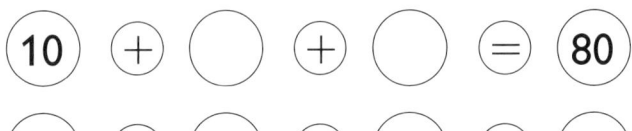

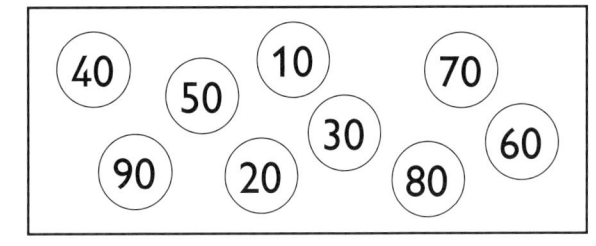

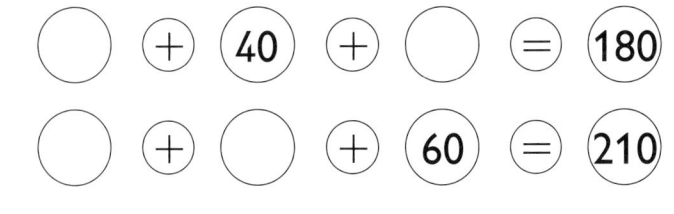

> This week we have been finding quick ways to add numbers.

1 Add these sets of numbers by looking for pairs which add up to 10.

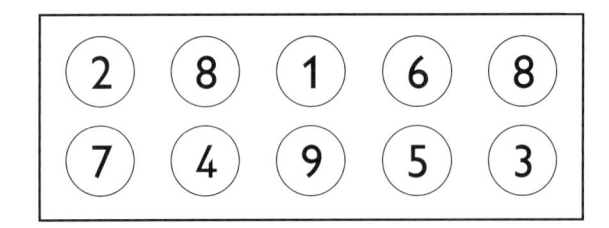

| 4 5 9 2 4 |
| 5 1 6 1 7 |

| 2 8 1 6 8 |
| 7 4 9 5 3 |

The total for this set is _____   The total for this set is _____

2 Use the numbers in the box to fill in the missing numbers in these sums.

10 + ◯ + ◯ = 80

90 + ◯ + ◯ = 120

| 40 10 70 |
| 50 30 60 |
| 90 20 80 |

◯ + 40 + ◯ = 180

◯ + ◯ + 60 = 210

Homework copymaster 12

> This week we have been doing adding and subtracting.

I can:
- Add money sums.
- Take away money sums.
- Tell you how much change I get.
- Work out money problems.

2p + 7p + 8p =   86p − 10p =
30p + 4p + 6p =   45p − 30p =
20p + 40p =   70p − 50p =
90p + 70p =   £1.00 − 20p =
70p + 25p + 30p =   £1.00 − 55p =

£ p	£ p	£ p	£ p	£ p
0.80	0.44	1.70	0.92	1.69
0.19 +	0.92 +	0.19 +	0.31 −	0.56 −

Write a sum to help you work out each of these.

John collects 5p coins. He has 20. How much has he got altogether?

Juli spends 60p. How much change does she get from £1.00?

Tiffany wants to buy a game costing £8.99. She has saved up £5.00. How much more does she need?

Ally has £10.00 to spend. He would like to buy a video costing £7.99 and a book costing £2.99. Has he got enough money?

Keiran wants a football which costs £16.00. He gets £2.00 a week pocket money. How many weeks will it take to save up enough to buy the ball?

Homework copymaster 13

> This week we have been measuring mass.

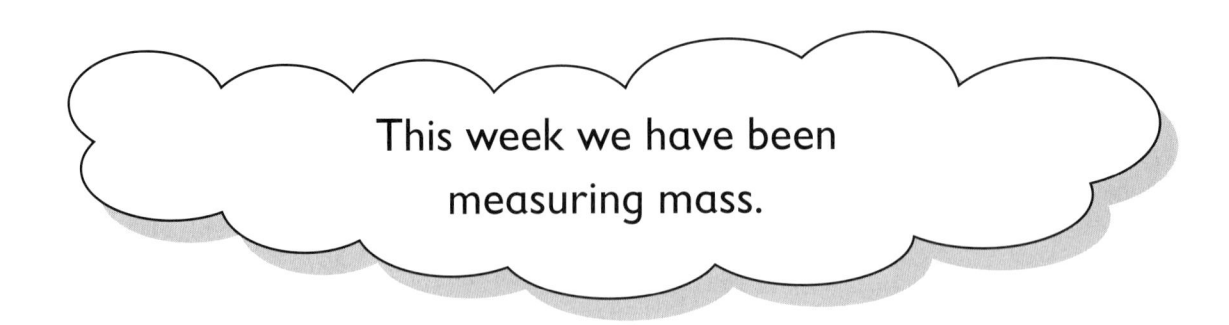

1 Write the mass shown on each of these scales. Write your answer in kilograms and grams.

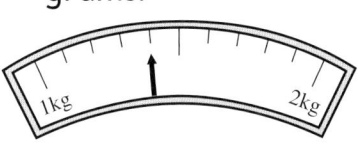

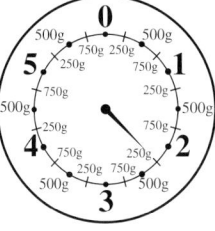

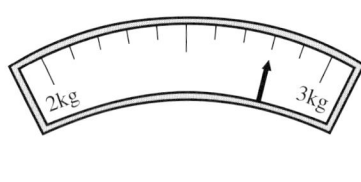

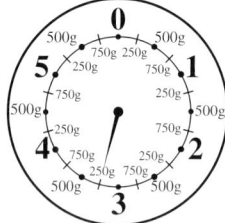

_____   _____   _____   _____

Now write the mass in grams.

_____   _____   _____   _____

2 Draw the pointer on each of these scales to show the weight of these two bags.

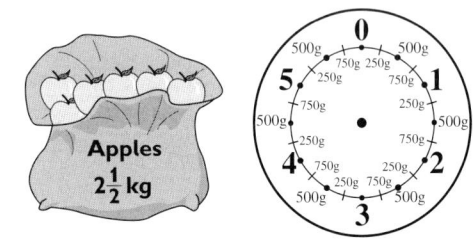

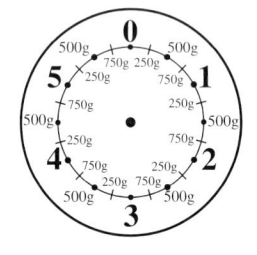

Apples 2½ kg

POTATOES 5 kg

3 How heavy is my shopping basket?

_____

Beans 420 G

JAM 450 G

CORN FLAKES 500 g

WHITE Bread 800 g

140

Homework copymaster 14

This week we have been learning about area.

1

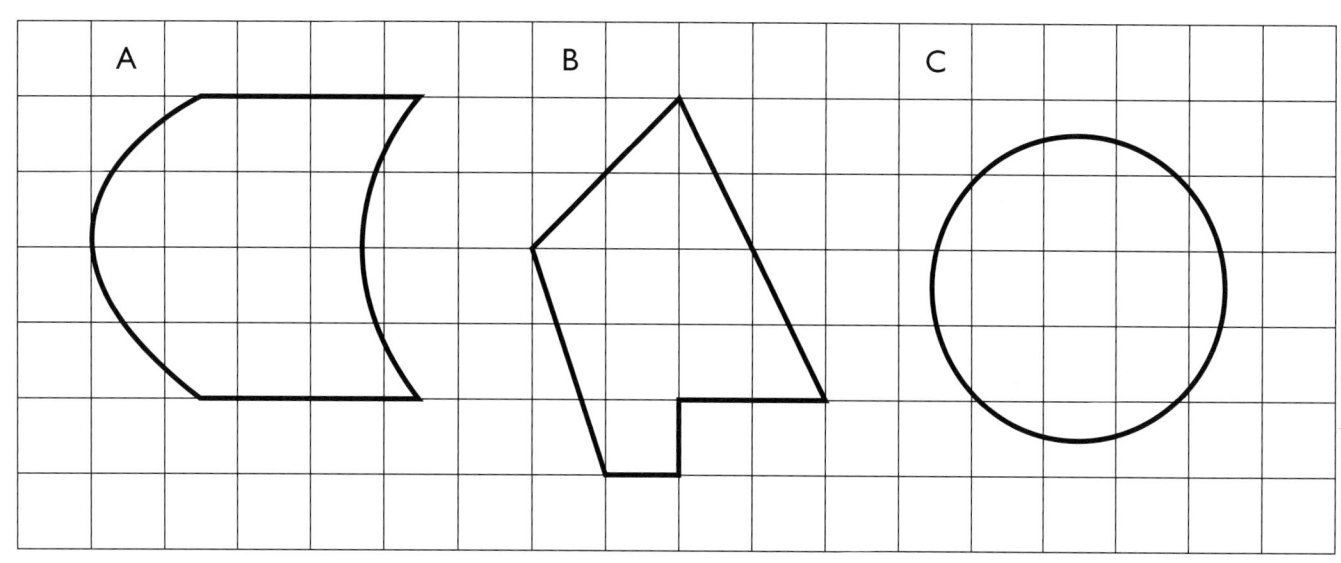

The area of shape A is _____

The area of shape B is _____

The area of shape C is _____

2 Draw any shape with an area of 24 cm².

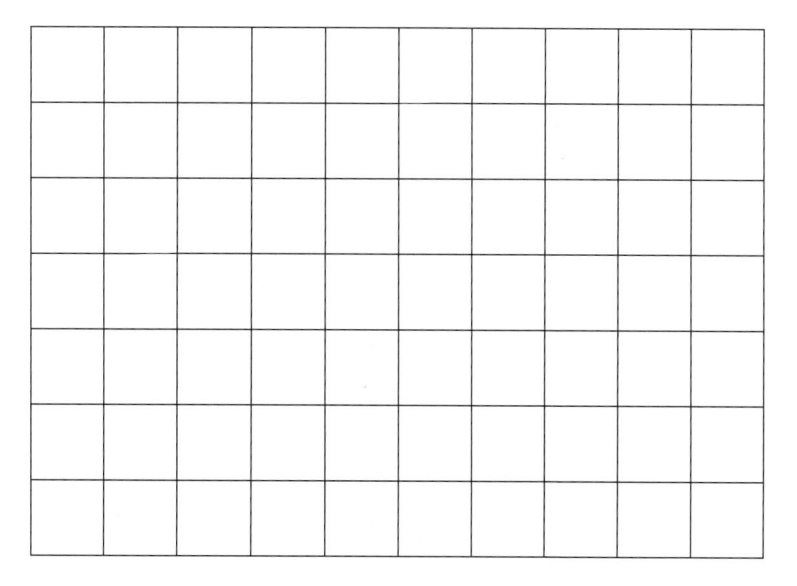

Homework copymaster 15

This week we have been learning about shape and movement.

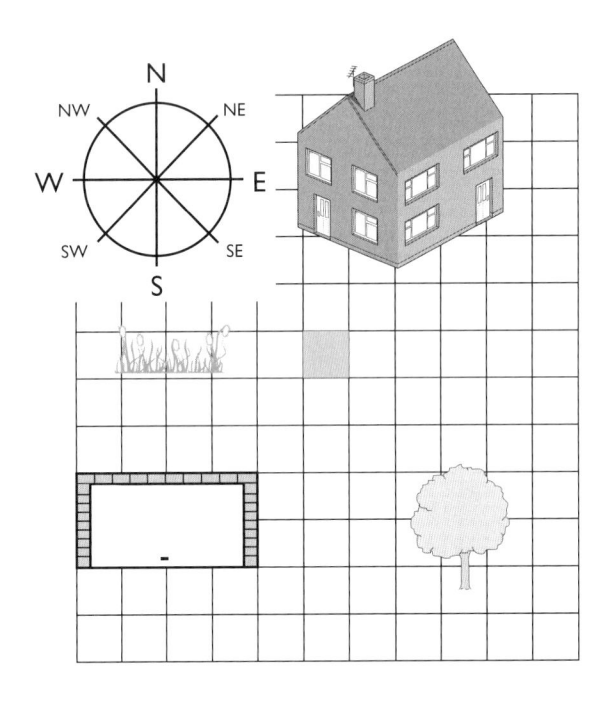

You are standing on the shaded square looking towards the house.

What direction is the door you can see in front of you? _____

What direction is the garage? _____

What direction is the flower bed? _____

If you make a half turn clockwise what direction are you facing? _____

You walk 4 squares to the east, then 3 squares to the north. Where are you standing? _____

142

Homework copymaster 16

This week we have been looking at number patterns.

1 Fill in the missing numbers in these number patterns.
Write the rule for each one.

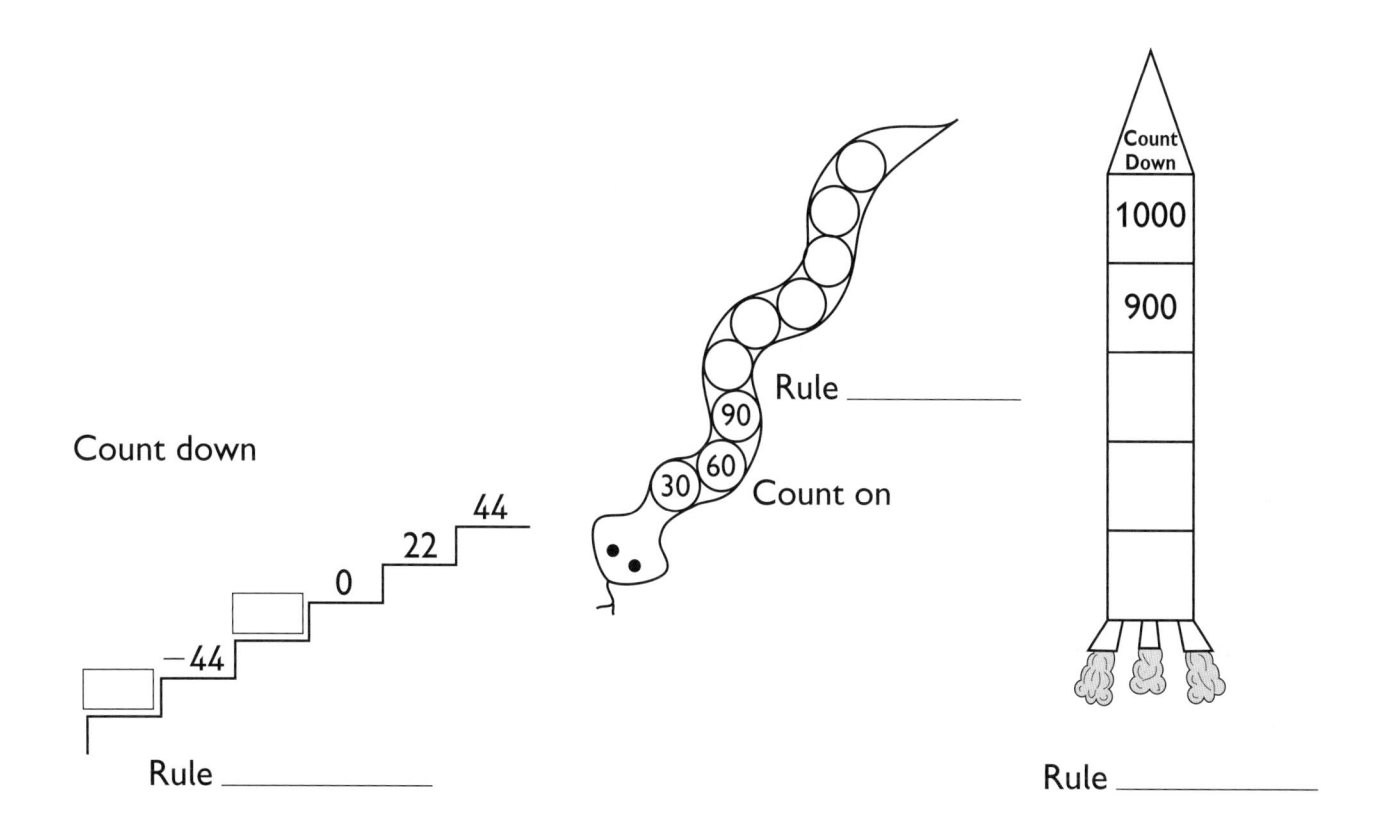

Count down

44
22
0
−44
☐

Rule _____

Snake: 30, 60, 90, ...
Count on
Rule _____

Rocket Count Down: 1000, 900, ...
Rule _____

2 These all show parts of a table square. Fill in the blank squares.

| 12 | 16 | 20 | | | |

4		
	9	
	16	
		25

| 7 |
| 8 |
| 9 |
| |
| |

4		
5		20

| 5 | 6 | | | 9 |
| | | | 18 | |

50	55
	77

143

Homework copymaster 17

> This week we have been working on multiplication and division.

I can:
  Find easy ways to multiply 2 numbers together, if one of the numbers is near 10.
  Find easy ways to multiply 3 numbers together.
  Multiply by splitting numbers.
  Divide money sums.

Times these numbers together.

| 8 5 2 | 2 2 6 | 10 5 2 | 6 5 5 |

Do these sums.

  46 × 9   39 × 9   91 × 11
  28 × 11   84 × 9   75 × 11

Do these sums.

  £4.00 ÷ 2   £8.00 ÷ 10   £8.00 ÷ 5
  £6.80 ÷ 2   £6.80 ÷ 4   £7.00 ÷ 2

Do these sums.

  [7|2] × 4 = [|] × □   [3|8] × 3 = [|] × □
           + □ × □   + □ × □
         =   =

Do these sums in the same way.

  54 × 5   73 × 3   62 × 4

144

Homework copymaster 18

> This week we have been learning about money problems.

1 Andy has this money. How much has he altogether?
Andy has _____

2 Gita has this money. How much has she altogether?
Gita has _____

3 Beth has this money. How much has she altogether?
Beth has _____

4 Andy, Gita and Beth want to buy some drinks.
They can buy a bottle of orange for 45p
or a can of cola for 38p.

Andy wants 2 drinks. What could he buy? _____
How much would his drinks cost? _____

Gita wants 10 drinks. Can she buy 10? _____
What is the greatest number of drinks she can buy? _____
How many bottles of orange can she buy? _____

Beth wants two bottles of orange and three cans of cola.
How much will her drinks cost? _____
How much money will she have left? _____

Homework copymaster 19

This week we have been learning about fractions and decimals.

1 You have these amounts of money in your pocket. What decimal fraction of a pound do you have?

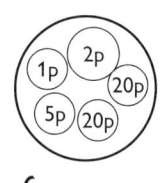

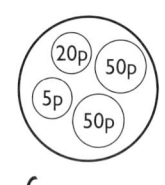

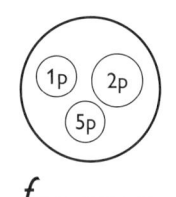

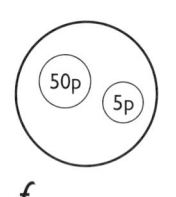

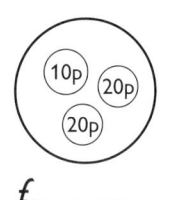

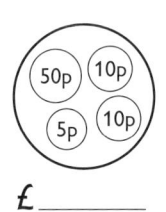

- (1p, 2p, 20p, 5p, 20p) £_____
- (20p, 50p, 5p, 50p) £_____
- (1p, 2p, 5p) £_____
- (50p, 5p) £_____
- (10p, 20p, 20p) £_____
- (50p, 10p, 5p, 10p) £_____

2 What decimal fractions of a metre are shown on these two tape measures?

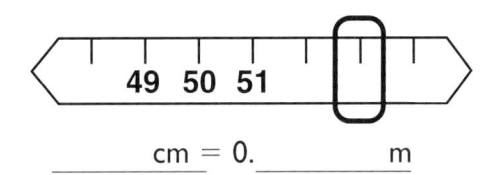

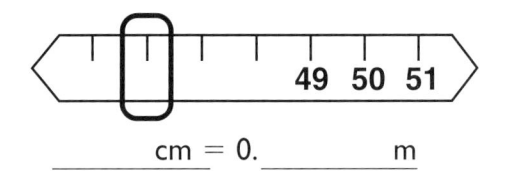

_____ cm = 0._____ m   _____ cm = 0._____ m

My bar of chocolate had 10 squares. I ate 5 squares. What fraction did I eat? What decimal was this? _____

Sean had 6 collecting cards to give away. He gave 1 to Aidan, 3 to Patrick and the rest to Nicki. What fraction did each person get?
Aidan _____   Patrick _____   Nicki _____

Write these decimals in size order. Start with the smallest.

0.7   0.1   0.5   _____

Write these decimals in size order. Start with the smallest.

0.62   0.25   0.3   _____

Homework copymaster 20

This week we have been learning about bar charts.

I can:

Draw a bar chart.

Read information from a bar chart.

A supermarket asked 500 people about their favourite drinks.
Here are the results.

Herbal tea	35
Tea	38
Coffee	57
Instant coffee	80
Decaffeinated coffee	71

Chocolate	65
Flavoured chocolate	62
Malted drinks	29
Instant chocolate	43
Mineral water	20

Draw a bar chart to show these results.

Homework copymaster 21

> This week we have been adding and subtracting.

1 How many 10s can you take away from these numbers?

150 ___   240 ___   309 ___   86 ___   550 ___

2 Add 1000 to each of these numbers.

180 ___   365 ___   695 ___   28 ___   1 ___

3 Now try these sums.

31 + 12 + 25 = ___   14 + 52 + 21 = ___   36 + 32 + 30 = ___

Can you explain a quick way to do these?

_____

Which of these sums can you do if you change the order of the numbers?
If you can find another way, write out the new sum and do it.
Is the answer always the same?

a) 14 + 13 + 19 = ☐

b) 86 − 34 = ☐

c) 29 + 58 = ☐

d) 75 − 28 = ☐

e) 25 + 46 + 75 = ☐

f) 21 + 94 = ☐

g) 37 − 19 = ☐

h) 143 + 12 + 8 = ☐

i) 52 − 49 = ☐

j) 63 − 18 = ☐

Homework copymaster 22

This week we have been learning about money problems.

1 Use a separate piece of paper for these problems.

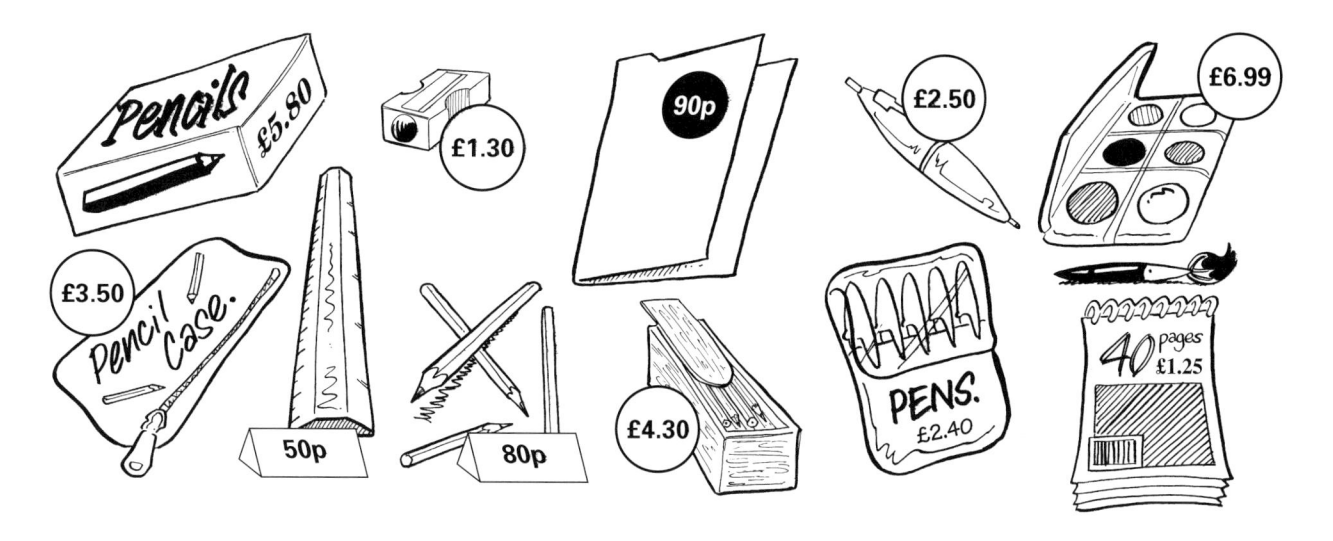

Pencils £5.80, Sharpener £1.30, Book 90p, Pen £2.50, Paints £6.99, Pencil Case £3.50, 50p, 80p, £4.30, Pens £2.40, 40 pages £1.25

If you had £10.00 to spend, which of these things could you buy?
How many different combinations can you make?

How much change would you get each time?

2 Sarah is having a party. She wants to buy these things. There will be 10 people at her party altogether.

Crisps 30p, 2 each
Cakes 10 for 90p, 2 each
Party poppers 10 for £2.00, 2 poppers each
Choc rolls 5 for £1.20, 1 roll each
Lemonade 75p, 1 bottle for 5 people
Cola 80p, 1 bottle for 5 people

How much will her party cost her?
How much would her party cost if there were only 5 people there?

Write out these sums in columns and do them.

Homework copymaster 23

> This week we have been learning to measure capacity.

1 Draw lines on these measuring jugs to show where these amounts of liquid would fill to.

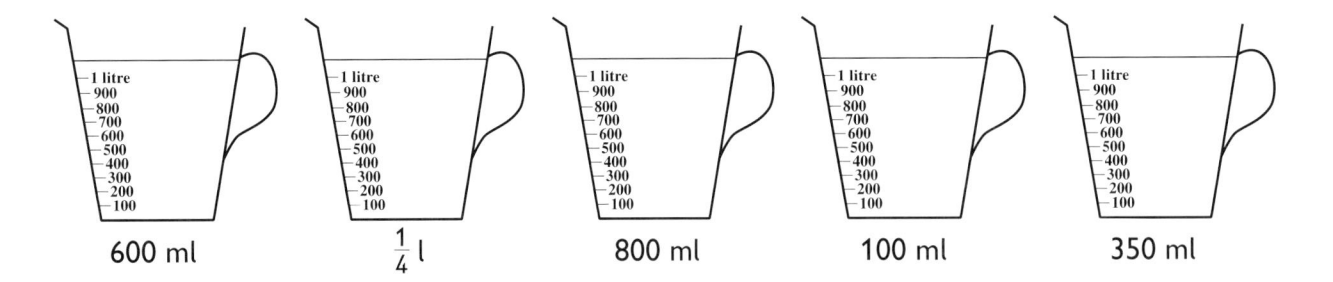

600 ml $\frac{1}{4}$ l   800 ml   100 ml   350 ml

2 How many times could you fill the measuring jug from each of these?

Milk 6 l   Lemonade 2 l   Squash $1\frac{1}{2}$ l   Mineral Water 3 l   Bath Foam 1 l

3 If you filled all these bottles with water, how much water would there be in total?

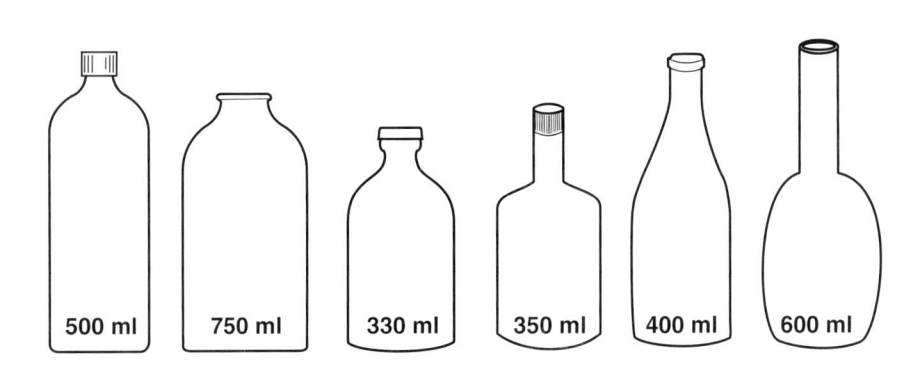

500 ml   750 ml   330 ml   350 ml   400 ml   600 ml

150

Homework copymaster 24

This week we have been learning about angles and reflections.

1 Draw the reflection of each of these two patterns.

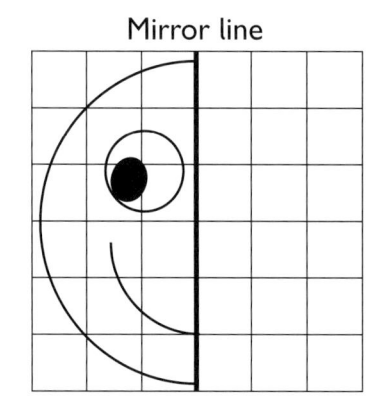

Mirror line

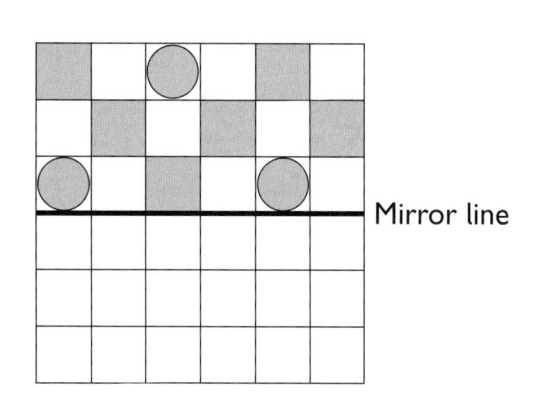

Mirror line

2 Here are some angles measured in degrees.
Match up each one with the right picture.

| 90° | 45° | 180° | 30° | 60° | 90° |

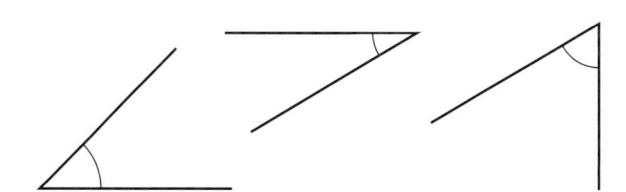

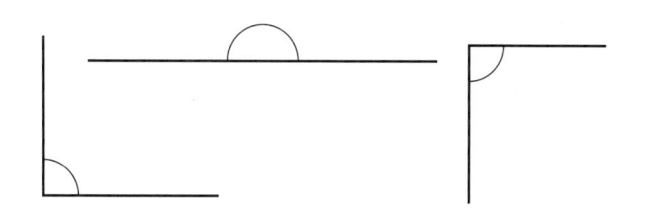

Which angle shows a half turn?
Which angles show a quarter turn?

151

Homework copymaster 25

> This week we have been working on multiples and solving number puzzles.

I can:
- Tell you a multiple of 2, 3, 4, 5 and 10.
- Solve number puzzles.
- Make up word puzzles to go with a sum.

Cut out these parts of the tables square and fit them together to make one big square.

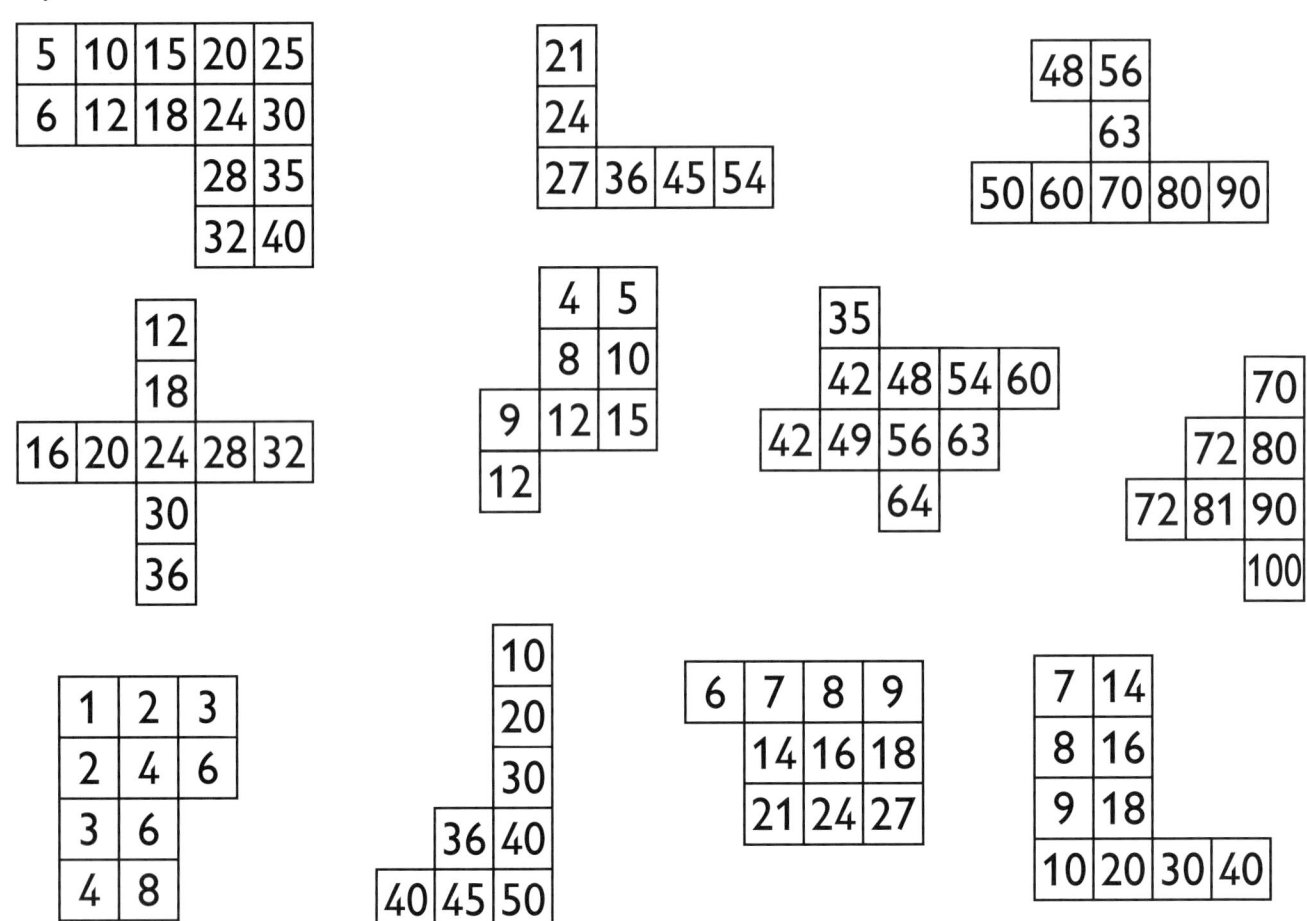

5	10	15	20	25
6	12	18	24	30
			28	35
			32	40

21
24
27 | 36 | 45 | 54

48	56			
	63			
50	60	70	80	90

12
18
16 | 20 | 24 | 28 | 32
30
36

4 | 5
8 | 10
9 | 12 | 15
12

35
42 | 48 | 54 | 60
42 | 49 | 56 | 63
64

70
72 | 80
72 | 81 | 90
100

1	2	3
2	4	6
3	6	
4	8	

10
20
30
36 | 40
40 | 45 | 50

6	7	8	9
	14	16	18
	21	24	27

7	14		
8	16		
9	18		
10	20	30	40

You can use any of these numbers and put them together in any of these sums.

| 1 | 2 | 4 | 8 | | + | − | × | ÷ |

How many different numbers can you make?

Hint: you can use the numbers on their own or put them together in TU.

152

Homework copymaster 26

This week we have been learning about multiplication and division.

1 Answer these questions as quickly as you can.

a How many tens are there in 70? _____

b How many tens are there in 92? _____

c Is 38 a multiple of 5? _____

d I put 5 pencils in each packet. How many packets will I need to put 48 pencils in boxes? _____
Will all the boxes be full? _____

e Share 50p between 4 people. How much will each person have? _____
How much money will be left over? _____

2 Use these number tiles to make some dividing sums.

| 60 | 36 | 51 | 17 | 32 | 25 |

You can use each tile as many times as you like, or not at all.

☐ ÷ 3 = ☐ No remainder   ☐ ÷ 3 = ☐ remainder 2

☐ ÷ 5 = ☐ No remainder   ☐ ÷ 2 = ☐ remainder 1

☐ ÷ 4 = ☐ No remainder   ☐ ÷ 10 = ☐ remainder 6

☐ ÷ 6 = ☐ No remainder   ☐ ÷ 4 = ☐ remainder 3

Homework copymaster 27

> This week we have been working on solving problems.

1 We bought some multi-packs of sweets.

How much did one bar of each sort cost?

Chunky Choc _____

Crispy Bars _____

Mighty Munch _____

Chocky Fingers _____

Mighty Munch 5 for 80p
Chunky Choc 10 bars for £1.60
Crispy Bars 10 for £1.80
Chocky Fingers 20 for £3.80

2 One apple weighs 140 g.
How much would 4 apples weigh? _____
Explain why your answer might be wrong.

3 We want to measure the length of the kitchen. Our rule measures 50 cm. How many times do we need to move the rule if the kitchen measures 4 m?

_____

4 Steve had £20.00 birthday money to spend. He bought a jigsaw puzzle for £7.99 and a pack of colouring pens for £2.49. How much did he spend? What change did he get?

_____

5 In a sale the colouring pens were being sold at half price.
What is half price to the nearest penny?

_____

Homework copymaster 28

> This week we have been learning about fractions and decimals.

I can:
    Find a decimal and fraction which are the same.
    Find a decimal of money.
    Put decimals in order of their size.

What decimal fraction does each grey line show?

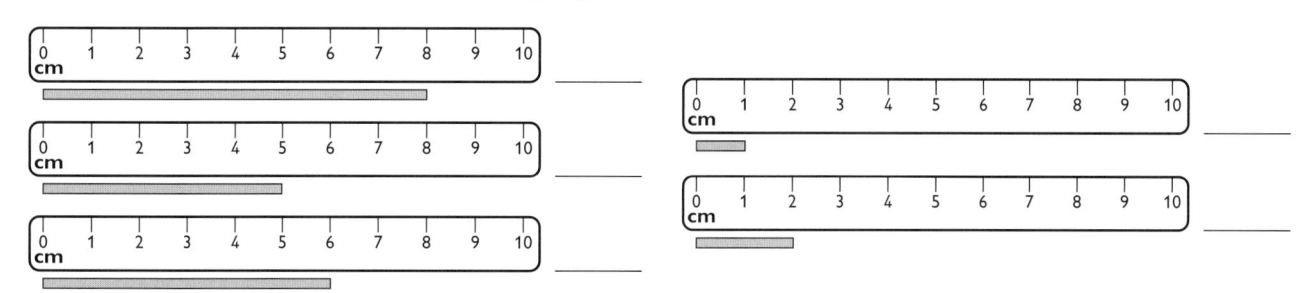

What decimal fraction is shaded on each of these jugs?

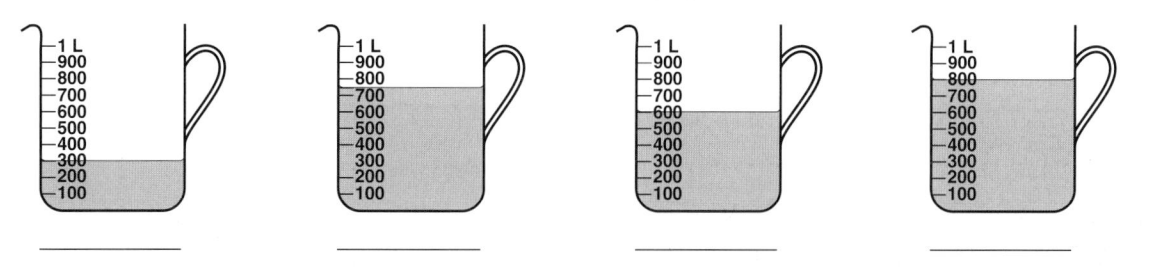

Shade in these jugs to show these decimals.

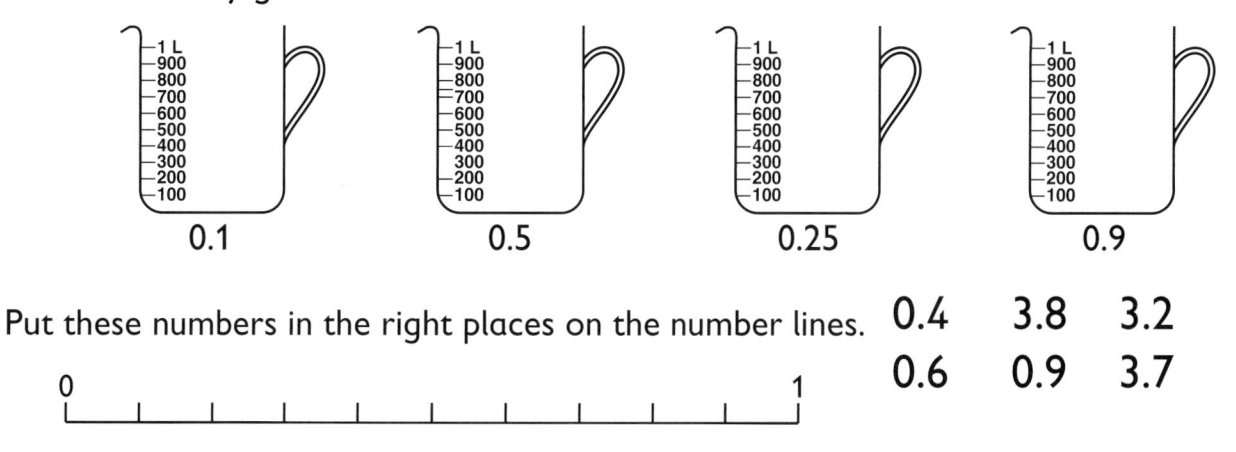

    0.1   0.5   0.25   0.9

Put these numbers in the right places on the number lines.   0.4   3.8   3.2
   0.6   0.9   3.7

0   1

3   4

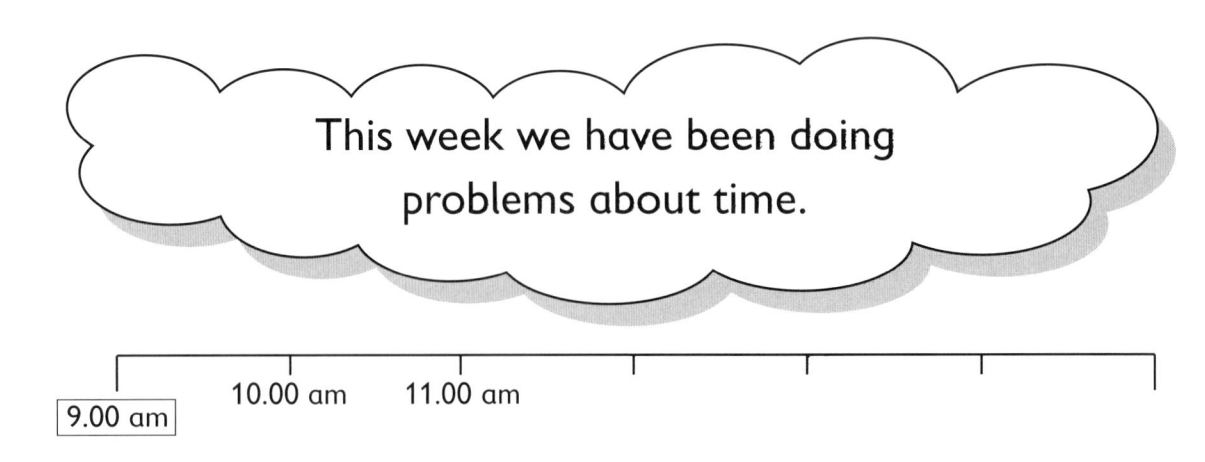

Homework copymaster 29

This week we have been doing problems about time.

| 9.00 am | 10.00 am | 11.00 am | | | |

On Saturday Matt had a busy day. Read his diary and write in what he did on the time line.

> Got up at 9.00 o'clock. A bit late because I had to meet Simon at half past.
> We went to the shopping centre with Simon's mum. We got stuck in the traffic so it took half an hour.
> We went to the library and we were there for half an hour. Then we looked round the shops for another 45 minutes. We had to wait three quarters of an hour then we had lunch.
> Then we went and played football in the park until it was time to go home.
> We left the park at 3 o'clock.

What time did Matt and Simon get to the shopping centre? _____

What time did they leave the library? _____

What time did they have lunch? _____

Lunch took them an hour and it took 15 minutes to reach the park.

What time did they get to the park? _____

How long did they stay in the park? _____

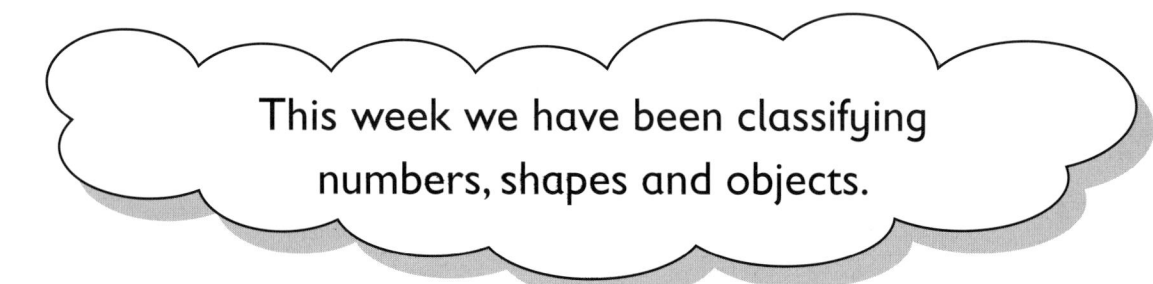

Homework copymaster 30

> This week we have been classifying numbers, shapes and objects.

I can:
- Put numbers on a Venn Diagram.
- Put numbers on a Carroll Diagram.
- Put things into a tree diagram.
- Collect and organise data.

Write a label for each circle.

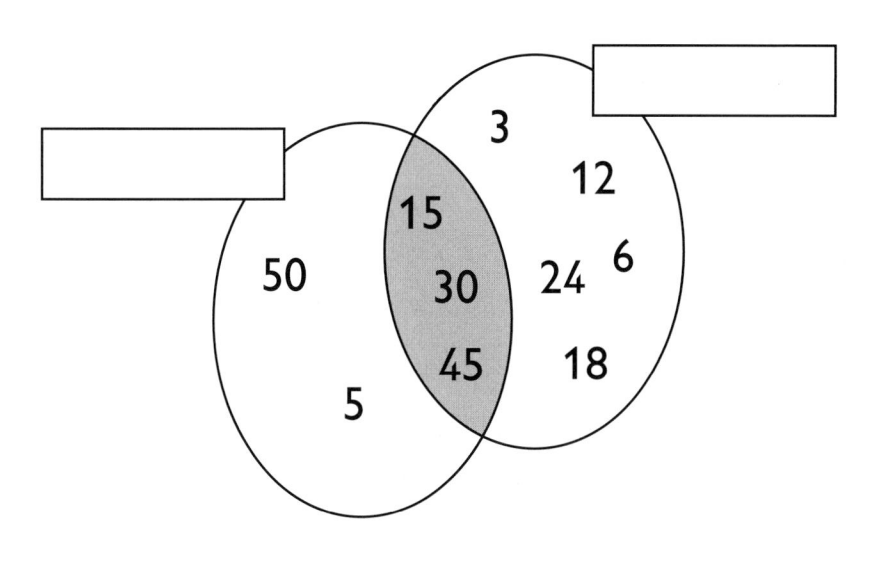

What label could you give to the shaded part?

(Venn diagram: left circle contains 50, 5; intersection (shaded) contains 15, 30, 45; right circle contains 3, 12, 24, 6, 18)

How many labels can you find for shapes in this group?

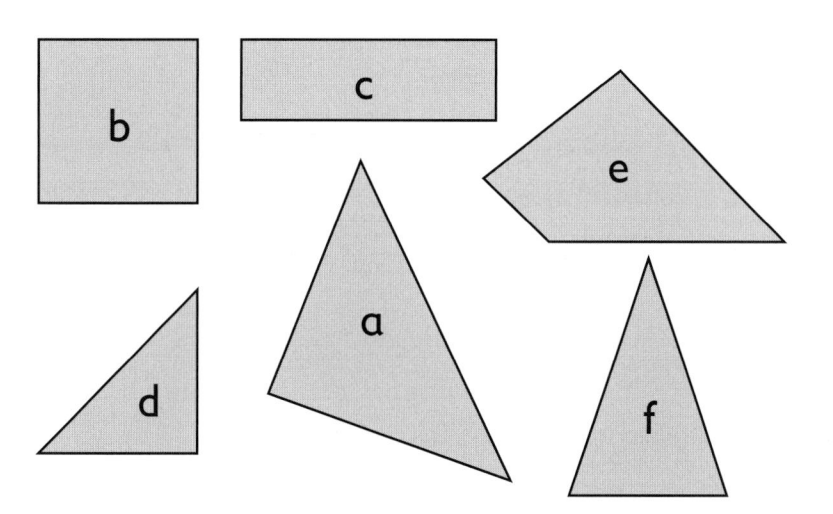

(Shapes: b – square, c – rectangle, a – triangle, e – triangle, d – right triangle, f – triangle)

Choose 2 of your labels and draw a Venn Diagram. Show where each shape should go.

Draw a tree diagram to classify these shapes.

157

Year 4
Answers

Copymaster number	Title	Answers
1	Doubles – patterns and puzzles	16, 160, 18, 180, 48, 64, 122, 56, 148, 70, 172, 184, 264, 438, 704 30, 20, 35, 15, 25, 42, 31, 38, 16, 60, 120, 90, 132, 214, 252 12 11 28 16 36 25 45 28 50 160
2	Missing Numbers	68, 68, 174, 95 11, 11, 97, 38 85, 85, 106, 106 17, 100 − 83 = 17 or 100 − 17 = 83, 141, 100 + 41 = 141, 78, 78 + 22 = 100 or 22 + 78 = 100 74, 100 − 74 = 26 or 100 − 26 = 74, 17, 17 + 58 = 75 or 58 + 17 = 75, 21, 21 + 18 = 39 or 18 + 21 = 39 107, 107 − 94 = 13 or 107 − 13 = 94, 58, 58 + 9 = 67 or 9 + 58 = 67, 91, 132 − 41 = 91 or 132 − 91 = 41
4	Money Problems	3 × 80p = £2.40 6 × 20p = £1.20 £18.00 + £7.00 = £25.00 4 × £10.00 = £40.00 £2.50 + £0.99 + (2 × 60p) = £4.69 £2.00 + (6 × £1.00) = £8.00 (10 × 40p) + (10 × 50p) + (10 × 25p) + (4 × 30p) = £12.70 £29.99 + £9.99 + £4.99 + £4.99 = £49.96
5	Maps	Q1 – Ambury to Deanside = 9 km, Ambury to Edgeworth = 8 km, Edgeworth to Fellmouth = 12 km, Fellmouth to Castletown = 19 km, Castletown to Banford = 17 km, Banford to Deanside = 5 km, Deanside to Fellmouth = 11 km. Q2 – 12 km + 8 km + 9 km + 21 km + 19 km = 69 km Q3 – Banford Q4a – 411 miles Q4b – 222 miles Q4c – Edinburgh to Southampton Q4d – Oxford to Southampton
6	Real Life Measuring	Q1 – Bill and Giles Q2 – 1$\frac{1}{2}$ m Q3 – 20cm, 320cm Q4 – yes Q5 – 40 cm Q6 – Leo, Joseph, Laura Q7 – Sarah, Sam, Ellie, Leo, Joseph, Laura Q8 – 15 cm Q9 – 283 cm
7	Perimeters	A – 18 cm B – 17.5 cm C – 20 cm D – 12 cm E – 16 cm F – 16 cm G – 30 cm H – 12 cm I – 20 cm J – 11 cm K – 12 cm L – 12 cm M – 17 cm N – 18 cm O – 13 cm
9	Shapes	cylinders pyramid circle octagon hexagonal prism circle, cone cuboid square, rectangle cube
10	3D Shapes	Cube, square Cuboid, rectangle Triangular pyramid, triangle Square pyramid, square Cylinder, circle Octahedron, triangle Hexagonal prism, hexagon Triangular prism, rectangle
11	Number Snakes	13, 23, 33, 43, 53, 63, 73, 83, 93 – add 10 210, 180, 150, 120, 90, 60, 30, 0 – subtract 30 1, 2, 4, 8, 16, 32, 64, 132 – double each number 18, 27, 36, 45, 54, 63, 72, 81, 90, 99 – add 9 78, 73, 68, 63, 58, 53, 48, 43, 38 – subtract 5 105, 305, 505, 705, 905, 1105, 1305, 1505, 1705, 1905 – add 200
12	Number Puzzles	**Square 1** – 4, 9, 2 3, 5, 7 8, 1, 6 Magic number – 15 Numbers used – 1, 2, 3, 4, 5, 6, 7, 8, 9 Sequences – 4, 5, 6 – add 1 3, 5, 7 – add 2 2, 5, 8 – add 3 **Square 2** – 7, 6, 11 12, 8, 4 5, 10, 9 Magic number – 24 Numbers used – 4, 5, 6, 7, 8, 9, 10, 11, 12 Sequences – 5, 8, 11 – add 3 4, 8, 12 – add 4 7, 8, 9, – add 1 **Square 3** – 11, 12, 7 6, 10, 14 13, 8, 9 Magic number – 30 Numbers used – 6, 7, 8, 9, 10, 11, 12, 13, 14 Sequences – 8, 10, 12 – add 2 7, 10, 13 – add 3 6, 10, 14 – add 4 **Target Numbers** – examples 24 = 20 + 4, 30 − 6, 48 ÷ 2, 6 × 4 60 = 6 + 54, 90 − 30, 60 ÷ 1, 4 × 15 36 = 1 + 35, 37 − 1, 3 × 12, 360 ÷ 10 110 = 109 + 1, 111 − 1, 110 ÷ 1, 2 × 55
13	Tens and Units	Q1 – 92, 72, 32 92 × 3 = 276 72 × 3 = 216 32 × 3 = 96 Q2 – 44, 46, 49, 43 44 × 2 = 88 46 × 2 = 92 49 × 2 = 98 43 × 2 = 86 Q3 – 16, 11, 14, 18 16 × 5 = 80 11 × 5 = 55 14 × 5 = 70 18 × 5 = 90
14	Number Tile Sums	6 × 3 = 18, 18 ÷ 3 = 6 10 × 2 = 20, 20 ÷ 2 = 10 e.g. 4 × 4 = 16, 16 ÷ 4 = 4 7 × 2 = 14, 14 ÷ 7 = 2 8 × 4 = 32, 32 ÷ 8 = 4 e.g. 2 × 6 = 12, 12 ÷ 6 = 2 5 × 7 = 35, 35 ÷ 7 = 5 5 × 6 = 30, 30 ÷ 5 = 6 e.g. 10 × 10 = 100, 100 ÷ 10 = 10 5 r 3 4 r 1 7 r 2 8 r 1 7 r 4 6 2 r 1 10 10 r 1 10 r 3 5 r 1 5 r 2 3 r 1 6 8
15	Fractions	$\frac{1}{2}, \frac{1}{5}, \frac{1}{6}, \frac{1}{4}$ $\frac{1}{6}, \frac{1}{8}, \frac{1}{3}$ $\frac{2}{4}$ or $\frac{1}{2}, \frac{2}{12}$ or $\frac{1}{6}$, $\frac{2}{6}$ or $\frac{1}{3}$ $\frac{6}{8}$ or $\frac{3}{4}, \frac{2}{4}$ or $\frac{1}{2}$ $\frac{2}{4}$ or $\frac{1}{2}, \frac{3}{10}, \frac{2}{6}$ or $\frac{1}{3}$
16	Fractions	9, 9, 25, 10, 5, 9, 4 9, 7, 10, 30, 15, 18, 8 8, 8, 11, 35, 20 20 wildlife park – 112 pupils sea-life centre – 56 pupils country park – 56 pupils $\frac{4}{32}$ or $\frac{1}{8}$ 6 beetles $\frac{5}{6}$ or 10 cm $\frac{3}{18}$
17	Clocks	A – quarter past nine B – five minutes to eleven C – half past twelve D – quarter past two E – twenty minutes past six F – quarter to nine G – ten minutes to two H – quarter past eight I – five o'clock J – half past three K – quarter to eight L – ten minutes past one h l g j i k
18	Time Puzzles	Seven o'clock Quarter to four 11 o'clock 2 hours and 10 minutes ten to four quarter to eleven half past five twenty past 4 twenty past 3 1$\frac{3}{4}$ hours
19	Pictograms	Reading – 15 Playing – 11 Watching TV – 5 Swimming – 2 Maths – 20 English – 23 Technology – 14 History – 6 PE – 25
20	Traffic Surveys	Carl
21	Totalling 10	e.g. 1 + 2 + 3 = 6 5 + 4 + 6 = 15 8 + 7 + 4 = 19 4 + 5 + 2 = 11 7 + 9 + 1 = 17 8 + 3 + 5 = 16 4 + 9 + 1 = 14 8 + 2 + 6 = 16 1 + 9 and 9 + 1 2 + 8 and 8 + 2 3 + 7 and 7 + 3 4 + 6 and 6 + 4 5 + 5 17, 13, 17, 20, 14, 15, 15, 26, 23, 25

158

Answers

Copymaster number	Title	Answers
22	Number Cards	81 is 80 + 1, 85 is 80 + 5, 87 is 80 + 7 24, 28 e.g. 74 + 66 = 140, 15 + 35 = 50, 81 + 59 = 140, 33 + 37 = 70, 28 + 62 = 90 15 + 85, 37 + 63, 52 + 48, 13 + 87, 19 + 81, 59 + 41 35, 37, 41, 48, 52 63 is 60 + 3, 62 is 60 + 2, 66 is 60 + 6 91, 94, 97 37, 35, 33 or 19, 17, 15
23	Money	13p, 17p, 25p, 29p, 44p, 17p, 18p, 55p, 120p or £1.20, 150p or £1.50 £1.00, £0.85, £0.91, £0.84, £0.96 £3.70, £9.70, £6.27, £14.87, £32.23 50p, 32p, 42p, 20p, 65p, 28p, £1.05, 90p, 50p £4.20, £5.24, £1.31, £3.10, £4.21 £5.05, £2.55, £2.79, £3.64, £4.01
24	Money Problems	1a – 50p, 20p, 10p, 5p, 2p 1b – No 2a – £3.02 2b – £1.98 3a – £2.55 3c – e.g. baked potato and tea = £2.75 3b e.g. sandwiches and tea = £1.75
25	Scales	1 kg 750 g, 3 kg, 5 kg 750 g, 4 kg 250 g, 1½ kg, 4 kg 300 g, 6 kg 100 g 2000 g, 5000 g, 2500 g
26	Weight Problems	1. in half 2. 800 g 3. weigh the full packet and subtract 25 g 4. Weigh the bowl, water and goldfish, then the bowl and water, and subtract to find the weight of the fish. 5. Weigh herself and the cat, then herself and subtract to find the weight of the cat. 6. Weigh 5 kg of potatoes, then another 5 kg of potatoes = 10 kg. Put 13 kg in one balance, 11 kg in the other balance. Weigh 2 kg of potatoes to make the scales balance, to make 12 kg in total.
27	Area	4 cm² + 8 cm² = 12 cm² 2 cm² + 8 cm² = 10 cm² 6 cm² + 5 cm² = 11 cm² 9 cm² + 5 cm² = 14 cm² 12 cm² + 24 cm² + 16 cm² = 52 cm² 24 cm² + 24 cm² + 12 cm² = 60 cm²
28	Area of Garden	20m² 20 squares 20 35m² The lawn can be any shape as long as it covers 35 squares in total
31	Number Sequences	1000, 900, 800, 700, 600 100, 80, 60, 40, 20 0, −1, −2, −3, −4 0, −5, −10, −15, −20 5, 0, −5, −10, −15 2, 1, 0, −1, −2 16, 8, 0, −8, −16 5, Fives, 10, 15, 20, 25, Tens, 35, 45, 55, 65, Fours, 61, 57, 53, 49 6, Threes, 9, 12, 15, 18, Twos, 20, 22, 24, 26, Tens, 16, 6, −4, −14 2, 12, 22, 32, 42, 45, 48, 51, 54, 34, 14, −6, −26 −5, −4, −3, −2, −1, 0, 1, 2, 3, 0, −3, −6, −9
32	Number Sequences	25, 31, 37, 43, 49, 55, 61, 67, 73, 79 5, 3, 1, −1, −3, −5, −7, −9, −11, −13 4, 8, 12, 16, 20, 24, 28, 32, 40, 44 92, 87, 82, 77, 72, 67, 62, 57, 52, 47 1, 2, 4, 8, 16, 32, 64, 128, 256, 512 50, 40, 30, 20, 10, 0, −10, −20, −30, −40 3, 2, 1, 0, −1, −2, −3, −4, −5, −6 67, 55, 43, 31, 19, 7, −5, −17, −29, −41 33, 44, 55, 66, 77, 88, 99, 110, 121, 132 0, 9, 18, 27, 36, 45, 54, 63, 72, 81
33	Table Square	2, 4, 6, 8, 10, 12, 14, 16, 18, 20 3, 6, 9, 12, 15, 18, 21, 24, 27, 30 4, 8, 12, 16, 20, 24, 28, 32, 36, 40 5, 10, 15, 20, 25, 30, 35, 40, 45, 50 6, 12, 18, 24, 30, 36, 42, 48, 54, 60 7, 14, 21, 28, 35, 42, 49, 56, 63, 70 8, 16, 24, 32, 40, 48, 56, 64, 72, 80 9, 18, 27, 36, 45, 54, 63, 72, 81, 90 10, 20, 30, 40, 50, 60, 70, 80, 90, 100 (2 × 5) × 7 = 70 (2 × 2) × 9 = 36 (6 × 5) × 4 = 120 (2 × 3) × 8 = 48
34	Adding or taking away	24 × 10 = 240, 240 − 24 = 216 83 × 10 = 830, 830 − 83 = 747 54 × 10 = 540, 540 − 54 = 486 37 × 10 = 370, 370 − 37 = 333 66 × 10 = 660, 660 − 66 = 594 41 × 10 = 410, 410 + 41 = 451 73 × 10 = 730, 730 + 73 = 803 86 × 10 = 860, 860 + 86 = 946 58 × 10 = 580, 580 + 58 = 638 92 × 10 = 920, 920 + 92 = 1012 (50 × 5) + (1 × 5) = 255 (30 × 4) + (2 × 4) = 128 (70 × 3) + (3 × 3) = 219 (60 × 3) + (5 × 3) = 195 (30 × 2) + (9 × 2) = 78 (20 × 3) + (5 × 3) = 75 (10 × 5) + (6 × 5) = 80 (50 × 4) + (3 × 4) = 212 (10 × 4) + (8 × 4) = 72 (20 × 5) + (9 × 5) = 145
35	Doubles and multiples	Q1 – 3, 5, 9, 10, 7 Q2 – 78, 110, 184, 206, 152 Q3 – 16, 24, 36, 42, 27, 15, 24, 24 Q4 – 66, 284, 186, 85, 136, 244, 117, 282, 340, 114
36	Money Problems	10 × 38p = £3.80 4 × 50p = £2.00 75p ÷ 3 = 25p 99p + (2 × £1.20) = £3.39 45p + 45p = 90p £1.90 ÷ 5 = 38p 80p × 6 = £4.80, £1.50 × 3 = £4.50, £2.80 × 1 = £2.80, 75p × 6 = £4.50, £2.30 × 2 = £4.60 (2 × 50p) + £1.30 + 85p + £1.00 = £4.15, not enough money left. £10.00 − £8.70 = £1.30 – clown card or flower card bought flower card £1.30 − £1.20 = 10p change
37	Fractions	1/2, 1/4, 1/6, 1/16 or 1/3, 1/12 or 1/4 2/4 or 1/2, 2/12 or 1/6, 1/12 or 1/2, 3 1/2 = 2/4, 3/6, 4/8, 5/10, 6/12 etc. or 10/20, 100/200, 45/90 etc. 1/2, 1/4, 1/8, 1/12, 1/16, 1/20 etc. or 1/10, 40/160, 17/68 etc. 1/3, 2/6, 10/30, 30/90 etc. Fraction wall – 1/2, 1/3, 1/4, 1/5, 1/6, 1/10. 5 bricks, 2½ bricks and 7½ bricks should be shaded in.
38	Decimal Fractions	£0.01 , 0.01 m £0.50, £0.30, £0.80, £0.10, £0.60 £0.25, £0.55, £0.02, £0.21, £0.28 50 cm = 0.50 m, 20 cm = 0.20 m, 85 cm = 0.85 m, 37 cm = 0.37 m 28 cm = 0.28 m, 73 cm = 0.73 m, 55 cm = 0.55 m, 99 cm = 0.99 m
39	Handling Data	Strawberries and bananas 50 81
41	Subtraction sums	11, 12, 11, 8, 3 4, 4, 3, 5, 6 7, 11, 9, 6, 13 18, 37, 10, 29, 35 63, 16, 33, 17, 12
43	Money questions	£3.86, £5.16, £2.12, £7.51, £8.30, £14.00 £7.20, £6.27, £7.77, £12.53, £35.03 £0.60, £0.75, £3.01, £2.00, £2.90 £2.99, £0.66, £2.50, £3.67, £1.58 £2.14, £3.12, £4.30, £0.92, £7.01
44	Money Problems	£1.30 ÷ 10 = 13p £8.25 + £6.44 + £85.39 = £100.08 £5.00 × 24 = £120.00 6 × 28p = £1.68 35 × 4p = £1.40 £2, £1, 50p, 20p, 2p, 1p 10 × £1.30 = £13.00 £26.00 ÷ 10 = £2.60 (90p × 3) + £2.10 = £4.80 (£2.00 × 2) + (£3.00 × 2) = £10.00, saves £5.00 in the last week
45	Measuring Capacity	draw marks against 300, 250, 500, 150, 50 and 1 litre. How much left? 500 ml, 3 litres, 1 litre.
46	Volume Problems	250 ml + 500 ml + 1 litre = 1750 ml 3000 ml ÷ 20 = 150 ml 18 litres + 18 litres = 36 litres 40 ml ÷ 5 ml = 8 4 litres ÷ 2 = 2 litres ½ × 5 litres = 2½ litres 500 ml − 350 ml = 150 ml 1 litre + 1 litre + 250 ml + 500 ml = 2750 ml 15 litres − 12 litres 800 ml = 2 litres 200 ml (1 × 330 ml) + (2 × 330 ml) = 990 ml
47	Right Angles	6, 4, 3, 4, 4, 16, 28 30°, 180°, 60°, 90°
48	Angles	60°, 50°, 90°, 30° 90°, 60°, 30°, 90° 90 ° 30°, 50°, 45°
49	Multiples	Q1 – 14, 20, 8, 2 Q2 – 20, 45, 30, 50, 35 Q3 – 20, 80, 100, 50 Q4 – multiples of two – 18, 16, 20, 50, 28 multiples of five – 15, 20, 50, 35 Q5 – 20 and 50 Q6 – 3, 3 and 8, 4, 2 and 3, 5

159

Answers

Copymaster number	Title	Answers
50	Number Puzzles	Q1 – 3 and 4, 3 and 5, 17 and 18, 10 and 6 Q3 – Chloe's sweets and 24 ÷ 2 = 12 Brian's cards and 20 – 7 = 13 Gary's socks and 14 + 3 = 17 Mum's buns and 5 × 6 = 30
51	Data Handling	Q1 – 9 × 4 = 36, 30 × 2 = 60, 50 ÷ 5 = 10, 26 ÷ 3 = 8 r 2, so 9 boxes Q2 – 15 counters in each circle 29 9 2 48 16 0 16 5 1 90 30 0 48 16 0 23 7 2 33 11 0 69 23 0
52	Division Problems	Q1 – 6, 12, 18, 24, 30, 36, 42, 48, 54, 60 7, 14, 21, 28, 35, 42, 49, 56, 63, 70 8, 16, 24, 32, 40, 48, 56, 64, 72, 80 9, 18, 27, 36, 45, 54, 63, 72, 81, 90 Q2 – 4, 7, 5, 4, 9, 9, 3, 2, 6, 10 Q3 – 17, 24, 27, 12, 13, 13 r 3, 11 r 5, 15 r 1, 19 r 1, 10 r 4 Q4 – 84 ÷ 6 = 14 Q5 – 42 ÷ 6 = 7 No. Only enough for 7 tables. Q6 – 75 ÷ 7 = 10 r 5, 10 weeks and 5 days
53	Length Problems	Q1a – 240 cm Q1b – 20 cm, 60 cm Q1c – 3 × £2.25 = £6.75 Q2 – Phil 160 cm, Janie 184 cm, David 240 cm, Fran 120 cm Q3 – (1 × £24.00) + (2 × £16.80) = £57.60
54	Measure Problems	Monday £5.83, Wednesday £5.94, Friday £2.27 Monday 500 g, Wednesday 3980 g (assuming 330 ml cola weighs 330 g), Friday 4200 g £14.04 8680 g 3.50 pm 1 hour 35 minutes
55	Measure Problems	$\frac{1}{2}, \frac{1}{5}, \frac{3}{4}, \frac{1}{2}, \frac{1}{2}, \frac{1}{10}$ Shade against 2 cm, 5 cm, 2.5 cm, 7 cm, 5 mm, 4 mm, 9 mm and 1 mm.
56	Fractions	9, 6, 10, 100, 20p 25p, 31p, £1, 4p, 4 cm 15 cm, 60 cm, 60 cm, 100 g, 100 g $1\frac{4}{10}, \frac{5}{10}, 2\frac{5}{10}, 1\frac{1}{10}, \frac{2}{10}, 3\frac{3}{10}, 3\frac{5}{10}$ Shade 13 squares, 24 squares, 8 squares, 37 squares, 11 squares, 46 squares, 39 squares, 13 squares and 21 squares.
57	Timetables	7.52, 8.01, 8.05 5 minutes 3.34, 3.43, 3.55, 4.00 4.05, 4.10, 4.22, 4.31, 4.35 half past 7 five minutes past 8
58	Calendars & Timetables	September, October, November or April, May, June Sunday Sunday Saturday B 9.55, 10.01, 10.10, 10.30 7 2.45pm 10.45 am 8.45 pm
59	Venn Diagrams	Multiples of 10 coloured in red – 40, 30, 20 Multiples of 2 coloured in blue – 34, 40, 42, 30, 18, 20 In blue circle – 34, 42, 18 In intersecting circle – 40, 30, 20 Outside circle – 25, 29 In intersecting circle – 70, 60, 80 In multiples of 5 circle – 35, 55, 65 Outside circle – 58, 42 In numbers bigger than 100 circle – 150, 120 In intersecting circle – 265, 189 In odd numbers circle – 45, 27, 95 Outside circle – 80, 38
60	Tree Diagram	1st butterfly, 3rd butterfly, 2nd butterfly, worm, ladybird, beetle, spider

Homework copymaster number	Title	Answers
1	Adding and Subtracting	64, 111, 110 10 94 = 120 – 26 14 = 26 ÷ 2 + 5 – 4 3 = 5 – 2 150 = 120 + 26 + 4 10 = 5 × 2
2	Money	900p, £3.00, 1380p, £5.92, £8.06, 7200p, £20.59, 2865p Q1 – £3.99 + £600 = £9.99 Q2 – 99p × 5 = £4.95 Q3 – £1.80 + £2.30 + (5 × 20p) = £5.10 Q4 – £10.00 – £7.50 = £2.50 Q5 – £5.00 – (6 × 70p) = 80p Q6 – 1p, 2p, 5p, 10p, 20p, 50p, £1.00, £2.00
3	Units of Measurement	millimetres, centimetres, metres, kilometres cm km cm mm m m km 18 cm 6.5 cm 12 cm 9 cm, 100 cm, 250 cm, 10 cm, 2.5 cm 75 cm, 500 cm, 100 cm, 25 cm, 2000 cm
4	Perimeters	The sides 12cm
5	Shapes	Pentagon, equilateral triangle, octagon, rectangle, heptagon, isosceles triangle, hexagon Shapes to draw – circle, semi-circle, square, quadrilateral Hexagon, rectangle Equilateral triangle, kite or rhombus Quadrilateral, hexagon 3, 3, 8, 6
6	Number Patterns	Colour 45, 723, 55, 121, 555, 917, 63 e.g. 45, 55 is add 10 or 428, 528 is add 100 4, 8, 12, 16, 20, 24, 28, 32, 36, 40, 44, 48 2, 3, 4, 6, 12 140, 240, 340, 440, 540 1000, 850, 700, 550, 400 78, 116, 154, 192, 230 6, 4, 8 and 8, 7, 3, and 3, 9, 6 e.g. 5 = 4 + 1 10 = (4 × 3) – 2 11 = (4 × 2) + 3 12 = 4 × 3 20 = (3 + 2) × 4
7	Multiplication & Division	Q1 – 80 Q2 – 16 and 32 Q3 – 18, 99, 51 Q4 – 51 Q5 – 95, 25, 65 Q6 – 73, 62, 53
8	Fractions	$\frac{3}{6}$ or $\frac{1}{2}, \frac{1}{4}, \frac{1}{3}, \frac{1}{6}, \frac{0}{12}, \frac{3}{4}$ Shade 3 rectangles, 5 triangles, 3 rectangles, 7 squares and 1 triangle. $\frac{1}{2} = \frac{4}{8}, \frac{3}{6}, \frac{5}{10}, \frac{2}{4}, \frac{6}{12}$ $\frac{1}{10}, \frac{1}{8}, \frac{1}{7}, \frac{1}{4}, \frac{1}{3}, \frac{1}{2}$ $\frac{2}{3}, \frac{1}{2}, \frac{1}{1}, \frac{1}{3}$
9	Time	Q1a – quarter past eleven Q1b – five minutes past four Q1c – twenty five minutes to ten Q1d – two minutes to seven Q3 – 20 minutes 30 minutes 65 minutes 30 minutes 18 minutes
11	Adding Numbers	44, 53 e.g. 10 + 40 + 30 = 80 90 + 20 + 10 = 120 90 + 40 + 50 = 180 80 + 70 + 60 = 210
12	Adding & subtracting	17p, 40p, 60p, 160p, 125p 76p, 15p, 20p, 80p, 45p £0.99, £1.36, £1.89, £0.61, £1.13 20 × 5p = £1.00 £1.00 – 60p = 40p £8.99 – £5.00 = £3.99 £7.99 + £2.99 = £10.98. No. 98p short £16.00 ÷ £2.00 = 8 weeks
13	Mass	1 kg 400 g, 2 kg 250 g, 2 kg 800 g, 3 kg 250 g 1400 g, 2250 g, 2800 g, 3250 g 2 kg 170 g
14	Area	Shape A is 12cm² Shape B is 10.5cm² Shape C is 12.5cm²
15	Shape and Movement	North Southwest West East At the back door of the house
16	Number Patterns	44, 22, 0, –22, –44, –66 rule is subtract 22 30, 60, 90, 120, 150, 180, 210, 240, 270 rule is add 30 1000, 900, 800, 700, 600 rule is subtract 100 12, 16, 20, 24, 28, 32 4, 6, 8, 10, 6, 9, 12, 15, 8, 12, 16, 20, 10, 15, 20, 25 7, 8, 9, 10, 20, 30, 11, 22, 33 4, 8, 12, 16, 5, 10, 15, 20 5, 6, 7, 8, 9, 10, 12, 15, 18 50, 55, 60, 66, 70, 77, 80, 88